Mining and Social Transformation in Africa

After more than three decades of economic malaise, many African countries are experiencing an upsurge in their economic fortunes linked to the booming international market for minerals. Spurred by the shrinking viability of peasant agriculture, rural dwellers have been engaged in a massive search for alternative livelihoods, one of the most lucrative being artisanal mining.

While an expanding literature has documented the economic expansion of artisanal mining, this book is the first to probe its societal impact, demonstrating that artisanal mining has the potential to be far more democratic and emancipating than preceding modes.

Delineating the paradoxes of artisanal miners working alongside the expansion of large-scale mining investment in Africa, *Mining and Social Transformation in Africa* concentrates on the Tanzanian experience. Written by authors with fresh research insights, focus is placed on how artisanal mining is configured in relation to local, regional and national mining investments and social class differentiation. The work lives and associated lifestyles of miners and residents of mining settlements are brought to the fore, asking where this historical interlude is taking them and their communities in the future. The questions of value transfers out of the artisanal mining sector, value capture by elites, and changing configurations of gender, age and class differentiation all arise.

Deborah Fahy Bryceson is a Reader at the Geographical and Earth Sciences School of the University of Glasgow.

Eleanor Fisher is Associate Professor in International Rural Development at the University of Reading.

Jesper Bosse Jønsson as Head of Development Planning and Environment for COWI Tanzania.

Rosemarie Mwaipopo is a Senior Lecturer in the Department of Sociology and Anthropology, University of Dar es Salaam, Tanzania.

Routledge Studies in Development and Society

Mining and Social Transformation in Africa

Mineralizing and democratizing trends in artisanal production

**Edited by Deborah Fahy Bryceson,
Eleanor Fisher, Jesper Bosse Jønsson
and Rosemarie Mwaipopo**

Routledge
Taylor & Francis Group

LONDON AND NEW YORK

First published 2014
by Routledge
4 Park Square, Milton Park, Abingdon, Oxon OX14 4RN
605 Third Avenue, New York, NY 10017

Routledge is an imprint of the Taylor & Francis Group, an informa business

First issued in paperback 2014

British Library Cataloguing in Publication Data
A catalogue record for this book is available from the British Library

Library of Congress Cataloging-in-Publication Data
Mining and social transformation in Africa : mineralizing and democratizing trends in artisanal production / [edited by] Deborah Fahy Bryceson, Eleanor Fisher, Jesper Bosse Jønsson, and Rosemarie Mwaipopo.
pages cm. – (Routledge studies in development and society)
Includes bibliographical references and index.
Gold mines and mining–Social aspects–Africa. 2. Democratization–Africa.
I. Bryceson, Deborah Fahy, editor of compilation. II. Fisher, Eleanor, editor of compilation. III. Jønsson, Jesper Bosse, 1971– editor of compilation.
IV. Mwaipopo, R. A., editor of compilation.
HD9536.A352M56 2014
338.2'741096–dc23
2013013514

ISBN: 978-0-415-70972-9 (pbk)
ISBN: 978-0-415-83370-7 (hbk)

Typeset in Times New Roman
by FiSH Books Ltd, Enfield

Contents

List of illustrations

List of figures

List of tables

Appendices

List of contributors

Editors

Deborah Fahy Bryceson is a Reader at the Geographical and Earth Sciences School of the University of Glasgow. Her research in Africa over the past 20 years has focused on changing work patterns as rural dwellers actively seek alternatives to agriculture. In the process, she has explored an array of labour activities, notably alcohol production, trade and most recently artisanal mining. She is currently coordinating a research programme studying the interaction between mining and urbanization in Sub-Saharan Africa. Her published books include *How Africa Works: Occupational Change, Identity and Morality in Africa* (Practical Action Publishing, 2010); *Disappearing Peasantries? Rural Labour in Africa, Asia and Latin America* (Intermediate Technology Publications 2000 with Cristobal Kay and Jos Mooij) and *Farewell to Farms: De-Agrarianization and Employment in Africa* (Ashgate, 1997 with Vali Jamal).

Eleanor Fisher is Associate Professor in International Rural Development at the University of Reading: she has conducted extensive research on African livelihoods, exploring the significance of non-agricultural activities – including artisanal mining, beekeeping and fisheries – and the dynamics of rural change. She has also been an observer of the development of the fair trade movement since the 1990s – as researcher, policy maker and practitioner – and is interested in how contemporary ideas on ethical trade and voluntary standards are applied to markets for African mineral products. Her publications include articles in *Development and Change, Resources Policy, Journal of Southern African Studies, International Journal of the Sociology of Agriculture and Food, Human Organization, Journal for International Development, Journal of Agrarian Change,* and *Social Enterprise Journal.*

Jesper Bosse Jønsson is Head of Development Planning and Environment for COWI Tanzania. He has 14 years of professional experience, most of which has been spent working on artisanal mining and rural livelihood transformation in Tanzania. He worked for rural NGOs in capacity building positions before doing a PhD on the organizational practices, livelihood strategies, and career trajectories of artisanal gold miners in Tanzania. He subsequently held positions as Coordinator of the Centre for Sustainable Artisanal and Small-Scale Mining located at the University of Copenhagen and International Field Coordinator in the 'Urban Growth and Poverty in Mining Africa' (UPIMA) research programme at the University of Glasgow, before moving to COWI Tanzania in early 2013. Jesper has published journal articles in, among others, *World Development, Resources Policy, Geography Compass, Natural Resources Forum, Journal of Cleaner Production*, and *Development and Change*.

Rosemarie Mwaipopo is a Senior Lecturer in the Department of Sociology and Anthropology, University of Dar es Salaam, Tanzania. As a senior social development specialist, her key areas of expertise include social analysis, livelihoods, and gender and poverty issues. She has extensive experience undertaking research and consultancy work on the mining sector, having conducted analyses of community-related issues in gold, diamond, uranium and gemstone mining in different parts of the country over the past 15 years. She has published an article entitled 'Rural-Urban Transitions in Northwestern Tanzania's Mining Frontier' (2010) in Agergaard, J., N. Fold and K. Gough (eds) *Rural Urban Dynamics – Livelihoods, Mobility and Markets in African and Asian Frontiers*. London: Routledge. She was a researcher in the Mwadui Community Diamond Partnership Project and researched Tanzanian mining for the UK's Department of International Development Research Report and the Tanzanian Research on Poverty Alleviation Organization.

Authors

France Bourgouin is affiliated to the Centre Interdisciplinaire de Recherché en Développement International et Société (CIRDIS) at the Université du Québec à Montreal. During the past 12 years, France has been conducting research and doing consulting on the political economy of extractive industries and mining policy in a development context. She has worked on mineral governance, including liberalization of extractive industries, MNC-artisanal mining relations, cross-sector collaboration, socio-economic impacts of mining development, corporate social responsibility, human rights, impacts risk, political risk, institutional and regulatory reform, and local procurement. She is co-editor and participating author of *Resource Governance and Developmental States: Critical International Political Economy Perspectives* (Palgrave Macmillan, forthcoming 2013).

John Childs is a Lecturer in International Development and Natural Resources at the University of Lancaster and former London School of Economics Fellow in Environment. His work focuses on politics of environmental governance in sub-Saharan Africa. With a particular interest in the political dimensions of natural resource use, notably the study of minerals and precious metals, he is currently researching the extent to which Fairtrade can solve the problems of social and environmental injustice in artisanal and small-scale gold mining. He has published on the topic in *Resources Policy* and the *International Journal of Environment and Pollution.*

Niels Fold is Professor of Geography at the University of Copenhagen. He has published extensively on resource utiliization and global value chains in *Geography Compass, Land Use Policy, Geoforum, Global Networks, Transactions of the Institute of British Geographers, Natural Resource Forum, Journal of Agrarian Change* among others.

Richard Sherrington holds a PhD in Social Anthropology and was formerly post-doctoral research fellow at Darwin College, University of Cambridge. He has undertaken research on mining and social development issues in Tanzania since 2000 and since 2006 he has worked as a social development specialist with extractive sector companies.

Hannelore Verbrugge is a PhD student at the Institute for Anthropological Research in Africa (IARA), University of Leuven, Belgium. Her research interest centres on women's economic and social lives in Tanzania's gold mining settlements.

Acknowledgements

This edited collection has been several years in the making. Tracing the economic and social innovation associated with artisanal mining's expansion has involved help from countless people along the way. We can mention only a few here. Multiple research permits, kindly issued by the Tanzania Commission for Science and Technology (COSTECH), were the vital first step in data collection. In the field, John Wihalla and Peter Buhabi provided invaluable research assistance. Alex Magayane and Juma Sementa from the Ministry of Energy and Minerals were generous with their time and expertise.

GEOCENTER Denmark funded Jesper Bosse Jønsson's fieldwork. Financial support from the UK's Department for International Development (DfID) and the Economic and Social Research Council (ESRC) RES-167-25-0488 facilitated the completion of the book. Some chapters of the book have been condensed from previous journal articles in *Development and Change*, *Journal of Modern African Studies*, *Natural Resources Forum* and *World Development*. We are grateful for permission to use this material, which is acknowledged in the specific individual chapters. The book has been enormously enhanced by the cartographic expertise of Mike Shand of the University of Glasgow. Finally, Mathias de Alencastro, Mathew Anderson, Alberto Arce, Niels Fold, Terry Garde, Siri Lange, Kate Meagher, Guy Standing and Gisa Weszkalnys kindly took time to comment on our draft chapters. We have benefited from their perceptive observations, while taking full responsibility for the contents of the chapters.

Above all, we wish to thank the many Tanzanian miners and residents of mining settlements who were willing to engage in discussion with us and answer our many questions about their lives in artisanal mining. We dedicate this book to their uncharted future.

1 Mineralizing Africa and artisanal mining's democratizing influence

Deborah Fahy Bryceson and Jesper Bosse Jønsson

The twenty-first century has witnessed Sub-Saharan Africa's re-emergence on the world stage of commodity export. A dramatic surge in mining is catalyzing fundamental change with the potential to transform or trammel personal and national destinies. As the continental economy expands, virtually everyone is affected in one way or another, most of all mineworkers and residents of mining settlements who are riding the crest of opportunity and risk associated with a global commodity boom. They are at the vortex of profound social transformation.

At present, juxtaposed to decades of entrenched economic recession, the current exploitation of Sub-Saharan Africa's rich mineral wealth is generating increased prosperity for some and impoverishment for others. Rape or redemption? There is an extensive literature on mineral booms of this nature discussing the so-called resource curse, Dutch disease and a paradox of plenty (Sachs and Warner 2001; Robinson *et al.* 2006). For better or worse, foreign direct investment has been on an upward trajectory, spurred by rising prices for gold and other valuable metals, along with diamonds and other precious stones (Bush 2008).

This volume, however, extends well beyond the world of foreign investment and corporate mining to an exploration of the artisanal mining sector, especially its core, the excavation of minerals by African mine claim owners, pit holders and diggers and its effects on local settlements. In several respects, artisanal mining averts the pitfalls of the mineral resource curse that has preoccupied economists, boosting labour absorption in national economies, raising purchasing power and enhancing the multiplier effect in local economies of mineral resource-rich areas.

We define artisanal mining as individual or collective labour-intensive mineral extraction with limited capital investment using basic tools, manual devices or simple portable machinery. Overwhelmingly, artisanal mining pits constitute a male domain but women are close at hand, engaged in panning, mineral processing and service sector activities. We use the term 'mineralizing' to denote the alteration in both the form and content of the African continent's social, political and cultural foundations arising from the growing importance of mining in national, local and household economies. The word mineralization used in biology, geology and soil science refers to chemical processes altering the organic or inorganic composition of original base substances. The analogy is apt for the continent's political economy and society. Over the past thirty years, a swathe of

African countries have experienced deepening agricultural malaise, most apparent in smallholder commercial crop production, leading to marked deterioration in the productive and exporting capacity of nation-states and rural households (Bryceson 2002).

Artisanal mining has appeared as one potentially lucrative alternative to agriculture, gaining in momentum over the last two decades (e.g. *Benin*: Grätz 2002; *Burkina Faso*: Luning 2006; *Democratic Republic of Congo*: De Boeck 1999; *Ghana*: Hilson and Potter 2005; *Madagascar*: Walsh 2003; *Sierra Leone*: Richards 1996; Maconachie and Binns 2007; *Zimbabwe*: Mabhena 2012; *Continental*: Jønsson and Fold 2011; Werthmann and Grätz 2012). Wherever it commences in the African countryside, artisanal mining is transformative and organizationally distinct from the economic principles and social ties that pervade smallholder agriculture and pastoralism.

Five salient and interrelated themes have emerged in the African artisanal mining literature: first, debate about the significance of artisanal mining livelihoods for poverty alleviation; second, contentious relations between artisanal and large-scale mining with regards to land, mineral rights and labour; third, artisanal miners' extraction of so-called conflict minerals; fourth, legal aspects of artisanal mining production and exchange; and fifth, the environmental hazards associated with artisanal mining.

Our edited collection probes the largely undocumented social and cultural dimensions of African artisanal mining, which are altering the form and content of relations within the household, local community and nation-state, using Tanzanian case study material for illustration. At the centre of this trajectory is the emergence of new occupations and lifestyles within the mining settlements. We draw inspiration from Sennett's (2008) analytical insights into the evolution of artisanal craftsmanship and its reverberations for the wider society. His focus is on those who work primarily with their hands and hand-held tools through world history. Sennett's depiction of their visceral relationship to their materials and tools in the process of craft production and trade, the changing nature of skill acquisition, relationships with their work colleagues and not least their motivation and professional commitment directed at accomplished work performance and valued product output provides conceptual insight for comprehending African artisanal miners.

Tanzania, a country that typifies the current movement of primarily agrarian national economies towards mineral-driven political economies taking place across the African continent, affords us a panoptic view of the social transformation and the ensuing tangled web of cultural innovations reconfiguring social dynamics at local, regional and national levels. The Tanzanian experience is indicative of the circumstances of many mineral-endowed African countries spurred by the dramatic ascent of global mineral prices. The early stages of mineralization have represented enormous opportunities for people, mostly men, to enter artisanal mining as mineral extractors, generally producing interdependently in association with one another rather than working on their own. As artisanal mining takes shape, both democratic and autocratic tendencies may surface. The chapters in this book interrogate opposing tendencies in the artisanal labour process and more widely in the daily lives of mining settlement residents, and at the national level as states become increasingly involved in channelling mining revenues in the larger economy.

Throughout this book, we are seeking to advance a new theoretical understanding of the role of artisanal miners in society, which may be generalizable to several countries in Sub-Saharan Africa. We have chosen to provide a detailed concrete example of the nature of artisanal mining in Tanzania to demonstrate the multi-faceted complexity of artisanal mining's impact on social transformation. By way of contextualization, the next section of this chapter reviews the broad historical trajectories of Sub-Saharan Africa's colonial and post-colonial mining, followed by the basic outline of our conceptualization of the embryonic democratic character of artisanal mining in current African mineralization. Thereafter, we move to Tanzania's historical background to illustrate the present nature of mineralizing and democratizing processes in preparation for the case study chapters that follow.

The final chapter of the book will return to these themes to review the significance of the Tanzanian case study findings, taking into account the creeping inequalities, injustice and autocratic tendencies revealed in the case study chapters and the reality of mineralization's non-renewable mineral resource base. In the conclusion, we reiterate our question as to whether a democratizing trend is generalizable to Sub-Saharan Africa.

Mining eras in Africa

Before embarking on an in-depth interrogation of African artisanal mining it is useful to review twentieth century history of African mining more generally, precisely because African mining narratives have tended to dramatize the themes of authoritarianism, on the one hand, and anarchy and violence, on the other. Both narratives are inclined to distract attention from alternative histories where mining was instrumental to economic development and social change in post-colonial transition, as exemplified by Ghana and Zambia.

The African continent's known mineral wealth was a significant lure for European colonial annexation during the scramble for Africa in the late nineteenth century. Subsequently, most of the colonial economies of Southern Africa, as well as the Belgian Congo and the Gold Coast (now Ghana), were dominated by large-scale mining, while artisanal mining was relatively rare and in most cases illegal. The following sub-sections outline the dominant patterns of African mining during the twentieth century to the present.

Apartheid mining in Southern Africa

South African construction of the infamous apartheid regime centred on a racist division of labour that enhanced profits in the mining sector at the expense of the black labour force's wages, housing and rights of residence in urban areas and was influential throughout Southern Africa. European colonial governments and mine corporations fine-tuned a production system that relied on temporary African mine labourers and the creation of labour reserves. Most workers were rural recruits who were housed in mining compounds and obliged to return to their home areas at the completion of their work contracts (Wolpe 1972; Jeeves 1985; Moodie 1994). Coercive control and a racist ideology removed the possibility of collective politics (Gordon 1977; Crush 1994).

The separation of men from their wives and children had deleterious effects on home life. Over the latter half of the twentieth century, the South African labour reserve was characterized by increasing reliance on foreign labour from neighbouring countries, declining numbers of recruited labourers, amidst continued racist labour stratification. Rising public concern over the societal effects of circular migration, surging political protest against the fiction of an agrarian fallback in the miners' rural homelands and the indignities of apartheid permeated South Africa and spread new norms that affected the policies of neighbouring countries (Crush *et al.* 1991; Moodie 1994; Wilson 2001).

On the Copperbelt of Northern Rhodesia (later Zambia), the mining economy acted as a melting pot for rapid social change and urbanization. With markedly different labour organization from the racist stratification dominating mining compounds in South Africa and Namibia, trade union activism and organized politics challenged tribal identities, generating a politics of class that stimulated nationalist and pan-African thinking (Epstein 1958; Bates 1971; Burawoy 1972; Kapferer 1976).

Elsewhere political transition and its relationship to mining took a more violent turn. In the 1970s, the growing momentum of African nationalist resistance transformed into armed struggle bent on overthrowing the racist regimes of Anglophone Zimbabwe and Namibia and Lusophone Mozambique and Angola. Since the European colonial governments of these countries were aligned with mining industry interests, the armed struggles were inevitably confronting the economic order of large-scale mining as well as colonial state power (Phimister 1988; Pearce 2004, 2005; Larmer 2011). After years of protracted conflict, African national rule was achieved in one country after another, culminating in the downfall of apartheid in South Africa and introduction of black majority rule in 1994.

Conflict mineral mining

National independence did not always ensure peace as demonstrated in Angola where contestation over national leadership led to continuation of armed struggle between the MPLA ruling party and UNITA rebel movement led by Jonas Savimbi. So too the Democratic Republic of Congo's (DRC) and Sierra Leone's weak governing regimes, were unable to stem political and economic breakdown arising from contending rebel factions. In each of these cases, mineral wealth became pivotal to the war.

The rebel armies operating in mineral-rich areas increasingly resorted to financing their armed struggle on the basis of illegal artisanal mining of diamonds, gold and other valuable minerals that took on the appellation of 'conflict minerals'. This term surfaced after the Cold War during the 1990s, as external financing for African political secessionist movements by rival super-powers, the Soviet Union, China and the United States ebbed away. Seeking alternative sources of funding, some rebel armies succeeded in gaining access to mineral wealth through infiltration of trade channels and direct production. Besides local populations participating in the mining activities, labour recruit-ment was sourced from: i) men, often youth, seized in war-affected areas and coerced by soldiers to work as artisanal miners, or ii) alternatively people from cross-border areas, attracted to potential diamond or gold earnings, who devel-oped business ties with the rebel army or private military companies, as was the case of Congolese diamond miners, as well as traders associated with UNITA in Angola (De Boeck 1999; Dietrich 2000; Pearce 2005; Rodrigues and Tavares 2012).[1]

Artisanal mining of conflict minerals remains relatively undocumented given the remote locations and typically dangerous conditions under which it has been conducted (Campbell 2004; Gilmore *et al.* 2005; Le Billon 2008; Pearce 2004; Bleischwitz *et al.* 2012). Angola's and Sierra Leone's conflict mineral production has ended with the cessation of war, although intimidation and exploitation of artisanal miners by the state army and private military companies in Angola's Lundas continues. What remains most salient at present is the export of conflict minerals including gold, cobalt and tantalum from parts of the Eastern DRC (Raeymakers 2010; Geenen 2012; Global Witness 2012).

New era of mineralization

Against the historical background of apartheid-influenced large-scale mining in Southern Africa and rebel-imposed artisanal mining dotted around the continent, the twenty-first century is witnessing a distinctly new mining era, marking a reprieve from exploitative conditions and inhumane labour control. The primary catalyst for change is the global market. China's hyperactive quest for raw mate-rials to fuel its economic ascent is unfolding in tandem with western countries' recessionary slide (Brautigam 2009; Alder *et al.* 2009). Global mineral prices, notably for gold and copper, have risen to unprecedented heights, triggering the mineralization of many African countries, several having never previously been known for mineral production (Bryceson and MacKinnon 2012). In this context, both artisanal and large-scale mining have surged over the past decade. Corporate investment from Chinese and western countries has imparted dynamism to African economies that have been slumbering since the late 1970s global oil crisis. Most of the investment has been directed to the extractive industry.

Appendix 1.1 lists African countries by their rating in a 'metallic mining contri-bution index', which refers to metallic mineral-producing countries with economies where metallic mineral production and export constitute a large and expanding part of the national economy. African countries account for over a third of the index's top 50 countries. An equivalent global index for diamond-producing countries does not exist. However, in 2010, out of the 20 largest diamond producers, African countries constituted 60 per cent of the total and produced 62 per cent of the recorded carats (Appendix 1.2). This is remarkable amidst the decline of South Africa as a major mineral exporter. It should be borne in mind that the above statistics relate to officially recorded production of metals and diamonds, which primarily emanate from large-scale production. Artisanal mining output, on the other hand, is usually exported through informal channels and inevitably goes under-counted.

While total recorded industrialized mineral exports supersede recorded artisanal exports by an enormous margin, the reverse is the case for labour absorption and livelihood generation. Artisanal mining offers income-earning opportunities to vast numbers of people. The African continent has an estimated 9 million people engaged in artisanal mining and another 54 million who depend on the sector as an indirect livelihood source (Hayes 2008). Statistical estimates of total employment in African large-scale mining do not exist.[2] Furthermore, the common observation that the extractive industries makes only a small direct contribution to employment creation only takes statistics on large-scale mining into account (e.g. UNCTAD 2007: 133). Country-level comparison suggests a vast differential between the numbers of people employed in large-scale as opposed to artisanal mining, given significant employment creation in the latter. In Tanzania, approximately 685,000[3] people worked in artisanal mining in 2012 (roughly two-thirds in gold) whereas the estimated directly employed operational labour force at the country's four major large-scale gold mines numbered 3,100, a number only likely to double when formal sub-contractors are counted (Roe and Essex 2009)[4] (Figure 1.1 and Appendix 1.3).

Artisanal mining's enhanced purchasing power has dynamized the surrounding countryside, creating employment opportunities for hundreds of thousands in easy-entry service sector and trade activities. The economic stimulus to resident populations in the mining regions is readily observable. Given these circumstances, African artisanal mining warrants careful consideration, both as a form of livelihood and a catalyst for democratizing tendencies, as discussed in the next two sections.

The artisanal mining labour process

Although most current mining literature refers to 'small-scale miners', we have chosen to avoid that label, given that scale of operation criteria limits perception of the fundamentally different nature of artisanal mining relative to large-scale production. The concept of 'artisanal miners' affords more analytical insight by drawing attention to the nature of workers' social interaction and their specialized performance of transformative processes on specified minerals using hand-held tools. Sennett's (2008) treatise on craftsmen refers to the artisan's work as that of 'hand and head', we extend this term to encompass miners' coordination of 'hand, head and heart' in their mining excavation, refining and marketing of mineral output. In other words, we are concerned with the integration of the miners' work

Figure 1.1 Map of estimated numbers of artisanal miners

Source: CASM 2008; Hayes 2008. See Appendix 1.3 for the country listing of estimated numbers, which predates the establishment of Southern Sudan, hence, the perforated boundary line

motivation and decision-making as well as the associational social ties of occupation, community and conjugal relations that congeal in the mining settlement and beyond, binding mining activities as an economic livelihood with a distinctive cultural way of life.

The artisanal miner is a largely self-propelled agent from the initial decision to migrate to a mineral site and throughout the course of his career to retirement. His work life begins with an informal, on-site apprenticeship (Chapter 2). From the outset, the miner must weigh the opportunity for financial gain and the identity and pride he has in being a miner against the challenges of acquiring the requisite skills, enduring physical hardship and taking on financial and physical risk

(Chapter 3). As *Homo faber*, man as maker of work with a moral life in common with others, the artisanal miner exercises autotelic agency in what Sennett (2008: 6) describes as 'becoming and being a craftsman'. In the African artisanal mining context, this generally necessitates the individual breaking out of the labour ascription of his agrarian origins. In becoming a miner the term 'occupationality' is relevant, defined as a 'process of skill acquisition, economic exchange, psychological orientation and social positioning through which an individual becomes actively engaged in specific work and identifies with it as an extension of his or her social being' (Bryceson 2010: 4).

The autotelic journey of becoming self-made miners, takes place largely independent of government, NGOs, aid agencies and other developmental institutions. But the journey is a social rather than solitary experience (Chapter 5). As their numbers grow throughout the continent, artisanal miners have been reflexively forming shared economic and social norms among themselves and in relation to mining settlement residents, thereby creating their own sense of mining identity and accomplishment. Occupying a frontier setting, they are devising a social etiquette and economic customs that suit their daily lives and reflect current global and local market demands, mineral supply availability and state impositions on their activities.

The social and financial risks of artisanal mining are high. Many fail in terms of their original expectations and objectives and for some failure extends to being unable to achieve a basic subsistence. They may be forced to look for another location or occupation to survive or return to their home areas with embarrassment. Others, however, succeed as miners, some earning large sums of money, albeit erratically, and gaining respect and power, upon which they consolidate their social position (Chapter 3).

In contrast, miners in large-scale corporate mines work as wage labourers under standard capitalist contractual conditions and under a management chain of command which leaves little scope for independent decision-making about how they work, or even where and how they live if company housing is provided for them. Their working lives are likely to be more regularized and secure, whilst in the employment of the mining company.

Large-scale mine workers tend to have a higher level of formal education and be engaged in machine-facilitated labour in which they do not exercise the same 'hand, head, heart' decision-making as artisanal miners. Their sense of being miners is contingent on conforming to the mining company's work regime. Less self-made and more a cog in the wheel of the global mining industry, they represent the mechanized, industrialized face of African mining. The contrast is stark, skilled workers are employed by large-scale companies on a salaried basis, subject to corporate production plans versus artisanal miners who face uncertain daily returns. As craft producers, they use their hands, heads and hearts, inadvertently fashioning a new local economy and society as they work.

This book is centred on African artisanal miners whose evolving lifestyles and work trajectories have been barely documented, an ironic and regrettable situation given their far greater numbers relative to those employed in large-scale mining and their pivotal political significance to the mineralization of the continent at present. The next section focuses on their social freedom and political assertiveness as autotelic craftsmen and advances our argument for the recognition of democratic tendencies in African artisanal mining.

Democratizing artisanal miners

Almost a half-century ago, Barrington Moore (1991 [1966]) in his book *Social Origins of Dictatorship and Democracy*, ambitiously traced the role of rural peasantries and landlord classes in the transition from agrarian feudalism to industrial capitalism, showing how democracy and dictatorship are both possible outcomes of a complex, contingent history of transformation. This collection is far less ambitious in scale but is nonetheless interested in similar contradictory historical processes at local and regional levels. The book's case study chapters focus on artisanal miners as 'autotelic agents', who have coalesced in specific circumstances, and are becoming and being miners with an internalized *raison d'être* individually and collectively. Constituting an artisanal mining fraternity, they evince strong democratic leanings related to the nature of their labour process, migration histories and the opportunity to create new settlements and occupational norms in a mineralizing context.

Democracy, derived from the Greek word *demos* (translated: the people), commonly refers to popularly elected representative government embedded in the ideals of freedom and equality (Robinson 2004: 3). We have adopted a related but far broader meaning suitable for exploring the social dynamics of artisanal mining. We define democratization as a process of occupational and residential community formation around the principles of freedom of movement, egalitarian opportunity and representative governance. At the local level, this takes the form of an effervescent amalgam of socially aspirant associational relations, emergent egalitarian-leaning occupational work practices and tendencies towards collective self-governance. At the national level, democracy is evidenced in free and fair elections, the rule of law embedded with principles of justice, state commitment to its citizenry's equality of opportunity, and the performance of bureaucratically impartial state agents. In effect the chapters that follow can be considered as baseline snapshots of a rapidly changing frontier generating a new potentially democratic narrative, not unlike De Tocqueville's (2003 [1835]) early observations about frontier America's democratizing tendencies.

Physical labour exertion and skill acquisition, rather than formal educational qualifications and privileged birth, are key to artisanal mining proficiency. A putative ethos of equality of opportunity pervades most mining sites. While there is generally a hierarchical division of labour (Chapters 3 and 7), the pit has a levelling egalitarian influence since everyone is subjected to the same uncertainty and danger. Throughout Africa, diggers generally share the mineral output on an agreed basis. Most operations are organized as two- to four-tier hierarchies, which involve some or all of what we term financiers, claim owners (formal and informal), pit holders, and diggers (Hilson and Potter 2005; Jønsson and Fold 2011).

Relative to the patriarchal norms of the surrounding agrarian countryside, artisanal mining settlements have a comparatively large measure of self-governance, owing to their remote locations. On new mineral rush sites, miners usually popularly choose their local leaders, who will interface with national, regional and district level government officialdom (Grätz 2002; Luning 2006; Spiegel and Veiga 2009). But democratizing influences do not stop there. The formation of the artisanal mining occupational identity in mineralizing Africa is negotiated and networked under conditions of high risk.

Occupational norms, codes of practice and ethics are evolving on the job in an *ad hoc* manner through intense social interaction (Bryceson 2010). An etiquette for cooperative and competitive relations amongst fellow miners has emerged. Artisanal miners' heavy physical exertion, the frequent, if not dominant, necessity for teamwork and the enormous uncertainties of their occupation tend to generate loose cooperative bonds between miners and a strong occupational identity that lends corporate strength to their self-governance. Miners' readily appreciate the pitfalls of non-cooperation. Trust in one's mine team colleagues' personal integrity and skill is vital to survival in the pit (Chapter 3).

Beyond miners' occupational identity formed through on-the-job interaction, there is the empathy and shared camaraderie arising from similar decision-making pathways. Most have journeyed from rural homelands and peasant farming seeking a distinctly different occupation and lifestyle. Their choice to mine in remote locations and pioneer the creation of frontier urban settlements imparts a compelling foundation for a shared collective identity, setting them apart from farmers in the surrounding countryside, government officials with regular salaried income and urban populations in regional towns and the capital cities (Walsh 2003). Mining lifestyles are usually characterized by greater openness to eclectic and foreign influences, most likely derived from their encounters with external mineral buyers, their generally superior purchasing power relative to agrarian communities, and not least, the experience of relatively frequent movement from one mining site to another where they continually meet people of diverse tribal and national origins. These shared experiences provide miners with both a collective identity and a communal identity that imparts a sense of purpose and cohesion, which they are likely to draw on when they confront problems necessitating negotiation or prompting retaliatory action vis-à-vis external non-mining institutions.

In arguing for recognition of the democratizing tendencies of artisanal miners in current mineralizing Africa, we are not suggesting that this is an entirely new phenomenon. Artisanal mining in the 19th century frontier of the western world evinced similar characteristics (Elkins and McKitrick 1954; Johnson 2000; Steffen 1983; Mitchell 2009). A dramatic historical illustration is that of the Ballarat gold rush miners' uprising of 1854 in Victoria Australia, which involved thousands protesting against the imposition of a mining license tax. Their demands centred on every citizen having a democratic voice in law-making. The Eureka Stockade uprising is seen by many as a defining moment in the development of Australian democracy.[5]

Artisanal miners' democratic leanings take shape within the local community and through engagement with the state and market. The collective identity of miners imparts confidence and strength, vital for struggles against predatory states and exploitative markets. Often artisanal miners, particularly highly mobile ones, are dormant politically, but when the state reduces miners' field of operation or market agents raise their margins of profit at the expense of miners to draining proportions, miners are likely to demand their rights as a collective. The definition of artisanal miners' spatial, temporal and functional boundaries of operation remains contestable at all times, given the non-renewable nature of the mineral supply and its inevitable diminishing returns.

Tanzanian mineralization

Moving from African mineralization and artisanal mining's democratizing tendencies continentally, we turn to Tanzania. A single-country focus affords in-depth analysis of the intricacies of social, economic, and cultural transformation taking place in artisanal mining. Tanzania, provides an especially useful illustration of change, since its mineralization has been very pronounced from a base of almost no mineral production in 1990 to mineral export dominance a mere 20 years later. Mining sites now dot most regions of the country (see Figure 1.2), but the preponderant majority have been gold sites located along the contours of the East African rift valley in what we refer to as Tanzania's 'ring of gold' (Bryceson *et al.* 2012). This section briefly reviews the major trends in Tanzanian colonial and post-colonial mining history.

Colonial mineral discovery and excavation

Contrary to other mineral-rich countries like Ghana, Mali, Zimbabwe, and South Africa, nothing points towards significant pre-colonial mining activities in Tanzania. In the 1890s, mineral prospecting by German colonialists revealed that Tanzania had a large variety of minerals (Lemelle 1986). Eighty years later, an aerial geophysical survey identified promising gold and uranium deposits, among other minerals (Kassum 2007). Since the German colonial period mining activities have been carried out on different scales and varying levels of intensity, primarily involving gold, gemstones, and diamonds, but it was not until the 1990s that the mineral riches of Tanzania started attracting serious international interests (Kulindwa *et al.* 2003; Phillips *et al.* 2001). Today the country is known for its large gold deposits, currently making it the fourth largest gold producer in Africa, its diamonds and large variety of gemstones including tanzanite, only found in Tanzania, and numerous industrial minerals including coal, nickel, iron, copper, and uranium (Yager 2010). Artisanal miners are responsible for the extraction of a wide range of minerals and metals, precious as well as industrial. The case study chapters in this book concentrate on precious minerals of high value, notably gold and diamonds. Gold is traded throughout the world and is the mineral extracted by most artisanal miners in Tanzania, followed by a variety of gemstones, and diamonds.

Figure 1.2 Map of Tanzania's 'ring of gold' mining sites

Source: Shand and Jønsson 2013. UPIMA unpublished project data compiled from Jønsson's
        updated Tanzanian inventory of artisanal mining locations

Between the late 1880s and World War I, the Germans in what was then
German East Africa registered numerous claims to gold and other minerals and
commenced production at several locations. However, it was not until after World
War I, under British administration of a League of Nations mandate, that mining,
in what had become Tanganyika, took off. Gold was the leading extracted mineral
and was predominantly mined at two centres, one was Lupa Gold Fields in the
southwestern part of the territory, where a gold rush of primarily artisanal miners
began in 1922 and continued through the 1930s. By 1936, Lupa had thousands of
Africans and more than a thousand European miners. While Africans initially

worked for their European bosses, a 1929 Mining Ordinance gave them the opportunity to acquire prospecting rights, hence the birth of Tanzania's artisanal mining tradition. The other centre, at the Lake Victoria Gold Fields, was the site of several gold mines, operating during the world depression in response to rising gold prices. The mines ranged from semi-mechanized family operations to East Africa's largest industrial gold producer, Geita Mine.

In the late 1930s, Tanganyika's gold exports (four tonnes in 1938) became a large contributor to the territory's economy, constituting close to 20 per cent of export earnings (Lemelle 1986). The world market price for gold stagnated between 1934 and 1967. Mining continued in the first years of World War II, but prospecting activities were banned from 1941, and existing mines had problems with labour shortages and accessing essential spare parts and supplies from overseas, resulting in a significant decrease in gold production, which was down to two tonnes by the end of the war.

In 1940, John Williamson, a Canadian geologist discovered a large diamond-bearing kimberlite pipe 160 kilometres south of Lake Victoria and Williamson Diamond Mine commenced production. By 1950 the mine contributed three per cent to GDP and 15 per cent of export earnings (Lemelle 1986). After Williamson's death in 1958, De Beers bought the mine in a partnership with the government of Tanganyika (Chachage 1995).

Post-colonial mining stagnation

Tanzania gained independence in 1961. With the continuing stagnation of the gold price, gold mines had faced difficulties for decades, leading to mine closures with the Geita Mine closing in 1966 as one of the last mines. From 1967 the country embarked on a path of central planning and nationalization of the mining sector. Development emphasis was on agriculture, which the Arusha Declaration of 1967 mentioned as the foundation for the country's development (Kassum 2007). Nyerere is quoted by Chachage (2010: 4) for having expressed the sentiment: 'We will leave our mineral wealth in the ground until we manage to develop our own geologists and mining engineers'. The performance of the formal mining sector declined with official gold exports falling to ten kilos in the early 1970s (Kulindwa *et al.* 2003).

Small but increasing numbers of Tanzanians, most being farmers with some experience of working in mines run by foreigners, realized the prices that gold and gemstones could earn at international markets, shifted into extra-legal artisanal mining during the 1960s and 1970s. Their output was smuggled out of the country. Meanwhile, a number of gemstone discoveries took place during those decades, notably tanzanite in 1967.

Foundations of artisanal mining

By the late 1970s, Tanzania's state-led mining was seriously under-performing. Meanwhile the 1970s oil price rises had pushed the Tanzanian agrarian economy into a state of indebtedness and dire need for foreign capital. The state sought remedial solutions, one of which was an attempt to stimulate the economic potential of mining. Tanzania's first post-independence mining legislation, the Mining Act of 1979, allowed Tanzanians to register mining claims in areas designated for prospecting and mineral mining and to engage in mining activities that did not require large investment expenditures and specialized equipment. This legislation was a vital boost to artisanal miners. Although informal artisanal mining had grown from independence to 1979, the new act coupled with increased international gold prices, saw the sector expand dramatically in the 1980s resulting in multiple discoveries of gold and gemstones throughout the country.

In 1986 Tanzania reluctantly began to implement an IMF-instigated structural adjustment programme, followed by economic liberalization policies in the 1990s, which had the effect of weakening the national economy, with particularly debilitating effects on the peasant agrarian sector, which experienced the removal of agricultural subsidies, the dismantling of agricultural marketing boards and the introduction of user fees for education and health services. These developments put increasing pressure on the livelihoods of already strained rural families. Decreasing global agricultural commodity markets had already left many people in a situation where they failed to make a living from cash cropping. As a consequence, they started to look for alternative income sources (Bryceson 2002). In mineral-rich areas, artisanal mining – especially of precious minerals – constituted a feasible, and sometimes attractive, alternative. Thus, in the mid-1990s Tanzania had an estimated 550,000 people directly involved with artisanal mining, mainly of gold and gemstones (Tan Discovery 1996). Similarly, an International Labour Office study from 1999 set the figure between 450,000 and 600,000 (ILO 1999).

Mining boom

In the late 1990s, Tanzania's government approved new mining legislation, which both provided the country's artisanal mining sector with the opportunity to embark on a process of consolidation, but simultaneously paved the way for substantial foreign mining investments (Butler 2004; Emel and Huber 2008). Mineral exports, primarily from large-scale gold mining companies increased from constituting less than one per cent of export revenues in the late 1990s to 50 per cent in 2005 (World Bank 2006). Thus, in reality, instead of strengthening the artisanal mining sector, the legislation left artisanal miners in a situation where they had to compete with international mining companies for access to the minerals; a contest they, in the decade following the legislation, often lost, as argued by Bourgouin (Chapter 9) and Lange (2008).

The boom in foreign exploration and mining investments, which came out of the investor-friendly mining legislation of the late 1990s, resulted in severe criticism of the government's capacity to govern the country's natural resource base. Discussions of limited national benefits from large-scale mining, unjust resettlement schemes of farmers, and coercion of artisanal miners dominated the mineral sector debate. The advancement of exploration and mining companies in mineral-rich areas, where artisanal miners had been operating for decades, was believed by some observers to have a negative effect on the numbers of artisanal miners, although estimates of what these numbers are remains contentious (Lange 2006; Hayes 2008).

The intensity of the debate on Tanzania's mineral sector led to yet new legislation, encompassing the Mineral Policy of 2009, and the Mining Act and Mining Regulations of 2010 (Keeler 2009; Tanzania 2009; 2010a; 2010b). This most recent mining act has attempted to counter increased voter dissatisfaction with the mining industry while maintaining a continuous in-flow of foreign investments into the mining sector (Chapter 7 and 9). As investor-friendly legislation, it does, however, extend the mining licences intended for artisanal mining from five to seven years, designating certain areas only for artisanal mining purposes, and most importantly, making it more difficult to speculate in mining licences. This is intended to curtail large and medium-scale interests obtaining exploration licences without engaging in active exploration thereafter; a practice that has reduced artisanal miners' areas of operation, pushing them into more extreme extra-legal mining activities.

Today the Tanzanian mining sector consists of one medium-scale and six large-scale gold mines and a number of proposed gold mining projects in the pipeline. The Williamson Diamond Mine (which De Beers sold to Petra Diamonds in 2008) is still producing, and Tanzania has one of the world's most advanced gemstone mines extracting tanzanite. Moreover, the country has advanced mine preparation projects targeting uranium, coal, and nickel respectively. In between these mining ventures and the country's hundreds of thousands of artisanal miners are a number of the so-called 'juniors', which are small and medium-sized exploration companies with a high skills base and professionalized management structure registered often at stock exchanges in Canada, USA, South Africa or UK. By far the largest population of miners are artisanal. A World Bank survey in 2011 estimated a total of 685,000 artisanal miners operating in the country.[6] It is their activities that we endeavour to illuminate in this edited collection.

Tanzanian artisanal miners as autotelic prime movers

Besides work by the editors of this volume, much of what has been written so far on Tanzania artisanal mining focuses on: the conflict between large-scale and artisanal mining over land and mineral entitlements (e.g. Carstens and Hilson 2009; Lange 2008, 2011); discussions on the impact of mining growth on the national economy (e.g. Chachage 1995; Emel and Huber 2008; Kulindwa *et al.* 2003; Phillips *et al.* 2001); and the environmental impact of artisanal mining (e.g. Ikingura and Akagi 1996; Kitula 2006; Taylor *et al.* 2005). While touching on these topics, our focus in this volume is on the agency of the artisanal miners, their relationship to minerals, each other, their settlements, and their working context. In Part II, we probe miners' occupationality, their migration patterns and career progression, family formation and neighbour, kin and gender relations within newly urbanizing settlements.

Tanzanian artisanal miners share an *esprit de corps* and frontier ethos. They see themselves as breaking new ground not only in the literal sense of mineral excavation, but also economically and socially, as they carve out occupational patterns and lifestyles that differ radically from the labour regimes and village communities presided over by agrarian patriarchs. In a relatively short period of time, they have asserted their presence on the Tanzanian landscape and in the interstices of the nation's political economy.[7]

It is too easily forgotten that many of Tanzania's present mining sites (Figure 1.2) were discovered by artisanal miners (Chachage 1995; Phillips *et al.* 2001). During the economically depressed days of the 1980s, as peasant farmers sought to diversify their income sources, many in Tanzania's mineral-rich regions, and particularly in the country's 'ring of gold' took to exploratory digging. As their numbers gained momentum and they began to travel further afield in their search for mineral strikes, they have pioneered new occupational norms and spatially established scores of urban settlements in far-flung areas of Tanzania (Bryceson *et al.* 2012).

Tanzanian artisanal gold miners, engaged in panning as well as digging pits, are known to shoulder exceptionally heavy risks (Chapters 2, 3 and 7). Those with agrarian roots know the hardships of agrarian uncertainty, especially food insecurity (Bryceson 1990). There is inevitably an overhang of beliefs and psychological mechanisms for coping with vagaries that somewhat incongruously surface at mining sites. Miners' association with a spate of albino murders is illustrative. The demand for albino-associated charms to ensure mining success emerged as a new variant of belief in witchdoctors' power to alter the future (Chapter 6).

However, this tragic chain reaction to the uncertainties of mining should not cloud the fact that the narrative of traditional agrarian beliefs and pre-ordained occupational destinies has largely been ignored or repudiated by the decision to mine. In the following chapters, the authors will be interrogating the decision-making of miners and residents of mining settlements at work, in family and community life and during leisure-time pursuits. Our agency approach focuses on miners' navigation through the economic hurdles, social opportunities, cultural ambiguities and political dynamics of Tanzania's rapidly expanding artisanal mining settlements. It also traces creative encounters with external agents in negotiation or confrontation over access to land and mineral resources (Chapter 5). In so doing, we provide abundant evidence to challenge notions of artisanal miners as economically irrational, socially destabilizing, and politically dissociated.

Recognizing the experimental autotelic process involved in becoming and being a miner centring on a relatively mobile life (Chapter 2) is foundational to understanding miners' career trajectories (Chapter 3) and the high incidence of fractured domestic family lives and open-ended sexuality in mining settlements (Chapter 4). The material outcomes and moral dilemmas arising from unequal distributions of land, mineral rights and economic opportunities are analyzed in Chapter 5. Contestation over land and mineral rights amongst migrant miners and longer-term residents of mining settlements involves collaborative and sometimes collusive relations. Miners' spiritual beliefs and sense of morality in the high-risk environment of mining settlements are interrogated in Chapter 6.

Part III delves into the institutional constructs surrounding mining communities, probing marketing infrastructure and ethical trade, and the policy context enveloping artisanal mineral production and distribution. Chapter 7 documents the evolution of organizational conventions in artisanal mining production and the innovative decision-making taking place at mining sites. Chapter 8 discusses aspects of the global market for minerals, focusing on the expansion of ethical trade initiatives in tandem with the rise of voluntary standards and the potential these initiatives have for realizing development benefits for artisanal miners. Thereafter, the interface between large-scale and artisanal mining is discussed at a policy level (Chapter 9). National policies often pay lip service to artisanal miners but nonetheless the actual implementation of such policies tends to constrain rather than encourage artisanal mining, posing the question of the future of artisanal mining as foreign direct investment in large-scale mining grows. Chapter 10 is an in-depth analysis of the practice of *ubeshi* in which the removal of diamond tailings from a large-scale diamond mine by nearby artisanal miners, results in a complex interplay of intrigue and accommodation between artisanal and large-scale mining.

The authors of the case study chapters represent an array of social science disciplines comprising geography, sociology, anthropology and politics. Methodologically, their data collection varies with respect to its emphasis on qualitative interviewing or quantitative survey data collection. So too, their conceptual approaches differ, but all the chapters are centred on documentation and analysis of current occupational and lifestyle transformation in Tanzania's mining settlements.

Our concluding chapter returns to the issue of miners as autotelic craftsmen, picking up on the question of autocratic or democratizing tendencies in artisanal mining, and suggesting ways in which democratic forms of production and consumption are expanding as well as being challenged within the mining settlement and nationally. Gazing into the future, democratic challenges are particularly apparent in relation to the spatial limits of the artisanal mining frontier – the point at which mineralizing and democratizing trends bifurcate and the all too finite nature of mineral resources appropriate for artisanal extraction becomes exposed. We end with a delineation of four African mining complexes as a way of juxtaposing the democratic and autocratic tendencies that exist across Sub-Saharan Africa's varied mining contexts.

While it is readily apparent to those who visit Africa's mineral-rich regions that artisanal mining has cohered as an occupation and way of life, the topic of mining in Africa nonetheless inevitably conjures up the image of large-scale corporate production. It is myopic if not perilous to ignore the significance of artisanal mining for the miners, their families, the mining settlements and African nation-states in which artisanal mining is proliferating. Therefore, this collection is directed at enhancing awareness of artisanal mining's contribution to the social, political and economic future of the African continent.

Notes

1   Personal communication with Mathias de Alencastro, 22 January 2013.
2   Estimated worldwide employment at 13 out of the 20 corporate members of the International Council on Mining and Metals totalled 674,625 (namely Alcoa, AngloAmerican plc, AngloGold Ashanti, BHP Billiton, Freeport McMoRan, Goldfields, Goldcorp, Lonmin, Mitsubishi Materials, Newmont, Rio Tinto Group, Xstrata and Vale) Available from http://en.wikipedia.org/wiki/International_ Council_on_Mining_and_Metals (accessed 12 February 2013).
3   Provisional estimate according to Professor Crispin Kinabo of the Geology Department, University of Dar es Salaam.
4   The mines were: Resolute's Golden Pride, Geita Gold Mine, Bulyanhulu and North Mara. Tellingly Roe and Essex (2009) estimate that Tanzania's mining future could account for: 60–90 per cent of foreign direct investment, 30–60 per cent of national exports, 3–20 per cent of government revenues, 3–10 per cent of national income and only 1–2 per cent of employment (Roe and Essex 2009: 11).
5   The miners' struggle has been seen as anti-colonialist, championing a diggers' charter demanding the democratic rights of the working man. Three years later, a bill was passed that granted universal manhood suffrage in the Victorian parliament. Twenty-two miners and six soldiers died in the uprising (Cassin 2004; Mckenry 2008).
6   See endnote 3 above.
7   Hortense Powdermaker (1965) documented a similar process of change on the Rhodesian Copperbelt in the 1950s.

References

Alder, C., Large, D. and De Oliveira, R.S. (2009) *China Returns to Africa: A Visiting Power and a Continent Embrace*. New York: Colombia University Press.

Barrington Moore, Jr (1991 [1966]) *Social Origins of Dictatorship and Democracy*. London: Penguin Books.

Bates, R.H. (1971) *Unions, Parties and Political Development: A Study of Mineworkers in Zambia*. New Haven, CT and London: Yale University Press.

Bleischwitz, R., Dittrich, M. and Pierdicca, C. (2012) 'Coltan from Central Africa: International trade and implications for any certification'. *Resources Policy* 37: 19–29.

Brautigam, D. (2009) *The Dragon's Gift: The Real Story of China in Africa*. Oxford: Oxford University Press.

Bryceson, D.F. (1990) *Food Insecurity and the Social Division of Labour in Tanzania, 1919–1985*. London: Macmillan.

Bryceson, D.F. (2002) 'The scramble in Africa: Reorienting rural livelihoods', *World Development* 30(5): 725–39.

Bryceson, D.F. (2010) 'Africa at work: Transforming occupational identity and morality', in Bryceson, D.F. (ed.) *How Africa Works: Occupational Change, Identity and Morality*, Rugby: Practical Action Publishing. pp. 3–26.

Bryceson, D.F. and MacKinnon, D. (2012) 'Eureka and beyond: Mining's impact on African urbanisation', *Journal of Contemporary African Studies*. 30(4): 513–37.

Bryceson, D.F., Jønsson, J.B., Kinabo, C. and Shand, M. (2012) 'Unearthing treasure and trouble: Mining as an impetus to urbanisation in Tanzania'. *Journal of Contemporary African Studies* 30(4): 631–49.

Burawoy, M. (1972) *The Colour of Class on the Copper Mines: From African Advancement to Zambianisation*. Manchester: Manchester University Press.

Bush, R. (2008) 'Scrambling to the bottom? Mining, resources and underdevelopment'. *Review of African Political Economy* 35(117): 361–8.

Butler, P. (2004) 'Tanzania: Liberalisation of investment and the mining sector analysis of the content and certain implications of the Tanzanian 1998 Mining Act'. in Campbell, B. (ed.) *Regulating Mining in Africa: For Whose Benefits?* Uppsala, Sweden: Nordic Africa Institute. pp. 67–80.

Campbell, G. (2004) *Blood Diamonds*. New York: Basic Books.

Carstens, J. and Hilson, G. 2009. 'Mining and grievance in rural Tanzania'. *International Development Planning Review* 31(3): 301–26.

CASM (Communities and Small-scale Mining) (2008) 'Miners' map'. Available from www.artisanalmining.org/casm/minersmap (accessed 30 December 2012).

Cassin, R. (2004) 'The Eureka project is unfinished', 3 December, 2004. Available from www.theage.com.au/news/Opinion/The-Eureka-project-is-unfinished/2004/12/02/1101923263712.html (accessed 22 November 2012).

Chachage, C.S.L. (1995) 'The meek shall inherit the earth but not the mining rights: Mining and accumulation in Tanzania'. in Gibbon, P. (ed.) *Liberalised Development in Tanzania*. Uppsala, Sweden: Nordic Africa Institute. pp. 37–108.

Chachage, C. (2010). 'Mwalimu in our popular imagination: The relevance of Nyerere today'. in Cassam, A. and Chachage, C. (eds). *Africa's Liberation: The Legacy of Nyerere*. Oxford: Pambazuka Press. pp. 3–6.

Crush, H., Jeeves, A. and Yudelman, D. (1991) *South Africa's Labor Empire: A History of Black Migrancy in the Mines*. Cape Town, South Africa: David Philip.

Crush, J. (1994) 'Scripting the compound: Power and space in the South African mining industry', *Environment and Planning D: Society and Space* 12: 301–24.

De Boeck, F. (1999) 'Domesticating diamonds and dollars: Identity, expenditure and sharing in Southwestern Zaire (1984–1997)'. in Meyer, B. and Geschiere, P. (eds) *Globalisation and Identity: Dialectics of Flow and Closure*. Oxford: Blackwell Publishers. pp. 177–209.

De Tocqueville, A. (2003 [1835]) *Democracy in America* (Translator Bevan, G.E.). London: Penguin Books.

Dietrich, C. (2000) 'Power struggles in the diamond fields' in Cilliers, J. and Dietrich, C. (eds) *Angola's War Economy: The Role of Oil and Diamonds*. Pretoria, South Africa: Institute of Social Studies. pp. 173–94.

Elkins, S. and McKitrick, E. (1954) 'A meaning for Turner's frontier: Part I: Democracy in the old Northwest'. *Political Science Quarterly* 69(3): 321–53.

Emel, J. and Huber, M.T. (2008) 'A risky business: Mining, rent and the neoliberalization of "risk"'. *Geoforum* 39(3): 1393–407.

Epstein, A.L. (1958) *Politics in an Urban African Community*. New York: Humanities Press.

Geenen, S. (2012) 'A dangerous bet: The challenges of formalizing artisanal mining in the DRC'. *Resources Policy* 37(3): 322–30.

Gilmore, E., Gleditsch, N.P., Lujala, P. and Rød, J. (2005) 'Conflict diamonds: A new dataset'. *Conflict Management and Peace Science* 22: 257–72.

Global Witness (2012) 'Civilians caught in crossfire as M23 rebels take Goma'. 20 November 2012. Available from www.globalwitness.org/library/civilians-caught-crossfire-m23-rebels-take-goma (accessed 10 January 2013).

Gordon, R.J. (1977) *Mines, Masters and Migrants: Life in a Namibian Mine Compound*. Johannesburg: Raven Press.

Grätz, T. (2002) 'Gold mining communities in Northern Benin as semi-autonomous social fields' [Working paper no. 36]. Halle, Germany: Max Planck Institute for Social Anthropology.

Hayes, K. (2008) *Artisanal and Small-scale Mining and Livelihoods in Africa.* Amsterdam: Common Fund for Commodities.

Hilson, G. and Potter, C. (2005). 'Structural adjustment and subsistence industry: Artisanal gold mining in Ghana'. *Development and Change* 36(1): 103–31.

ICMM (International Council on Mining and Minerals) (2012) *The Role of Mining in National Economies.* London: ICMM.

Ikingura, J.R. and Akagi, H. (1996) 'Monitoring of fish and human exposure to mercury due to gold mining in the Lake Victoria Goldfields, Tanzania'. *Science of the Total Environment* 191(1–2): 59–68.

ILO (International Labour Organization) (1999) 'Social and labour issues in small-scale mines: Report for discussion at the tripartite meeting on social and labour issues in small-scale mines'. Geneva: International Labour Organization.

Jeeves, A. (1985) *Migrant Labour in South Africa's Mining Economy: The Struggle for the Gold Mines' Labour Supply, 1890–1920.* Johannesburg: Witwatersrand University Press.

Johnson, S.L. (2000) *Roaring Camp: The Social World of the California Gold Rush.* New York: W. W. Norton.

Jønsson, J.B. and Fold, N. (2011) 'Mining from below: Taking Africa's artisanal miners seriously'. *Geography Compass* 5(7): 479–93.

Kapferer, B. (1976) 'Conflict and process in a Zambian mine community'. in Aranoff, M. (ed.) *Freedom and Constraint.* Amsterdam: Van Gorcum, Assen. pp. 50–82.

Kassum, A.N. (2007) *Africa's Winds of Change: Memoirs of an International Tanzanian.* New York: I.B. Tauris.

Keeler, R. (2009) *Tanzania Mining Industry: Revenues, Resentment and Overregulation?* Available from www.ratio-magazine.com/20090721815/Tanzania/Tanzania-Mining-Industry-Revenues-Resentment-and-Overregulation.html (accessed 14 December 2012).

Kitula, A.G.N. (2006) 'The environmental and socio-economic impacts of mining on local livelihoods in Tanzania: A case study of Geita District'. *Journal of Cleaner Production* 14(3–4): 405–14.

Kulindwa, K., Mashindano, O., Shechambo, F. and Sosovele, H. (2003) *Mining for Sustainable Development in Tanzania.* Dar es Salaam: Dar es Salaam University Press.

Lange, S. (2006) 'Benefit streams from mining in Tanzania: Case studies from Geita and Mererani' [Report R2006.1]. Bergen, Norway: Christian Michelson Institute.

Lange, S. (2008) 'Land tenure and mining in Tanzania'. Bergen Norway: Chr. Michelsen Institute.

Lange, S. (2011) 'Gold and governance: Legal injustices and lost opportunities in Tanzania'. *African Affairs* 110(439): 233–52.

Larmer, M. (2011) *Rethinking African Politics: A History of Opposition in Zambia.* Farnham: Ashgate.

Le Billon, P. (2008) 'Diamond wars? Conflict diamonds and geographies of resource wars'. *Annals of the Association of American Geographers* 98(2): 345–72.

Lemelle, S.J. (1986) *Capital, State and Labor: A History of the Gold Mining Industry in Colonial Tanganyika 1890–1942.* PhD thesis, University of California, Los Angeles.

Luning, S. (2006) 'Artisanal gold mining in Burkina Faso: Permits, poverty and perceptions of the poor in Sanmatenga, the "land of gold"'. in Hilson, G. (ed.) *Small-scale Mining, Rural Subsistence and Poverty in West Africa.* Rugby: Intermediate Technology Publications Ltd. pp. 135–47.

Mabhena, C. (2012) 'Mining with a "Vuvuzela": Reconfiguring artisanal mining in Zimbabwe and its implications to rural livelihoods. *Journal of Contemporary African Studies* 30(2): 219–33.

Maconachie, R. and Binns, T. (2007) '"Farming miners" or "mining farmers"': Diamond mining and rural development in post-conflict Sierra Leone'. *Journal of Rural Studies* 23(3): 367–80.

Mckenry, K. (2008) 'The ballads of Eureka'. *Journal of Australian Colonial History* 10(1): 51–74.

Mitchell, T. (2009) 'Carbon democracy'. *Economy and Society* 38(3): 399–432.

Moodie, T.D. (1994) *Going for Gold: Men, Mines and Migration*. Berkeley: University of California Press.

Pearce, J. (2004) 'War, peace and diamonds in Angola: Popular perceptions of the diamond industry in the Lundas', *African Security Review* 13(2): 51–64.

Pearce, J. (2005) *An Outbreak of Peace: Angola's Situation of Confusion*. Claremont, South Africa: David Philip.

Phillips, L.C., Semboja, H., Shukla, G.P., Sezinga, R., Mutagwaba, W., Mchwampaka, B., Wanga, G., Kahyarara, G. and Keller, C. (2001) 'Tanzania's precious mineral boom: Issues in mining and marketing'. Washington, DC: USAID.

Phimister, I.R. (1988) *An Economic and Social History of Zimbabwe, 1890–1948: Capital Accumulation and Class Struggle*. Harlow: Longman.

Powdermaker, H. (1965) *Copper Town: Changing Africa – The Human Situation on the Rhodesian Copperbelt*. New York: Harper.

Raeymakers, T. (2010) 'Protection for sale? War and the transformation of regulation on the Congo-Ugandan border'. *Development and Change* 41(4): 563–87.

Richards, P. (1996) *Fighting for the Rain Forests: War, Youth and Resources in Sierra Leone*. London: Villiers Publications.

Robinson, E.W. (2004) *Ancient Greek Democracy: Readings and Sources*. Oxford: Blackwell Publishing Ltd.

Robinson, J.A., Torvik, R. and Verdier, T. (2006) 'Political foundations of the resource curse'. *Journal of Development Economics* 79(2): 447–68.

Rodrigues, C. and Tavares, A.P. (2012) 'Angola's planned and unplanned urban growth: Diamond mining towns in the Lunda Provinces'. *Journal of Contemporary African Studies* 30(4): 687–703.

Roe, A.R. and Essex, M. (2009) 'Mining in Tanzania: What future can we expect?' Paper presented at the ICMM Workshop on Mining in Tanzania, Dar es Salaam, 18 May, 2009 (revised 28 June 2009). Oxford: Oxford Policy Management.

Sachs, J.D. and Warner, A.M. (2001) 'The curse of natural resources'. *European Economic Review* 45: 827–38.

Sennett, R. (2008) *The Craftsman*. London: Penguin Books.

Shand, M. and Jønsson, J.B. (2013) 'UPIMA unpublished project data compiled from Jønsson's updated Tanzanian inventory of small-scale mine locations'.

Spiegel, S. and Veiga, M. M. (2009) 'Artisanal and small-scale mining as an extralegal economy: De Soto and the redefinition of "formalization"'. *Resources Policy* 34(1–2): 51–6.

Steffen, J.O. (1983) 'The mining frontiers of California and Australia: A study in comparative political change and continuity'. *Pacific Historical Review* 52(4): 428–40.

Tan Discovery (1996) 'Final report on baseline survey and preparation of development strategy for small scale and artisanal mining program'. Dar es Salaam: Ministry of Energy and Minerals/World Bank.

Tanzania, United Republic of (2009) *The Mineral Policy of Tanzania.* [Ministry of Energy and Minerals]. Dar es Salaam: Government Printers.

Tanzania, United Republic of (2010a) *The Mining Act 2010.* [Ministry of Energy and Minerals]. Dar es Salaam: Government Printers.

Tanzania, United Republic of (2010b) *The Mining Regulations 2010.* [Ministry of Energy and Minerals]. Dar es Salaam: Government Printers.

Taylor, H., Appleton, J.D., Lister, R., Smith, B., Chitamweba, D. and Mkumbo, O. (2005) 'Environmental assessment of mercury contamination from the Rwamagasa artisanal gold mining centre, Geita district Tanzania'. *The Science of the Total Environment* 343(1–3): 111–33.

UNCTAD (United Nations Conference on Trade and Development) (2007) *World Investment Report: Transnational Corporations, Extractive Industries and Development.* Geneva: United Nations.

United States Geological Survey (2010) *Mineral Commodity Summaries.* Available from http://geology.com/articles/gem-diamond-map/ (accessed 15 November 2012).

Walsh, A. (2003) '"Hot money" and daring consumption in a northern Malagasy sapphire-mining town'. *American Ethnologist* 30(2): 290–305.

Werthmann, K. and Grätz, T. (2012) *Mining Frontiers: Anthropological and Historical Perspectives* [Mainzer Beiträge zur Afrikaforschung, vol. 32]. Cologne, Germany: Rüdiger Köppe Verlag.

Wilson, F. (2001) 'Minerals and migrants: How the mining industry has shaped South Africa'. *Daedalus* 130(1): 99–121.

Wolpe, H. (1972) 'Capitalism and cheap labour power in South Africa: From segregation to apartheid', *Economy and Society* 1(4): 425–54.

World Bank (2006) 'Tanzania mining sector review' [Report No. AB2029]. Washington, DC: World Bank.

Yager, T.R. (2010) 'The mineral industry of Tanzania'. in *2010 Minerals Yearbook of the United States* Geological Survey. Available from http://minerals.usgs.gov/minerals/pubs/country/2010/myb3-2010-tz.pdf (accessed 12 December 2012).

Part I

Miners' agency and social relations

2 Going for gold

Miners' mobility and mining motivation[1]

Jesper Bosse Jønsson and Deborah Fahy Bryceson

Contracting global markets for African smallholder agricultural exports have triggered large-scale processes of de-agrarianization and a search for alternative sources of income for hard-pressed rural households since the late 1970s (Bryceson 2000). In the search, some have literally struck gold. Little, however, has been written about artisanal miners' mobility and their rush to mine following a mineral strike. Neither the artisanal mining literature nor the burgeoning field of migration studies has focused on the migration patterns of African artisanal miners. This contrasts with the deluge of analyses and legends associated with gold rushes of the past, notably those occurring in Northern California in the mid-19th century and the Canadian Yukon five decades later (Berton 1994; Brands 2003). Migrants flocked to these locations in the hopes of becoming wealthy.

Tanzanian gold miners are similarly motivated by a quest for riches in an otherwise depressed agrarian landscape. Over the last three decades, rushes to mining sites of gold have proliferated, often leading to massive influxes of people. Amidst the panoply of material outcomes for those involved, local service economies are dynamized with profound socio-economic and ecological implications (Bryceson and Mwaipopo 2009; Hentschel *et al.* 2002; Hilson 2002).

The mobility of Tanzanian artisanal gold miners is spurred by the availability of gold as a high value commodity, on the one hand, counterbalanced by the risks of a livelihood crisis in the absence of striking gold. The miners face, in an extreme form, migrants' essential trade-off between the security and knowledge of their *in situ* location as opposed to the uncertain outcome of venturing to a new, potentially far more promising, locality. Migrants' estimation of the risks as opposed to the rewards is thwarted by the lack of reliable information about the alternative site.

This chapter probes artisanal miners' livelihood and mobility decision-making by analyzing a relatively new gold strike location and an older, long-established mine site. The first section outlines how understanding gold miners' mobility patterns requires going beyond the existing livelihood and migration literature on Africa to highlight decision-making agency with respect to uncertainty and risk. This is followed by a description of our field methodology and an analysis of our survey findings on miners' mobility strategies and material outcomes. A narrative of a neophyte miner's early mining experiences illustrates several of our quantitative survey findings, before concluding with a summary and returning to the issue of how miners contend with livelihood and mobility decision-making in the face of high levels of uncertainty.

Economic migration with a different impetus and momentum

Sub-Saharan Africa's migration literature focuses primarily on urban migration (Baker and Aina 1995; Toure and Fadayomi 1992). Todaro (1969) weighed the opportunity costs of migrating against the expected wage earnings of prospective migrants, a calculation that does not relate to miners' circumstances. More recently, the migration literature has stressed forced movement of refugees and transnational brain-drain movement, neither of which sheds light on miners' mobility (Colson 2003).

What is missing in both literatures is a focus on risk, central to an understanding of gold miners' movements and how, on the basis of enormous uncertainty, they nonetheless have started building career paths in gold mining. Tanzanian miners have moved beyond the concerns of the mainstream livelihood literature in terms of coping, experimenting and adapting their work. They are instead concentrating on the pursuit of minerals in a window of opportunity afforded by high world market prices for gold and current liberalized Tanzanian government policies.

Ulrich Beck (1999) writes of increasing livelihood uncertainty, casualization of labour, the fragility of work and material insecurity worldwide. He rejects the concept of postmodernity, arguing instead for recognition of the existence of a neo-liberal 'second modernity' in which escalating risk and uncertainty drives decision-making. He contrasts the Western ideal of rational control and insurance in a 'man-made hybrid world' with the unintended consequences of modernization and the uninsured 'residual risk' world where material insecurity is the norm (Beck 1999: 53, 149). His concept of the sociology of risk and the calculus of realms of the known, the unknown and the unperceived are pertinent to our study of Tanzanian miners.

Beck's (1999) stress on the denial of the inability to know and loss of dualism between nature and culture in the Western world is illustrated by economists' risk decision-making models posited on the optimizing individual and neo-classical micro-scale economic analyses of rational behaviour. Game theory models based on the probability of outcomes in the sphere of the unknown assume that decision-making agents behave rationally by heuristically calculating their odds for success or failure (Harsanyi 1973; Myerson 1991). Amartya Sen (1998) argues that perceiving decision-making in a situation of partial knowledge with probability frequencies raises philosophical questions. Epistemologically, there may be a fuzzy distinction between calculable risk and incalculable uncertainty.

It is in this grey area that Beck's work affords greatest insight, questioning rational behaviour in the face of uncertainty, raising distinctions between types of uncertainty and the interaction of economic and sociological decision-making and its outcomes vis-à-vis the unknown. Risk regimes can be differentiated through historical time and space, leading to quite distinct epistemological premises about the known and unknown. Foucault (1970) observed that before the Enlightenment, magical knowledge and scientific knowledge in Europe were interchangeable. People relied heavily on symbolic representation and analogy to understand and act on reality. In place of probability calculations or authoritative assessment of risk by public bodies, decision-making agents sought meaning in symbols and supernatural signs to point them in the direction of the right decision. In making mining a livelihood and choosing mining sites to work, the inability to know and still less to control outcomes leads to various ways of rationalizing and coping emotionally with the uncertainty. It is within this risk framework that we trace Tanzanian miners' decision-making about their livelihood and mobility.

Tanzanian miners' decision to move to their first mining site is a livelihood choice based on restricted information. Subsequent decisions to move have the benefit of miners' greater knowledge about mining as well as heightened awareness of how much they do not know about the next site. The decision to migrate for gold mining contains multiple uncertainties of livelihood failure, family separation, accidents, physical attack, disease and destitution. Miners must be willing to endure these risks in their quest for striking gold.

Exploring the risk/reward calculus that has propelled Tanzanian artisanal miners to move, we probe their views about the role of mobility in achieving a gold strike given that in the majority of cases they have moved at least once and in many cases several times. To do this we examine miners' biographical profiles, their motivation to mine, calculable and incalculable risks and ways of coping with uncertainty, their pattern of movement between mining sites and their success as gold miners. We probe how miners locationally navigate a striking career in the face of great risk and uncertainty.

Comprehending strike behaviour: Getting there fast

A gold strike is difficult to conceal. Mining supplies need to be purchased and the minerals sold. Miners, bragging and inviting friends and relatives to join them, rapidly make the discovery a public secret. Once the rumours reach adjacent villages and the wider artisanal mining community, people arrive within days rather than months and small villages may balloon into settlements of thousands in a matter of weeks. Rising mobile phone use and coverage throughout rural Tanzania has accelerated the speed and numbers of people rushing to newly discovered sites. Clearly, for the lucky and knowledgeable ones, a mineral rush presents an opportunity to earn relatively large amounts of money. However, late arrival or what is termed lack of luck means that some miners return home empty-handed. The duration of mineral rushes varies depending on the extent of the gold deposit and the legal status of the artisanal miners. Most settle for longer periods of time only in the most mineral-rich areas, which will then develop into more permanent settlements (Bryceson and Mwaipopo 2009).

Tracing artisanal miners' mobility is greatly hampered by the lack of accurate population data in mining settlements. The dynamism of mining populations is not remotely hinted at in Tanzania's population censuses of 1988 and 2002.[2] While artisanal mining in Tanzania is legal, local government authorities are not required nor in a position to keep count of the incoming and outgoing migrant population of their settlements. Mine rushes are often distant from a pre-existing population and develop as settlements with limited official awareness let alone recognition as a settlement. Thus, our study was designed with these constraints in mind. The field research, upon which this and the following chapter as well as Chapter 7, is based, was conducted for twelve months within the 'ring of gold' at two artisanal gold mining settlements, Matundasi and Londoni (Figures 1.2 and 2.1), between July 2006 and February 2008.

The village of Matundasi, located in Chunya district of Mbeya region in south-western Tanzania, has been an active mining settlement since the 1930s (Roberts 1986). Back then, the present sub-village of Itumbi had several hard rock mines owned by Europeans, most of whom left around independence. Some artisanal

Figure 2.1 Location of Londoni and Matundasi research sites

miners continue to exploit the old pits and tunnels previously developed. The legalization of artisanal mining and rise in the price of gold has transformed Matundasi during the last two decades. Whereas the village had only one small shop in the early 1980s, with residents travelling 100 kilometres to the town of Mbeya for most supplies, present day Matundasi is a pulsating centre with several service facilities and, according to a 2007 village survey, 7,640 residents. At the time, the village had around 1,500 artisanal miners, who mined alluvial or hard rock gold deposits as their sole livelihood. Moreover, nearly all capable residents engage in seasonal alluvial gold mining in order to supplement their income from agriculture. Of the 1,500 active miners, only nine owned Primary Mining Licenses (PMLs) as most remaining land in Matundasi is held by commercial companies with prospecting licenses.

Londoni is a village located on the border between the districts of Manyoni and Singida Rural in Singida region in central Tanzania. After a herder with mining aspirations discovered gold in 2004, the news rapidly reached the Tanzanian artisanal mining community. People started arriving within weeks and Londoni expanded from a village with 1,600 residents involved in subsistence farming and two small shops into a lively settlement with a number of service facilities and an estimated population of over 10,000. Alluvial surface deposits were quickly depleted and since 2005, miners almost exclusively engaged in hard rock mining. As of 2009, miners held a total of 215 PMLs in Londoni, having secured a large area designated for artisanal mining by putting pressure on key politicians in 2004 and 2005, prior to the 2005 election. The gender ratio of Londoni was heavily biased towards men, of whom the preponderant majority was within the economically active ages of 20 to 40 years.

With the aim of gaining insight into miners' mobility patterns throughout their work life cycle, we conducted an age-stratified random sample survey of 45 miners[3] and 9 former miners[4] in each of the two study settlements for a total of 108 respondents.[5] Many artisanal miners are wary of and resistant to outsiders for various reasons. Whereas some are involved in illicit forms of mining, others are suspicious of potential rivals in pursuit of mineral-rich land. Thus, creating trust with miners was vital. This was done by getting familiarized with the communities through meetings and participation in various activities, which helped miners feel comfortable when discussing sensitive topics.

All of the 108 survey respondents in our sample were men.[6] Seventy-seven per cent originated from rural areas, which is exactly the same as the national average in the 2002 national census (NBS 2002). They came from 27 of Tanzania's approximately 125 tribes, with birthplaces spanning 19 of the 25 regions of mainland Tanzania. There was a heavy concentration coming from Tanzania's five traditional gold mining regions (79 per cent).[7] Although both study areas were situated far from the home area of the Sukuma tribe, the largest ethnic group (22 per cent) represented in the sample were Sukuma. The Sukuma's tribal area south of Lake Victoria is known for its longstanding gold discoveries and the mining skills of its people.[8] The tribe, being of agro-pastoralist origin, has traditionally been associated with high mobility and migratory expansion (Madulu 1998;

Sanders 2001). Some Sukuma miners travel great distances, including to neighbouring countries, in their quest for mining opportunities. However, they are not alone in their willingness to be mobile in pursuit of gold.

Miners' mobility strategies

In rural Tanzania, farming and livestock keeping have defined people's occupational identity. Their engagement in non-farm activities has in the past been largely perceived as resulting from adversity. Often, money earned from such activities was invested back in agriculture. At the outset of the mineral boom, mining was therefore seen as temporary employment until sufficient money was earned to return to farming (Madulu 1998). However, a growing disenchantment with farming as a way of life, particularly amongst the younger generation, has surfaced (Bryceson 1999; Mwamfupe 1998). Tanzania's rural population has been consciously diversifying its income-earning into non-agricultural activities. Artisanal mining is potentially one of the most lucrative activities: with easy entry that does not require starting capital investment on the part of mine workers.

Gold mining sites in Tanzania may be makeshift with infrastructural deficiencies but they are extremely cosmopolitan places inhabited by miners' who are highly mobile. The 108 survey respondents had chalked up 293 site visits to 70 different sites, spending an average of 3.4 years per site. Of the ten most visited sites, nine were well-known artisanal gold mining sites. On average, individual miners had worked in 2.7 sites: Londoni respondents reported 3.1 sites, while the more sedentary Matundasi respondents reported 2.4 sites.

A general pattern of movement was discernible (Figure 2.2). Most respondents began mining close to their place of birth. Of the miners who started to mine in another region, the majority had relations there or had worked close to the mining site. There was a distinct difference between respondents' behaviour pertaining to their first mining site and subsequent mining sites. Proximity and attachment to home played a significant role in miners' locational entry to mining.

The original motivation was centred on livelihood improvement. From their second mining site onwards, miners' decisions to move were driven by opportunities embedded in the collegial networks necessary for building a mining career, namely: new site information, pit access, and loan support. Miners tended to end up increasingly further away from the security of their home areas as they moved from site to site. Travelling considerable distances in their quest for gold, motivated by mineral rushes and other mining opportunities, they accepted continued material hardship and separation from family as part of their work. Significantly, the sources of information prompting their decision to move on were fellow miners instead of relatives and friends. Essentially, they were committing themselves increasingly to a mining lifestyle, becoming part of the mining fraternity with its own work norms and career path.

More time was spent at the first mining site compared to subsequent sites. Some were reluctant to move away from the security of mining close to home and only slowly built up the confidence and skills to move on. At the first site, people

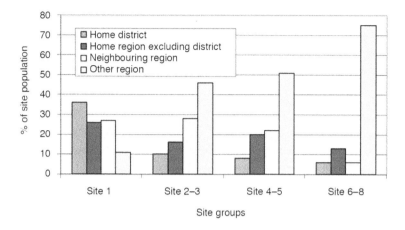

Figure 2.2 Location of miners' mining sites relative to their birthplace
Source: Authors' survey data, 2006–2002

learned how to mine and socially interact within the mining settlement, gradually identifying themselves as miners and becoming part of a miners' network. At the succeeding sites, they spent considerably less time, as they focused on the material rewards from mining and left when the gold was depleted or another site with higher prospects was found. Thus, whereas miners spent an average of 67 months in their first mining site, they spent only 37 months in other sites.

Table 2.1 shows the percentage of miners according to the number of sites they had worked. At the two extremes, over a third had worked one site whereas a tiny minority (4 per cent) were veterans of 7–8 sites. Given their extensive experience, they were usually known as experts (*wataalam* or *wabongosi*).

Table 2.1 Miners' number of sites worked

Sites worked	No. of miners	Percentage of total
1	39	36.1
2	19	17.6
3	18	16.7
4	14	13.0
5	8	7.4
6	6	5.6
7	2	1.9
8	2	1.9

Source: Authors' survey data, 2006–2008

We examine miners' site mobility with respect to their age and stage of career below. Miners do not move to new sites in a rash way but rather on the basis of calculated decision-making. After arriving at a mining site they concentrate their efforts there for some time to achieve economic gain. Outside of the initial alluvial panning for gold in a few sites, a miner must participate in teamwork to dig for gold, manoeuvring issues of land rights, equipment access, skill compatibility, work hierarchy, and inter-personal work compatibility that take time and effort to become viable.

Each successive site represents new opportunities as well as fresh problems. Survey responses revealed that the advantages of a new site were overwhelmingly weighted towards the productive opportunities of finding gold or other precious minerals (45 per cent) and achieving a viable or improved livelihood (39 per cent). Only seven per cent mentioned proximity to home as a main advantage. The remaining nine per cent gave an array of reasons including having fun, being with lots of people from their home area and getting married.

Respondents' main problems related to the declining productivity of the site (46 per cent), followed by tenure problems (19 per cent), bad working conditions (16 per cent) and limited security (10 per cent). These obstacles became catalysts for movement to another site. Low returns on the existing site (41 per cent) was the major push factor while news of a mineral strike elsewhere (23 per cent) was the major pull factor. Only 10 per cent mentioned the need to go home. Nonetheless, after leaving a mining site, 37 per cent went home, some with earnings from mining, others sick and penniless. They returned home for a variety of reasons: to recoup their position, wait for a gold strike elsewhere, see family, or recuperate from illness. Fifty-nine per cent of respondents went directly to another mining site, indicating their focused commitment to mining as a livelihood and occupational identity. A mere 3 per cent went elsewhere after their mining exit.

Open entry

Artisanal mining is an open-entry occupation. People join or disengage from it at any age. The men in our sample had on average started mining in 1995, with the earliest year being 1974 and the latest 2006. Youths began mining as early as 12 years old, but on average, miners started mining at the age of 24. To trace the nature of miners' mobility and its impact on the progression of their career, we have divided the respondents into five cohorts relating to the year[9] and age when they started mining (Table 2.2). It is notable that 'experienced adults' have spent the least time at each site before moving on. They may be on a trajectory of higher mobility than their older colleagues.

Table 2.3 reveals that the longer the respondents mined, the more sites they worked and the less time they spent at each site. Most miners were compelled to be mobile in order to continue their mining activities over a number of years. Mineral deposits get depleted and miners move on. However, the fact that the oldest miners (over 52 years) do not appear in the 6–8 site group may suggest that

Table 2.2 Career characteristics of mining age/experience cohorts

Mining cohorts	Cohort defining characteristics		No. of people	A Current average age	B Average entry age at Site 1 (years)	C Duration of mine work (years)	D % of lifetime as miner	E Average number of sites	F Average years at each site
	Age	Year mining started							
Beginner youths	<26	2004 onwards	16	20	19	1.1	5.5	1.2	1.0
Beginner adults	>25	2004 onwards	7	41	39	1.8	4.4	1.1	1.5
Experienced youths	<26	Before 2004	14	20	14	5.9	29.5	1.7	3.4
Experienced adults	>25	1990–2003	39	38	26	9.4	24.7	3.1	3.1
Old Timers	>25	Before 1990	32	48	26	16.5	34.4	3.8	4.3
Survey Average			108	36	24	9.3	25.8	2.7	3.4

Source: Authors' survey data, 2006–2008

Table 2.3 Comparison of age/experience cohorts with site cohorts

Sites worked	Number of people	Age	Duration of mine work (years)	Time at each site (months)	Beginner youths (%)	Experienced youths (%)	Beginner adults (%)	Experienced adults (%)	Old timers (%)
1	39	29	6	67	87.5	64.3	85.7	15.4	12.5
2–3	37	39	10	48	12.5	21.4	14.3	53.8	31.3
4–5	22	40	12	34	0	14.3	0	20.5	37.5
6–8	10	41	15	28	0	0	0	10.3	18.8

Source: Authors' survey data, 2006–2008

miners' mobility has started accelerating quite recently amongst proactive youths and middle-aged miners.

To understand miners' mobility, it is necessary to reflect on miners' overall motivations to mine. One fifth of the respondents saw mining as a way to provide a livelihood for their families. Thirty-seven per cent were consumption-oriented, seeking to raise their standard of living materially through mining. A third was primarily business-oriented, seeking profit and expansion. Less than five per cent saw mining as a means of supplementing their farming pursuits. 'Beginner youths' with limited material possessions were the most consumption-oriented (65 per cent), whereas adults were more apt to cite family needs and commercial business as their main motivation for mining.

Miners with a low number of site visits were consumption or family-oriented. As the number of sites mounted, commercial mining, business, and family support dominated and farming plans played an insignificant role. Over 50 per cent of miners with two or three site visits had 'building a business' as their ultimate goal. However, only some miners manage to achieve their commercial aspirations. In the next sections, we seek to identify who they are and why they succeed.

Assessing success

Few miners experienced an uninterrupted trajectory of success as they moved from site to site. They had hopes but no way of knowing how they would fare in the next site. Having to decide in the face of uncertainty, they took a calculated risk based on their knowledge of the condition of the site they were leaving relative to the potential opportunities of succeeding in the new site. Their knowledge of the latter is particularly imperfect and depends a great deal on the information they gather from others. Feelings of insecurity may lead them to supplement their network fact-finding with efforts to obtain 'luck' to be described below. If the new site is worse than the one they left behind, miners who are better off can always return to their former site. Those without sufficient means for transport run the risk of getting stuck in less productive settlements.

Time of arrival at the new site is critical. Respondents who arrived in the two study areas within the first month after the mineral strike earned an average monthly income of US$ 255 (Tanzania shillings 405,000). The ones arriving between one and three months earned US$ 228 (Tsh 363,000), between three months and one year, US$ 124 (Tsh 197,000), and over one year, US$ 85 (Tsh 135,000). The importance of early arrival is seen clearly in Tables 2.4 and 2.5. Except for one person, all who arrived within the first year came from Londoni, the new strike site, as opposed to the mature site at Matundasi. Table 2.4 shows various economic performance indicators based on the number of sites worked.

Mining's effect on livelihood and number of owned houses are positively related to the number of sites worked. The group with 4–5 site stays has the highest monthly earnings. Miners with 6–8 sites recorded present site earnings that were less than miners with 2–5 sites, but paradoxically, had the highest satisfaction with mining's effect on their livelihood. However, mining's livelihood effect

Table 2.4 Economic performance characteristics at last site based on number of sites worked and timing of arrival at site

Site group	Mining's overall effect on livelihood*	Owned houses	Monthly income at present site (Tsh)	Monthly income in Matundasi	Monthly income in Londoni	Arriving within 3 months after strike		Arriving more than 3 months after strike	
						No. of people	Monthly income	No. of people	Monthly income
1	2.36	0.41	84,000	100,000	65,000	3	63,000	36	85,000
2–3	2.24	0.84	218,000	177,000	278,000	5	401,000	32	189,000
4–5	2.18	0.91	350,000	306,000	370,000	8	594,000	14	210,000
6–8	2.00	1.00	132,000	67,000	176,000	1	27,000	9	144,000
Average	2.25	0.71	188,000	156,000	221,000	17	412,000	91	147,000

Source: Authors' survey data, 2006–2008

* Mining's overall effect on livelihood is based on the question: 'Overall, how has mining affected your livelihood?' with the answers: 'very positively' = 1, 'positively' = 2, 'negatively' = 3, and 'very negatively' = 4.

relates to the respondent's entire career whereas the monthly earning estimate refers solely to the current site where respondents with 6–8 sites arrived relatively late. Their mining career satisfaction is likely to have arisen from success at previous sites and the spin-off effects this created, whereas their relatively low earnings at the current site hints that timely mobility is key. Success is associated not only with high mobility but acting fast to get to strike sites early. Timely movement is linked to having a good flow of information about new strike sites and good social networking, which helps to reduce the uncertainty of risks associated with a new site. Economic performance indicators for the age/experience cohorts and the functional groupings are shown in Table 2.5.

'Old timers' own more houses than any of the other groups. 'Experienced youth' own more houses than 'Beginner youth' and 'Experienced adults' more than 'Beginner adults' despite the fact that these groups are of similar age. Amongst active miners, wealth increases with mining experience. In terms of respondents' own ranking of the sites, 'Experienced youth' appear better off than 'Beginner youth', 'Experienced adults' better off than 'Beginner adults', and 'Old timers' better off than all other cohorts. Moreover, their reported conditions at the last site are generally better than the average for all sites, suggesting that miners who persist are able to create better conditions for themselves and material gratification as their career unfolds.

Nonetheless, it is also indicative of the fact that amongst mining sites in the country, Matundasi and especially Londoni offer relatively good conditions and promising prospects. 'Beginner adults' view their mining outcome relatively negatively, suggesting that they become demoralized when they compare their situation with experienced miners of the same age. Respondents from the gold rush settlement of Londoni earned significantly more than respondents from Matundasi given the recent discovery and richness of the Londoni gold deposits. The fact that arrival time matters is further illustrated by the magnitude of earnings for those arriving close to the strike compared to average earnings.

Having reviewed the overall mobility and earning patterns of miners in our survey sites, the following section uses the oral history of a miner at the beginning of his career to illustrate the motivation and decision-making that faces Tanzanian miners on new sites.

Starting out: Learning while earning

Eliudi, a young 26-year-old miner from the Fipa tribe, began mining in 2007. His rural home in Sumbawanga district is a long way from the traditional mining areas. He migrated alone to Matundasi, a distance of 400 km.

> I was told by a relative who had recently returned from mining that there was money to be earned in Matundasi... When I arrived, I asked people about where to find the *Wafipa*... When I found them, I greeted them in *Kifipa* and they welcomed me, asking many questions and inviting me to stay... telling me that 'if you have come with peace, you are welcome to stay'. The next day, one

Table 2.5 Economic performance at last site

Mining categories	No. of owned houses	Mining site outcome*		Monthly income (Tsh)			Arrival within 3 months after strike		Arrival more than 3 months after strike	
		Site summary	At last site	At last site	Matundasi	Londoni	No of people	Monthly income	No of people	Monthly income
Age/experience mining cohort										
Beginner youth	0.06	2.78	2.88	53,000	52,000	54,000	3	73,000	13	49,000
Experienced youth	0.36	2.84	2.93	79,000	74,000	106,000	0	n.a.	14	79,000
Beginner adults	0.43	2.64	2.57	74,000	8,000**	85,000	0	n.a.	7	74,000
Experienced adults	0.82	2.87	2.95	274,000	187,000	350,000	11	565,000	28	160,000
Old timers	1.13	3.00	3.22	224,000	200,000	264,000	3	189,000	29	227,000
Average	0.71	2.88	2.99	188,000	156,000	221,000	17	412,000	91	147,000
Functional mining groups										
Mine workers	0.62	2.77	2.86	156,000	137,000	185,000	7	503,000	72	123,000
Pit holders	0.95	3.10	3.20	318,000	354,000	309,000	9	364,000	11	280,000
PML owners	1.25	3.00	3.25	191,000	188,000	200,000	1	200,000	3	188,000

Source: Authors' survey data, 2006-2008

* The condition is based on the question: 'How would you rate what you got out of the site?' with the answers: 'very poor' = 1, 'poor' = 2, 'OK' = 3, 'good' = 4, and 'very good' = 5

** One person

of them took me to a place close to the river and taught me alluvial mining. I helped him and that day we got a small gold nugget in the gravel we were washing. He told me that I had brought luck. We went back to the camp, changed our clothes, and went to sell the nugget to the local broker, Omari...The nugget was 3.2 grams and was sold for Tsh 64,000 (US$ 40) and I received half of that. I had a hard time comprehending how much the stone was worth. I had only seen such amounts of money back home during the harvest when the most successful farmers sold their crops. I used most of my gold money to buy a bag and clothes and was then left with Tsh10,000 (US$ 6).

In the coming days and weeks I kept on mining with my fellow *Wafipa*. We normally got enough to pay for our daily necessities...I lived with them and contributed to the household expenses. One day four of us got a 13.7 grams nugget and my share was Tsh 70,000 (US$ 44). I paid for a room for three months, bought new shoes and clothes. When the rainy season stopped, I went to ask for work in a *longabase* (hard rock) claim. I knew people who worked in one claim and went to introduce myself to the foreman and ask for work. I got work, but the first shift[10] I was part of did not bring anything but loss. The same was the case for the second shift. It rained a bit and I went back to trying my luck in alluvial mining. But soon the rains stopped. I had to go back to the hard rock claim. That shift took 45 days and only yielded Tsh 13,000 (US$ 8). The next shift took 30 days and brought nothing. At this stage my clothes were in tatters and I was getting desperate. I got work on another claim. Up until then I had been working as a *vutafelo* mine worker who removes the waste material and gold-bearing rocks out of the pit. At the next claim I worked, the pit collapsed. Fortunately, it happened at night when no one was working. We had failed to use sufficient timber to secure the pit, so I was unlucky yet again. I got a job washing tailings[11] and earned enough to eat for some weeks. I also did a bit of alluvial mining and got a few grams to buy some new clothes. Then I worked at a claim in Matundasi for three months without getting any proper payment as the gold was very limited. I was by that time working as a driller. I recently went back to doing alluvial panning, having found 7 grams one of the first days after my return. I will keep doing alluvial, which I prefer, as long as there is rain. I now work with three guys who are not Fipa. Me and my Fipa mates have gone our separate ways...Life in the mines is definitely better than back in Sumbawanga since I can always earn cash here.

(Interview at Matundasi, 6 February 2008)

This example illustrates many of our survey findings. Eliudi's home area was distant from the mines so he did not have the opportunity of local apprenticeship, but he did the next best thing. He found some tribal mates who gave him basic training in mining. He was exceptionally fortunate to strike gold on his first day. Thereafter he had to contend with the reality of uncertain earnings and hazards of the production process, including long, futile 'shifts' at hard rock mining operations. He, however, made good use of his time, gaining various mining skills and establishing the vital social networks, which would help him find work and facilitate team cooperation. His career from a *vutafelo* mineworker to a driller is indicative of a rise in the working hierarchy of artisanal miners. However, he also typically resorted to an array of job opportunities out of necessity, including washing of tailings, after a long period without earnings.

He moved away from reliance on his tribal mates. Without a wife or children to support, he used his earnings entirely for his own personal consumption, mostly on daily survival needs, although he splurged on clothing when he had sufficient cash in hand. It was difficult for him to generate savings. What appeared to be very large earnings when he struck gold were quickly spent on consumer goods at the inflated prices of the mining settlement. Despite the irregularity of payment and uncertainty, Eliudi preferred his life as a miner to that of farming in his home village.

Ingredients of success: Is mobility enough?

Having traced the mobility patterns of miners in relation to age, experience, the mining functional hierarchy and material outcomes, we turn to how miners view the role of mobility in striking gold and achieving material success. During in-depth interviews, we asked nine miners representing a spectrum of ages and mine experience to weight the importance of mobility, social networks and luck in finding gold.

Most agreed that mining required the interaction of all three components. A miner at Matundasi observed:

> Being ready to move when gold is found somewhere is very important...
> When you get to a new mining area, it is also important to have people who
> know the area to explain to you the way things work here.
> (Interview with David M., aged 22, at Matundasi, 6 February 2008)

While it is generally believed that the best chances come from rushing to a gold strike, some nonetheless seek stability, carefully choosing the best site vis-à-vis continuing gold availability and residence of their family:

> I was tired of always being on the road, then in Tanga, then Morogoro, then
> Mozambique and so I decided to stay in Matundasi, where I can concentrate
> on my family and alluvial mining. In Matundasi, one can always mine alone
> if there is no one to work with.
> (Interview with Zaidi A., aged 41, at Matundasi, 3 February 2008)

All the respondents in our sample acknowledged that mobility had a role to play, with youthful beginners according the most weight to it. Inexperienced youth who have hardly travelled, appreciate this more than others, as they venture beyond the security of their first mining settlement. Older, more experienced miners, on the other hand, are likely to discount the importance of mobility. They have come to accept movement from site to site as part of the job and proceed accordingly, following the availability of gold as it is struck, moving on as it dwindles to the depths beyond which, it becomes too costly – both financially and health-wise – for artisanal miners to mine.

Miners are known for their determination and ebullient personalities. It is likely that the inter-personal skills required to negotiate effective social networking after arrival at a site continue to be deployed throughout their stay and take considerable conscious thought. Getting accepted in social networks affords them the gold site access and teamwork necessary for mining successfully. By contrast, the imperative of mobility crops up more sporadically and requires soundings from other miners before weighing the wisdom of moving on or staying. Comprising a one-off decision, its role in finding gold on a day-to-day basis is likely to be discounted.

Interestingly, luck is something that most miners, young and old, experienced and inexperienced, believe is necessary.

> Luck is necessary, because it is difficult to know about the specific geology of a site.
>
> (Interview with Gilbert S., aged 37, at Matundasi, 3 February 2008)

Miners' mobility: Weighing the risks and coping with the uncertainties of rushing for gold

Tanzanian miners' mobility provides insight into livelihood decision-making in a coalescing work environment. Artisanal mining has become the main occupation for hundreds of thousands Tanzanians. The miners are highly mobile, moving considerable distances in their quest for mineral riches. After the basic mining instruction they receive at their first site, located generally close to their homes or amongst familiar people, those who are willing to take the risk start the peripatetic life of a miner. Each move involves high odds: the possibility of striking gold as opposed to the possibility of finding nothing and experiencing destitution, being involved in a mining accident,[12] getting ill or being robbed when one does strike gold.

While youthful beginners may be eager for adventure and make light of the risks, they soon become aware of the hazards and uncertainties of mining. Site movement cannot be taken lightly. This is suggested by miners' 'sticky' pattern of movement. On average, they stay at each site for 3.4 years, giving them ample time to establish social networks and a *modus operandi* for gold digging. The advantages of social networks range from gaining access to working on claims, being allocated one's share of gold proceeds within a mining team, having colleagues to spend one's leisure time with, and getting assistance when ill.

Mobility has accelerated quite recently, especially among proactive youth and middle-aged miners who are responding to successive gold strikes. Accordingly, the most mobile of our five cohorts were the 'Experienced adults' and not the 'Old timers'. They can offset their knowledge and skills in mining against a shorter time spent at each site.

In a context of high risk and uncertainty, it is readily evident that many miners do not go beyond the first site. And of those who migrate to a second, third or fourth site, tens of thousands become disenchanted and quit. However, as those who remain progress from site to site, their identity as miners solidifies, and they tend to become increasingly motivated by mineral rushes and mining opportunities. A willingness to move and an early arrival at a gold rush site are extremely important to success, supported by their mining skills, resistance to adversity, and participation in collegial networks. Satisfaction with site outcomes increases over successive sites as their mining skills improve and their social networks proliferate.

Miners have no way of knowing how well they will fare in their upcoming sites and take a calculated risk whenever they move to a new site. Persistence eventually brings many to a site where they succeed. Miners' belief in good and bad luck and the power of medicinal charms to bring luck and ensure against mining accidents is widespread amongst inexperienced, veteran and old timer miners. The Sukuma are especially known for their expertise in divination. At one level, this may be perceived as traditionalism, but it is clearly an existential attempt to surmount the uncertainty of the unknown. In the case of the miners, the big unknown is where precisely they should dig to strike gold. The geological knowledge as well as the economic and social barriers to finding the exact location are formidable given Tanzanian artisanal miners' restricted technical capacity.

In conclusion, our evidence indicates that the mobility of artisanal miners is economically optimizing at the same time as there is a strong sociology of risk influencing decisions on site movement. Miners' decision to mine is rational in view of the economic alternatives, their moves are logistically sound in that they move away from sites of diminishing returns to better prospects, and overall, those who continue to mine are doing so because sufficient numbers of them are finding gold and garnering material success. Tracing miners' migration paths, it is clear that the rush for gold does not entail rushed decision-making. Finally, for the vast majority of seasoned artisanal miners, mining is synonymous with moving, detaching oneself from the safety of home areas and the security of age-old agrarian pursuits.

However, rational behavioural models of optimizing individual decision-makers can take us only so far in understanding Tanzania's gold miners. Their awareness of the unknown and the unperceived with respect to the location of mineral outcrops in the natural rock formations as well as the dangers associated with mining and the inability to control the outcome of their mining efforts is expressed in their efforts to obtain luck through rituals, magic and charms. No matter how experienced a miner is, he sees luck as a vital ingredient in success. Along with Beck (1999), we would argue that such beliefs are far more realistic than rational behaviour models, which clinically treat the unpredictable and uncontrollable as a statistical probability. If you are a miner you must always be ready for the truly unknown, unperceived and unpredictable because your life can oscillate between rags and riches, regardless of how carefully you weigh your decisions.

Notes

1 This article is derived from following the article: Jønsson, J.B. and Bryceson, D.F. (2009) 'Rushing for gold: Mobility and small-scale mining in East Africa', *Development and Change* 40(2), 249–79.
2 The results of the latest 2012 national census were not available at the time of writing.
3 Survey sampling took place at off-work interview sites where a cross-section of miners of all ages, incomes, ethnic and educational backgrounds congregated. The advantage of off-work sites is that respondents are away from knowing ears and are likely to feel more relaxed. Each of the selected sites was divided into a 3 x 3 matrix with its own number. Respondents were selected from the square chosen through random drawing of its number. If more than one person was within the square, the respondent in the 12 o'clock position (from the interviewer's point of view) was chosen. The order in which the age categories were filled up indicated the age composition of the settlement. During the selection of respondents only five non-miners were encountered, indicating the extent of the mining activities within the settlements. Of the 45 miners interviewed in each settlement, nine were taken from each of the following categories: below 20 years, 20–29 years, 30–39 years, 40–49 years, and above 50 years.
4 The 18 ex-miners were selected purposively to get a cross-section of respondents of various ages and incomes.
5 Besides this survey, the overall fieldwork included semi-structured interviews with 41 PML owners and pit holders, 8 focus group discussions, 30 interviews with key informants and 9 oral histories.
6 We sampled miners in bars and recreational areas frequented mostly by men. It is likely that women's mobility is markedly different from men's in mining settlements but we have no data to substantiate that hunch.
7 The regions of Mbeya, Singida, Shinyanga, Mwanza, and Tabora.
8 For example, during a focus group discussion in Matundasi, miners agreed that most improved mining methods had been brought by people from around Lake Victoria and, in particular, the Sukuma.
9 The three cohort entry periods are before 1990 (pre-economic liberalization), 1990–2003 (economic liberalization) and 2004 onwards, when many young miners rushed to Londoni.
10 A shift consists of a cycle of blasting, hoisting and processing rocks, thereby extending the pit vertically or horizontally by a few metres. It typically lasts for a period of between one and four weeks.
11 Tailings are the residue sediments left over after processing that are reworked to extract any remaining gold.
12 Subsequent to our survey, four miners, including one pit holder from our sample, tragically died in Matundasi from gas poisoning from an irrigation pump, which they used in the pit to pump up water.

References

Baker, J. and Aina, T. A. (1995) *The Migration Experience in Africa*. Uppsala, Sweden: Nordic Africa Institute.

Beck, U. (1999) *World Risk Society*. Cambridge: Polity Press.

Berton, P. (1994) *Klondike: The Last Great Gold Rush, 1896–1899*. Toronto: McClelland and Stewart Inc.

Brands, H. W. (2003) *The Age of Gold: The California Gold Rush and the New American Dream*. New York: Anchor.

Bryceson, D. F. (1999) 'African rural labour, income diversification and livelihood approaches: A long-term development perspective', *Review of African Political Economy* 80: 171–89.

Bryceson, D. F. (2000) 'African peasants' centrality and marginality: Rural labour transformations'. in Bryceson, D. F., Kay, C. and Mooij, J. (eds), *Disappearing Peasantries: Rural Labour in Africa, Asia and Latin America*. London: Intermediate Technology Publications. pp. 37–63.

Bryceson, D. F. and Mwaipopo, R. (2009) 'Rural-urban transitions in Northwestern Tanzania's mining frontier'. in Agergaard, J., Fold, N. and Gough, K. (eds) *Rural Urban Dynamics: Livelihoods, Mobility and Markets in African and Asian Frontiers*. London: Routledge. pp. 158–74.

Colson, E. (2003) 'Forced migration and the anthropological response', *Journal of Refugee Studies* 16(1): 1–18.

Foucault, M. (1970) *The Order of Things: An Archaeology of the Human Sciences*. London: Tavistock Publications.

Harsanyi, J. C. (1973) 'Games with randomly-distributed payoffs: A new rationale for mixed-strategy equilibrium points', *International Journal of Game Theory* 2: 1–23.

Hentschel T., Hruschka, F. and Priester, M. (2002) 'Global Report on Artisanal and Small-Scale Mining'. London: International Institute for Environment and Development.

Hilson, G. (2002) 'The future of small-scale mining: Environmental and socioeconomic perspectives', *Futures* 34(9–10): 863–72.

Madulu, N. F. (1998) 'Changing lifestyles in farming societies of Sukumaland: Kwimba District, Tanzania' [Working paper, vol. 27]. Leiden, The Netherlands: Africa Studies Centre, University of Leiden.

Mwamfupe, D. (1998) 'Changing village land, labour and livelihoods: Rungwe and Kyela Districts, Tanzania' [Working Paper, vol. 29], Leiden, The Netherlands: African Studies Centre, University of Leiden.

Myerson, R. (1991) *Game Theory: Analysis of Conflict*, Cambridge, MA: Harvard University Press.

NBS (Tanzania, National Bureau of Statistics) (2002) *Population and Housing Census 2002: General Report*. Dar es Salaam: National Bureau of Statistics.

Roberts, A. D. (1986) 'The gold boom of the 1930s in Eastern Africa', *Journal of the Royal African Society* 85(341): 545–62.

Sanders, T. (2001) 'Territorial and magical migrations in Tanzania', in De Bruijn, M., van Dijk, R. and Foeken, D. (eds) *Mobile Africa: Changing Patterns of Movement in Africa and Beyond*. Leiden, The Netherlands: Brill. pp. 27–46.

Sen, A. (1998) 'Rational behaviour', *The New Palgrave Dictionary of Economics* (vol 4), London: Macmillan Press Ltd. pp. 68–76.

Todaro, M. P. (1969) 'A model of labor migration and urban unemployment in less developed countries', *American Economic Review* 59(1): 138–48.

Toure, M. and Fadayomi, T. O. (1992) *Migrations Development and Urbanization Policies in Sub-Saharan Africa*. Oxford: Codesria Book Series.

3 Pursuing an artisanal mining career

Downward success[1]

Deborah Fahy Bryceson and Jesper Bosse Jønsson

Traditionally African smallholder agriculture rested on family production units working the land usually on the basis of customary usufruct rights, in well-established local communities. Work tasks were generally allocated by age and gender within the confines of familial authority structures. Subsistence food production was given precedence. Cash cropping was primarily within the purview of the senior male in the family (Bryceson 2000a).

Labour at artisanal mine rush sites is radically different; being mobile and multi-ethnic, with a continually high turnover of people working in close contact with one another. In view of the recent surge in mining and recruitment of large numbers of mine labourers from agrarian and trading backgrounds in Tanzania, we need to ask how artisanal mining has coalesced so effectively, managing to achieve work efficiency and avoid mayhem in the production and processing of such a valuable commodity, despite the poverty of the Tanzanian countryside.

The existing livelihood literature does not directly address this question.[2] More revealing is current literature on labour restructuring and changing career patterns in the Western world, where analogous trends are occurring. De-industrialization has altered the traditional career structures of blue- and white-collar workers, casualization of labour has become pervasive in many sectors, and gender opportunities in the workforce are being reconfigured. The interaction between the sectoral change of de-industrialization, altered work opportunities and reconfigured career patterns, bears similarity to the process of de-agrarianization (Bryceson 2000b), the surge in new mining opportunities and the evolution of mining career patterns in Tanzania's artisanal mining sector.

There are innumerable definitions of careers. In general terms, a career comprises an occupation taken up for a significant period of one's life with opportunities for progress. This pertains to people who have worked in mining over a number of years. Kanter (1989) identified conditions for the existence of career trajectories: first, long-term employment, allowing for the eventual reward of sacrificing behaviour at the beginning of one's career and upward progression in a hierarchically ranked pyramid; second, sustained sectoral growth, allowing for the expansion of the pyramid; and third, a restricted number of competitive achievers with organizational and productive roles who maintain coherence and enforce the legitimacy of the production pyramid both internally and externally.

The length of occupational engagement, the level of concentration on mining activities and the willingness to move in response to the changing availability of minerals are key indicators of career commitment and progression, distinguishing career miners from African rural income diversifiers more generally. In this chapter, we define miners as people who are engaged in the active search and extraction of minerals. Those who have mined for more than two years and/or who proceed to another mining site can be considered to have broken ranks with rural income diversifiers and are on their way to becoming specialized producers. This article traces the path of deepening mine work specialization and career development marked by the bifurcation of career-minded miners from diversifying part-time miners who stay *in situ* and pursue mining alongside other income-earning and subsistence activities in agriculture, trade, etc.

Evolving organizational hierarchy of artisanal gold mining

In Tanzania, the division of labour within artisanal gold mining has developed in a layered pyramidal triangle (Figure 3.1). At the apex are the Primary Mining License (PML) owners who are responsible for mining activities conducted on their claim, including hiring and paying labour, organizing the mining, and endorsing safety and environmental regulations (Fisher 2007; Mwaipopo *et al.* 2004). But PML owners' active involvement in these matters rarely transpires given the history of artisanal mining. When Africans were initially granted *de facto* mineral rights in the 1930s, the geological uncertainties and expenses associated with mining meant that a system of informal sub-contracting and shareholding emerged (Chachage 1995). Today, the same principles of risk and profit sharing form the basis of most artisanal mining activities. The actual system depends on local conditions of labour availability, reef richness, and labour skills. However, in most mining sites a three-tier division of labour has developed between PML owners, pit holders and diggers.

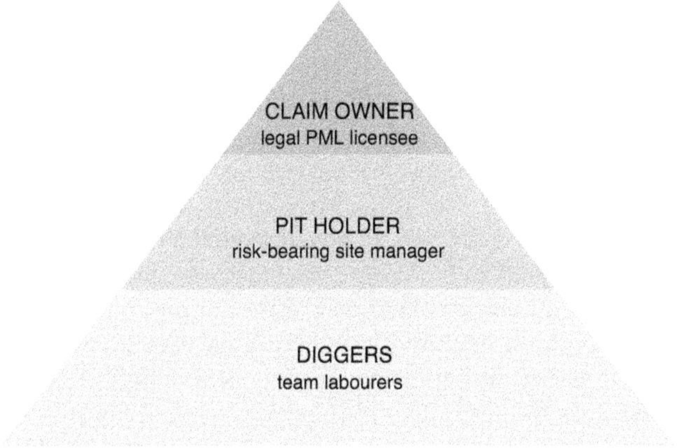

CLAIM OWNER
legal PML licensee

PIT HOLDER
risk-bearing site manager

DIGGERS
team labourers

Figure 3.1 Gold mining hierarchy
Source: Authors' depiction

A PML grants the right to exploit an area for seven years. The area can be mortgaged, renewed or transferred to another holder, including foreign firms. It is a widespread practice among PML owners to informally lease out mining activities to pit holders who organize procurement and sourcing of necessary inputs and labour and conduct the mining. Thus, capital investments and the risks and costs related to fruitless periods fall upon pit holders, who often run their activities in partnership with others, hence their local name of *wanachama* (members). Typically, diggers are provided only with food and medicine in periods of no mineral output. They can roughly be divided into traditional drillers, *waponjaji*, who work their way into the rock mainly with hammers and chisels, and *vutafelo*, who remove the waste material and gold-bearing rocks out of the pit. The former usually receive a larger share than the latter. In addition, artisanal mining sites have people occupied with various specialized tasks for which they are typically paid a specific amount of cash or quantity of rocks, e.g. security, pit supervision, blasting, electrical drilling, ore transportation, manual ore crushing, operation of ball mills, and separation of gold through washing and amalgamation.

Systems vary between mining settlements. Overall, PML owners typically take around 30 per cent of the output, the pit holders' share adds up to around 40 per cent, out of which production costs are usually covered, and diggers receive the remaining third to divide amongst themselves (Jønsson and Fold 2009). Subleasing of pits contradicts the mining legislation and if a PML owner chooses to sell his license, pit holders and diggers are likely to be evicted. Thus, internal forms of exploitation exist within the artisanal mining sector with PML owners topping the pyramid (Fisher 2007).

While the literature on African artisanal mining has proliferated over the last decade, there is surprisingly little on artisanal miners' decision-making and career trajectories. With the aim of studying the work and mobility patterns of artisanal miners, our field study involved interviews with miners of different ages and degrees of mining experience in the two contrasting gold sites of Matundasi and Londoni.

Profiling the miners

Biographical and socioeconomic profiles of artisanal miners are vital to understanding the miners' motivation and decision-making behaviour (Hilson 2005). All people sampled in the survey were men. In both of the two study sites, female miners did not appear in great numbers. Male miners argue that women entering the pits bring bad luck. The few female miners encountered throughout the fieldwork were either occupied with crushing, washing, panning, and transporting of sediments, or (in a few cases) had shares in PMLs or pits. Characteristics of the sample have already been reviewed in the previous chapter (see also Bryceson and Jønsson 2010). Here it is pertinent to mention that of the 108 respondents, 84 were diggers whereas 24 were either PML owners or pit holders. The latter were more mobile than the average respondent with 3.8 site stays each. Thus, being at the top of the artisanal mining pyramid, they were generally more mobile than the diggers (Jønsson and Bryceson 2009).

As described in Chapter 2, a digger's first mining site is effectively an apprenticeship where he learns how to mine and socially interact within the mining settlement. Some are reluctant to move away from this site, which is often located close to the home area, but many gradually build up the confidence and skills to move on. The mark of career aspirations begins with commencement of work at a second site. From here onwards, miners spend on average less time than at the first site, as they focus on the material rewards from mining and leave when deposits are depleted or a new promising site is discovered (Jønsson and Bryceson 2009).

As miners move from site to site, they increasingly distance themselves from their home areas, thereby weakening their family ties, but they compensate by forming attachments to households in mining sites or other localities. Individual miners depend on each other in informal, yet very systematic ways pertaining to roles, obligations, and shares. Miners' careers are essentially moulded by how they manage to access gold-bearing land, gold, mining teams, equipment, mining knowledge, markets, security, and credit. On arriving at a new site, miners need inter-personal skills to negotiate effective social networking, which is crucial for gold mining access and success.

Familial relations are deployed by successful PML owners, who tend to rely on relatives to manage their operations when they are not present. Outside of this property guardianship function, the importance of familial and tribal ties does not seem salient in mining. Ethnic and tribal boundaries are intersected by new cultural, political, and tenurial relations within the mining settlements (Godoy 1985). Miners are increasingly judged for their qualifications and competence instead of place of origin and tribal affiliation. Consequently, although some pit teams seemed to be formed on a tribal basis, these constituted a small minority.

To gain detailed insight into miners' work trajectories and comprehend the significance of timing in embarking on a mining career with respect to entry year and starting age, we have constructed three different category groupings. The 'mining entry year cohorts' (see Table 3.1) reflect the responsiveness of miners to changing government policies towards mining and gold strike information. The 'career entry age cohorts' (see Table 3.2) are constructed by comparing individual miners' entry age relative to their mining experience in years. Those who start at a younger than average age within each mining experience group are 'early starters'. Below average are 'delayed starters', followed by those starting very late. The aim is to shed light on miners' career decision-making with respect to the progression of their life cycle. We hypothesize that those who started early and persist are more likely to succeed than the latecomers. Finally, we group the miners with respect to their hierarchical function (see Table 3.3) – diggers, pit holders and PML owners – with the expectation that PML owners at the top of the pyramid will have the highest material rewards.

Table 3.1 reveals that from a very low number of entrants before 1985, there was an almost five-fold increase in the number of men starting mining in the late 1980s, coinciding with the government's initiation of economic liberalization policies. Thereafter there was a steady stream of men entering mining, generally

Table 3.1 Career characteristics of 'mining entry year' cohorts

Cohorts	Number of respondents (N = 108)	Average age	Average entry age	Number of sites worked	Years of mining experience	Mean months per site	< 5 years of school (%)	Rural origin (%)	Originating from traditional mining areas (%)
Pre 1979	5	49.6	21.0	5.0	18.4	44	20.0	80.0	60.0
1980–84	5	51.8	27.8	5.2	17.0	39	20.0	100.0	100.0
1985–89	23	46.3	26.4	3.2	16.0	60	34.8	78.3	56.5
1990–94	19	38.1	23.7	3.5	11.3	39	5.3	47.4	73.7
1995–99	18	32.4	22.9	2.7	7.9	35	22.3	83.3	44.4
2000–04	19	26.5	21.6	1.6	4.5	33	26.4	73.7	36.8
2005+	19	26.7	25.4	1.2	1.1	11	26.4	94.7	78.9
Mean average	—	36.0	24.2	2.7	9.3	41	23.2	76.9	60.1

Source: Authors' survey data, 2006–2008

Table 3.2 Characteristics of 'career entry age' cohorts*

Cohorts	Number of respondents (N = 108)	Average age	Average entry age	Number of sites worked	Years of mining experience	Mean months per site	< 5 years of school (%)	Rural origin (%)	Traditional mining areas origins (%)
Early starters	28	34.0	17.4	3.4	13.7	48.1	21.4	82.1	46.4
Average starters	47	33.3	22.2	2.5	9.2	43.4	29.8	74.5	66.0
Delayed starters	19	37.8	27.2	2.9	6.8	28.0	15.8	73.7	84.2
Late starters	14	46.5	40.2	1.6	4.6	33.6	14.2	78.6	35.7
Mean average	—	36.0	24.2	2.7	9.3	41.3	23.2	76.9	60.1

Source: Authors' survey data, 2006–2008.

* In analysing the career progression of men of widely varying ages in our sample, we grouped miners by their years of mining experience and mining entry age. Those in the modal group were 'average, starters', compared with 'early starters', later 'delayed starters' and very 'late starters'.

in their early to mid-20s. Although miners with many years of experience in mining have worked the most sites, there appears to be a general trend for duration of site stays to decline with later mining entry cohorts, hinting at increased inter-site mobility. The large cohort in 1985–89, which registers comparatively low mobility, is less educated than any other cohort. Those were years of economic distress and it is possible that many of these men entered mining as a coping rather than an optimizing strategy. The respondents who started mining in 1990–94, on the other hand, stand out as more urban and better educated than any other cohort, with three-quarters coming from traditional mining areas.

Table 3.2 reveals two, rather than one, career paths in mining. The 'early starters', 'average starters' and 'late starters' display a 'normal progression path', i.e. the earlier people started mining, the more sites they worked and the longer they stayed at each site. There is a logical pattern of decreasing number of sites and duration of each site for the average and late starters. The late starters spent approximately one year less at each site compared with early and average aged starters. The later the entry, the less time spent at each mining site before moving on. This could be a result of both increased pressure from commercial mining companies and the fact that the legalization of artisanal mining gave miners more freedom of movement to search for the most productive mining sites.

The 'delayed' starters break this pattern. They were five to ten years older than the early and average starters when they began mining but they 'geared up' very quickly and managed to work at more sites than average starters and spent far shorter periods at each site than any of the other cohorts. Table 3.2 shows that the overwhelming majority of them are from traditional mining areas, which may help to explain how they adjusted so quickly to mining. Furthermore, they tend to be the least rural of any of the groups. We will return to the significance of this later.

Distinguishing miners by functional hierarchy in Table 3.3, we see that all three groups have almost identical entry ages, but their current ages differ. Pit holders and PML owners are eight to nine years older than diggers, inferring that work experience is requisite to climbing the pyramid to its second and third tiers. A progression up the functional artisanal mining hierarchy exists. All but two of the 24 pit holders and PML owners started their mining careers as diggers and managed to work their way up to their current position.

Pit holders have a higher mobility than any other group, i.e. they have visited more sites and spend less time on each site. However, there is a big difference in mobility between miners from Matundasi with an average of 2.3 site visits, and Londoni miners with twice the number of site visits. The four PML owners, on the other hand, were the least mobile, with an average of 7.8 years per site, which accords with the fact that their ownership rights would require a more sedentary existence close to their site for supervision purposes. If a new gold rush occurs, PML owners are more confined to their claim, for which they hold the legal tender, than are pit holders to their existing pits. Education level may facilitate advancement: PML owners are better educated than the pit holders who are in turn better educated than diggers.

Professional career trajectories within artisanal mining

Compared with the multi-various *ad hoc* non-farm rural activities that have proliferated over the last few decades, artisanal mining has a readily identifiable career structure as outlined by Kanter (1989). The sector presents miners with the opportunity for career progression from 'early apprenticeship' to successive mining sites, requiring readiness to move, dedication to the work, and good inter-action with fellow miners.

This marks a step away from the non-farm employment experimentation of the last three decades in Tanzania, which was propelled by people trying to cope with material adversity and ensure physical survival (Bryceson 1999). Less than five per cent of respondents mentioned post-mining agrarian strategies. On the contrary, business initiatives, commercial mining, and consumption figured prominently as miners' ultimate saving goals (Jønsson and Bryceson 2009). It is increasingly apparent that multi-sited artisanal miners are no longer frustrated farmers-turned-miners for survival reasons. On the contrary, they evidence the emergence of career miners with mineral-led spatial mobility strategies, social mobility aspirations, and collective identity characteristics.

Miners accept continued material hardship and separation from family as part of their work. While their initial entry into the sector does not entail significant barriers, sustaining a career within artisanal mining involves enduring a number of hazards and uncertainties of livelihood failure, family separation, and occupational risks. Conditions in mining communities can be harsh and miners have to be resistant to adversity and persistent in the pursuit of their career. Many quit after experiencing or witnessing accidents or due to economic ruin, social demoralization or poor health. Despite the high intake of alcohol and marijuana, especially amongst youthful diggers, most artisanal miners are committed to hard work and display a strong work ethic.

Barret *et al.* (2001: 325) argue that 'substantial entry or mobility barriers to high return niches within the rural non-farm economy' exist. However, although artisanal mining is potentially one of the most lucrative non-farm activities, its initial barriers to diggers' entry are relatively limited in terms of required investments and skills. Estimates from Phillips *et al.* (2001) found average incomes within Tanzanian artisanal mining to be six times higher than in agriculture. Our rough estimate of respondents' monthly gold mining income averaged US$ 99 (158,000 Tanzanian shillings [Tsh]) at all sites, which supports the argument that income levels within artisanal mining as a whole are higher than in farming. The income estimate should be viewed as indicative for the purpose of comparing income differences between the mining cohorts. Covering a wide income spectrum, respondents earned from close to nothing up to one and a half million shillings monthly (US$ 900). Large differences between various cohorts exist with regard to performance and satisfaction (Tables 3.4 to 3.6). Monthly earnings increase with age up to 40 years and thereafter decline, which is likely to be indicative of decreasing amounts of time spent digging as the men age.

Table 3.3 Career characteristics of 'functional mining' cohorts

Cohorts	Number of respondents (N = 108)	Average age	Average entry age	Number of sites worked	Years of mining experience	Mean months per site	< 5 years of school (%)	Rural origin (%)	Traditional mining areas origins (%)
PML owners	4	43	26	2.0	15.4	93	0	50	75
Pit holders	20	42	25	4.1	11.4	33	10	65	75
Diggers	80	34	24	2.4	8.6	43	28	80	55

Source: Authors' survey data, 2006–2008

Table 3.4 Performance of 'career entry age' cohorts

Cohorts	Mean monthly salary	Total income (in mill)	Mining site summary outcome*	Mining's effect on livelihood**	PML owners (%)	Pit holders (%)	Diggers (%)	Matundasi/ Londoni respondent distribution
Early starters	152,305	27.0	2.91	2.07	7	32	61	18/10
Average starters	125,187	15.6	2.78	2.34	2	9	89	27/20
Delayed starters	276,854	30.0	3.15	2.11	—	32	68	3/16
Late starters	114,491	7.0	2.77	2.50	7	7	86	6/8
Mean total	157,513	20.0	2.88	2.25	4	18	78	54/54

Source: Authors' survey data, 2006–2008

* Based on the question: 'How would you rate what you got out of the site?' with the answers: 'very poor' = 1, 'poor' = 2, 'OK' = 3, 'good' = 4, and 'very good' = 5.
** Based on the question: 'Overall, how has mining affected your livelihood?' with the answers: 'very positively' = 1, 'positively' = 2, 'negatively' = 3, and 'very negatively' = 4.

Excluding the 'delayed starters', we see a logical career progression and the importance of early mining entry. The 'early starters' are materially better off and more satisfied with their situation than the 'average starters', who in turn have higher earnings and are more satisfied than the 'late starters', whereas the 'delayed starters' perform significantly better than all other cohorts. They are relatively well educated, several are pit holders, and 16 of the cohort's 19 respondents are from Londoni, where miners earned significantly more than miners from Matundasi due to the recent discovery and richness of the Londoni gold deposits. Moreover, as shown in Table 3.2, it is the cohort with the highest degree of mobility.

Familiarity with artisanal mining, obtained by people growing up in mining areas is an advantage. Eighty-four per cent of the 'delayed starters' came from traditional mining areas as opposed to only 36 per cent of the 'late starters'. Some of the 'late starters' may have been pushed by livelihood failure into travelling a long distance to start mining. Our data indicates a pattern of improving material reward and career progression as miners become more experienced, skilled and mobile, expanding their networks within the mining community. However, alongside this pattern of career progression, the geographical origin and educational level of miners are important factors of success. The 'delayed starters' have an advantageous sideways entry into mining, which pegs them higher than most others, possibly in response to the proximate opportunities they could observe from their urban locations in regional mining areas, as opposed to many who seek mining as a livelihood solution. The locational advantage of the 'delayed starters' is twofold: first, they have grown up in mining regions and second, many have lived in urban areas of mining regions, which gives them an overview perspective; they know promising areas and on the basis of such knowledge can arrive at gold strike sites in a timely fashion, which can make a large difference to earnings (Jønsson and Bryceson 2009).

Miners with long mining careers out-perform those who have recently entered mining, demonstrating the value of a mining apprenticeship and accumulated work experience. Miners who have started mining in the new millennium generally earn less than other miners. But it is not just years of experience that matter. The large mining entry cohort of 1985–1989 who responded to the exceptionally poor economic conditions of the time and in a sense were driven to mining are relatively poorly educated. Only 57 per cent of them originated from traditional mining areas. The majority of them work in Matundasi, where proceeds are generally lower than in Londoni, and tellingly, all arrived late at their last gold strike site. They were less satisfied with their situation compared to other cohorts. By contrast, the 1990–1994 mining entry cohort, who were the highest earning cohort, were overall the most satisfied with their situation. They were the best educated cohort with a high percentage of miners originating from traditional mining areas and more than two-thirds of them were mining in Londoni.

Finally, turning to the three functional groups, gold findings are unequally divided between the PML owners, pit holders and diggers. As expected, PML owners and pit holders earn more and are more successful with their mining

Table 3.5 Performance of 'mining entry year' cohorts

Cohorts	Mean monthly salary on all sites	Total income (in mill)	Mining site summary outcome*	Mining's effect on livelihood**	PML owners (%)	Pit holders (%)	Diggers (%)	Matundasi/ Londoni respondent distribution
Pre 1979	211,760	43.7	2.82	1.80	20	40	40	3/2
1980–84	293,116	41.0	2.92	2.00	—	40	60	2/3
1985–89	149,633	29.0	3.02	2.30	—	22	78	16/7
1990–94	239,642	32.1	2.96	2.11	11	42	47	6/13
1995–99	155,390	15.9	2.74	2.33	6	11	83	12/6
2000–04	144,537	8.3	2.95	2.37	—	5	95	11/8
2005+	49,951	0.7	2.68	2.32	—	—	100	4/15
Mean total	157,513	20.0	2.88	2.25	4	18	78	54/54

Source: Authors' survey data, 2006–2008
* See notes Table 3.4. ** See notes Table 3.4.

Table 3.6 Performance of 'functional mining' cohorts

Cohorts	Mean monthly salary	Total income (in mill)	Mining site summary outcome*	Mining's effect on livelihood**	Matundasi/ Londoni respondents' distribution
PML owners	230,000	41	3.00	1.75	3/1
Pit holders	311,000	44	3.10	1.95	4/16
Diggers	117,000	13	2.79	2.35	33/47

Source: Authors' survey data, 2006–2008
* See notes Table 3.4. ** See notes Table 3.4.

activities and livelihood than diggers. Seventy-five per cent of the pit holders and PML owners originate from traditional mining areas, as opposed to 55 per cent of the diggers. Interestingly, however, pit holders report higher earnings and better mining outcomes than PML owners. This may be because PML owners are differentiated on the basis of the perceived gold-bearing quality of their claim. Pit holders have more inter-claim mobility. A pit holder on a PML with rich deposits can easily earn more money than a PML owner whose area only has a few low-yielding pits. Many PML owners with mediocre claims struggle to get pit holders to work on their claims because the pit holders gravitate to the PMLs located on rich gold reefs.[3] Furthermore, 80 per cent of the pit holders interviewed were from the more productive gold-producing site, Londoni. The two cases below illustrate the upward career progression through the functional groupings as well as the importance of timely movement, apprenticeship, and technological investments and innovation.

Fifty-year-old Thomas S started mining in Itilima in Shinyanga in 1982 at the age of 25. He worked as a digger in other people's pits and sometimes during the rainy season also did alluvial mining. After four years he went to Matinje in Tabora, again being employed in other people's pits. After five years, he went to Mwagi Magi in Shinyanga, where gold had recently been discovered. After working other people's pits for nearly a year, he went on to Sekenke in Singida. By then, he had learned his trade and upon arrival, he instantly started his own pit, which he operated as a pit holder for the next seven years. When gold was discovered in Londoni in 2004 he obtained a pit. Nine months later the gold fever was on at Haydom in Manyara and he was one of the first to arrive. Again he had his own pit. But the produce was limited and after a year, he was back in Londoni operating a new pit (Interview at Londoni, 16 January 2007).

Forty-year-old Peter B started mining as a 12-year-old youngster at home in Ushirombo in Shinyanga. While schooling, he mined for gold in his spare time, either alluvial with friends or in other people's pits. After finishing school he became a full-time hard rock digger. When gold was struck in neighbouring Mwabomba, he went and started his own pit. After eight months, the gold-bearing reef became increasingly difficult to access. He bought a ball mill from his mine earnings and transported it the 700 kilometres to Matundasi. Here, the ball mill was the first of its kind, hence earning him good money from crushing other miners' rocks. After a while he started operating his own pit (Interview at Matundasi, 11 January 2007).

The fact that Peter B came from a traditional mining area and had 11 years of schooling is likely to have played a significant part in his skills acquisition and acumen to invest in processing equipment fairly early in his mining career and make timely moves to new mining sites.

Career consolidation

Given the unpredictable nature of gold mining, the long-term success of artisanal miners depends heavily on how miners use their earnings. Successful miners tend to cite their savings behaviour as an important element in generating their success, as illustrated in the following case:

> Omari M. arrived in Matundasi in 1983, starting as a digger. In 1987 he began to buy gold and a decade later moved his family to a new house in Mbeya town. Today he is one of the two main gold buyers in Matundasi. His children go to a private school and he owns a taxi and a small bus. He still spends most of his time in Matundasi running his business, but he is now assisted by a relative, who runs things when he is away. He attributes his success to discipline and his ability to save money when he was setting up his business, observing that 'one miner gets [Tsh] 50,000 and thinks it's barely enough for beer for one night for him and his buddies; another sees the same amount as the first step to a fortune'.
>
> (Interview at Matundasi, 5 February 2008)

Table 3.7 shows house accumulation and investment patterns of the cohorts at Londoni and Matundasi. As seen, especially in Table 3.7-B, wealth accumulation is heavily correlated with the passage of mining years and progression of the individual life cycle. Wealth increases with mining experience but the increase is not linear, as pit holders and especially PML owners own significantly more houses than diggers (Table 3.7-C). In general, building or improving one's house is a prioritized investment target because a house fulfils the miners' family housing needs as well as being a source of economic security and a status symbol that may constitute a significant increase in one's standard of living. Given miners' high mobility, the decision of where to build one's family home is significant. Bearing in mind that the vast majority of miners were not native to the two surveyed mining sites, it was interesting to see that some of the more sedentary miners of Matundasi chose to build in Matundasi, whereas none of the recent strike miners invested in modern housing in Londoni. House construction there was provisional and low cost. Londoni miners built or improved their houses elsewhere, typically building houses of local materials in their home areas, whereas windfall mining proceeds were invested in well-built modern houses or other property investments in regional centres.

The miners who failed to save anything or used their savings for entertainment are likely to consist both of those earning just enough for their daily requirements and miners choosing conspicuous consumption at the expense of investments or remittances – what Walsh (2003: 298) describes as 'immediate fulfilment of personal desires'. Nine per cent of all savings were used on land or livestock, which are easy to purchase, can be monitored and/or looked after elsewhere, and are generally sound investments. Business initiation was the focus of the more successful individuals, again underscoring their high earnings and farsightedness.

Artisanal mining settlements are rarely safe places for holding cash reserves or savings. The flimsy, temporary housing, absence of banks, fast dissemination of information about strikes, and presence of criminals discourage most miners from keeping cash in the settlement. As a result, many miners choose to go home

Table 3.7 Investment pattern for cohorts at latest site (% of miners)

	No. of savers (%)	No. of houses owned	House (%)	Land and livestock (%)	Business (%)	Family support (%)
		A – Career Entry Age Cohorts				
Early starters	54	0.79	7	4	11	21
Average starters	40	0.64	9	6	4	11
Delayed starters	68	0.79	11	26	16	—
Late starters	29	0.71	—	7	—	14
Average	47	0.71	7	9	8	12
		B – Mining Entry Year Cohorts				
Pre 1980	60	1.60	20	—	20	20
1980–84	40	1.40	20	—	—	—
1985–89	48	0.91	13	9	—	13
1990–94	58	0.89	—	11	26	11
1995–99	39	0.72	6	6	11	11
2000–04	53	0.37	11	11	—	21
2005+	37	0.21	—	16	—	5
Average	47	0.71	7	9	8	12
		C – Functional Mining Groups				
PML owner	75	1.25	—	—	25	25
Pit holder	70	0.95	15	20	20	10
Digger	39	0.63	5	8	4	11
Average	47	0.71	7	9	8	12

Source: Authors' survey data, 2006–2008

immediately after earning large sums of money in a major strike, thereby avoiding the security problem and being seen as ungenerous given the potlatch pressures to treat one's fellow miners to the good life.

> Philip M., 50 years old, had spent five months mining alluvial gold in Iluma in Singida in 1991–1992 when he one day found a very large gold nugget. The next day he left for Dar es Salaam where he sold it for Tsh 50 million. He went home to Mbeya, bought a modern house and a number of plots for investment purposes, after which he returned to mining, but at a different site where his earlier success was not known.
>
> (Interview at Londoni, 19 January 2007)

Beyond mining: ex-miners capitalizing on savings

It is revealing to consider what miners do after they retire from mining. Bearing in mind that the vast majority are untraceable, we, however, managed to interview

18 sedentary ex-miners in the two survey mining sites. On average, they were 39 years old, had mined for 12.5 years at 2.9 sites and were generally positive about what they had got out of mining. They were relatively well educated with all but one having finished primary school. They had capitalized on their earnings, by investing in various kinds of local service businesses.

Their reasons for drawing their mining careers to a close were wide-ranging and mostly connected with dissatisfaction with mine work: unhealthy, hard and risky work (45 per cent), loss of money on mining (17 per cent), lured to a new activity that paid better (21 per cent), or simply tired of mining (17 per cent). Thus, it seems, many miners stop mining due to weariness. The majority (61 per cent) stated that life had improved economically since their retirement. The main reasons were due to the increased stability and higher income of their current work, and the fact that some had been unlucky in mining recently. The rest were phlegmatic about their change in occupation, stating that there was little change in income level, but they appreciated that their present earnings were more stable. Their slightly higher educational level is likely to have given them the self-confidence to quit mining and strategically start a new occupation. Significantly, they had remained in the mining settlement where their knowledge of mining and social networks of the artisanal mining community gave them the navigational skills to facilitate making a living from non-mining activities within the mining settlements. Most viewed their current sedentary life with satisfaction, although a third still regretted not being able to follow new mineral rushes.

> Kiduta M., 38 years of age, stopped mining back in 2002 when a pit in which he was mining collapsed: 'I was half buried in gravel and stones, but luckily people were close by... They got me up, but my knee got severely injured'. He had been saving up and when he was able to walk again, he opened a clothes and shoe shop in Londoni. 'It is too uncertain to dig for gold... One risks one's life and limb... Today I earn more money selling clothes and shoes than I earned in the mines'.
>
> (Interview at Londoni, 7 February 2007)

Reflecting on their past mining careers, the ex-miners were divided about whether mining was a worthwhile occupation to pursue. Only a third mentioned that it had afforded them an improved livelihood and 11 per cent said that they had enjoyed the excitement of travelling. But many had deep regrets. Over 40 per cent felt that they had wasted their time and six per cent stated that mining had ruined their health. Another six per cent felt that they had frittered away their earnings on mindless conspicuous consumption and too much drinking. A third regretted that they had not left mining to do business earlier. However, half of the respondents were unequivocal about the fact that they would chose mining if they could start their work careers all over again.

Conclusion

Western literature on career structure tends to assume formal employment conditions such as those found in a civil service or corporation. But more broadly, careers encompass a lifetime work pattern, which can ideally be traced onwards and upwards (Ip 2008). It is in these terms that the concept of career is relevant to many Tanzanian gold miners. Remarkably, as artisanal mining has gained momentum within the last two decades, artisanal mining career trajectories have emerged despite miners' uncertainty of finding gold in any given locality combined with their shifting mine sites, casualized work teams, and *ad hoc* subsistence payments. Of those who persist onwards many rise upwards.[4] The latter's career commitment is reflected in their willingness to continually uproot themselves and dash to new gold strike sites. Experienced miners can be rewarded with progression from digger to higher earning pit holder and/or PML owner. In this way, miners' mobility, risk-taking and tenacity to carry on working for many years despite physically demanding labour and hardship pays off.

Uncountable numbers leave, most probably after the initial mine site, whereas others drop by the wayside finding alternative livelihood activities or are forced to stop mining due to injury or death. Mining accidents and high HIV prevalence rates take their toll. But those who stay are propelled by the possibility of being rewarded with larger incomes as pit holders and PML owners.

Climbing up the career pyramid is facilitated by one's origins near to a mining area, a comparatively higher education level, a willingness to move from site to site, and arriving early at strike sites (Jønsson and Bryceson 2009). Furthermore, lifestyle choices play a part. Those who avoid boom–bust expenditure patterns and are able to save and invest in houses and business are more likely than others to have the capital to become a pit holder or PML owner.

Tanzania's artisanal miners are often criticized for working on illegal mining sites and in illicit gold trade, engaging in heavy drinking and prostitution, and causing environmental degradation. They are frequently viewed by local farmers and government officials as misfits. On the other hand, their activities have a dynamic impact on the local economy and their work is highly labour-absorbing and productive. Furthermore, many of them have evolved a career trajectory through which they have gained professional competence and work incentives affording them the means to anticipate, plan and invest over the course of their work lives (Kanter 1989). This contrasts with the continuing amorphous nature of self-employed income diversification, more generally in Tanzania with its uncertainty of markets, supply and infrastructure. Mining opportunities at the base of the career pyramid afford the entry of massive numbers who try their hand at mining. Those who gain the skills and have the determination to mine believe with good reason that they will earn a livelihood that is likely to improve over time.

But the question is how long will this last? Artisanal miners face technical limits to the depths to which they can dig. Where mineral wealth is abundant, large corporate interests inevitably edge out artisanal producers. The Tanzanian gold diggers, pit holders and PML owners that we have focused on in this study have demonstrated personal initiative and collective creativity in evolving a career trajectory and professionalism, enabling them to be productive to the benefit of their families and the country as a whole. Their pyramidal career hierarchy has succeeded in providing them with valuable work skills and considerable self-governance.

As large-scale mining increasingly encroaches on artisanal mining areas, the onwards and upwards career movements of artisanal miners will be stymied and demoralization is bound to set in. Policy measures need to be devised and implemented in a timely fashion to preclude penalizing an exceptionally hard-working and creative segment of the Tanzanian workforce. Their prospecting work has in many cases pointed the way for large-scale mining. As Tanzania's mineral wealth accrues, the government and large-scale mining firms would be advised to design schemes to recruit labour and encourage service sector employment from the ranks of these mining pioneers.

Notes

1   This chapter is derived from the following article: Bryceson, D.F. and Jønsson, J.B. (2010) 'Gold digging careers in rural Africa: Small-scale miners' livelihood choices'. *World Development* 38(3), 379–99.
2   There are, however, a number of studies that provide important insights especially where livelihood diversification has led to combined mining and agricultural pursuits. See Banchirigah (2008), Maconachie and Binns (2007) and Hilson and Garforth (2013).
3   There may, however, have been some sampling bias. The wealthy PML owners of Londoni who make a lot of money did not appear in our sample, which included only one PML owner from Londoni and three from Matundasi.
4   We have noted in the title to this chapter, the metaphorical irony of upward success in an occupation directed at downward excavation.

References

Banchirigah, S.M. (2008) 'Challenges with eradicating illegal mining in Ghana: A perspective from the grassroots'. *Resources Policy* 33(1): 29–38.

Barret, C.B., Reardon, T. and Webb, P. (2001) 'Nonfarm income diversification and household strategies in rural Africa: Concepts, dynamics and policy implications'. *Food Policy* 26: 315–31.

Bryceson, D.F. (1999) 'African rural labour, income diversification and livelihood approaches: A long-term development perspective'. *Review of African Political Economy* 80: 171–89.

Bryceson, D.F. (2000a) Peasant theories and smallholder policies: Past and present. in Bryceson, D. F., Kay, C. and Mooij, J. (eds), *Disappearing Peasantries? Rural Labour in Africa, Asia and Latin America*. London: Intermediate Technology Publications, pp. 1–36.

Bryceson, D.F. (2000b) 'African peasants' centrality and marginality: Rural labour transformations'. in Bryceson, D. F., Kay, C. and Mooij, J. (eds), *Disappearing Peasantries? Rural Labour in Africa, Asia and Latin America*. London: Intermediate Technology Publications, pp. 37–63.

Bryceson, D.F. and Jønsson, J.B. (2010) 'Gold Digging Careers in Rural Africa: Small-scale Miners' Livelihood Choices'. *World Development* 38(3): 379–99.

Chachage, C.S.L. (1995) 'The meek shall inherit the earth but not the mining rights: Mining and accumulation in Tanzania. in Gibbon, P. (ed.), *Liberalised Development in Tanzania*. Uppsala, Sweden: Institute for African Studies, pp. 37–108.

Fisher, E. (2007) 'Occupying the margins: Labour integration and social exclusion in artisanal mining in Tanzania'. *Development and Change* 38(4): 735–60.

Godoy, R. (1985). 'Mining: Anthropological perspectives'. *Annual Review of Anthropology* 14: 199–217.

Hilson, G. (ed.) (2005) *The Socio-Economic Impacts of Artisanal and Artisanal Mining in Developing Countries*. The Netherlands: A.A. Balkema.

Hilson, G. and Garforth, C. '"Everyone now is concentrating on the mining": Drivers and implications of rural economic transition in the eastern region of Ghana'. *Journal of Development Studies* 49(3): 348–64.

Ip, C.Y. (2008) *The End of Careers? Changes of Male Employment Careers in Britain between 1955 and 2004*. DPhil thesis, University of Oxford.

Jønsson, J.B. and Bryceson, D.F. (2009) 'Rushing for gold: Mobility and artisanal mining in East Africa'. *Development and Change* 40(2): 249–79.

Jønsson, J.B. and Fold, N. (2009) 'Handling uncertainty: Policy and organizational practices in Tanzania's artisanal gold mining sector'. *Natural Resources Forum* 33(3): 211–20.

Kanter, R.M. (1989) *When Giants Learn to Dance: Mastering the Challenge of Strategy, Management and Careers in the 1990s*. New York: Simon and Schuster.

Maconachie, R. and Binns, T. (2007) '"Farming miners' or 'mining farmers"?: Diamond mining and rural development in post-conflict Sierra Leone'. *Journal of Rural Studies* 23(3): 367–80.

Mwaipopo, R., Mutagwaba, W., Nyanga, D. and Fisher, E. (2004) 'Increasing the contribution of artisanal and artisanal mining to poverty reduction in Tanzania'. London: Department for International Development.

Phillips, L.C., Semboja, H., Shukla, G.P., Sezinga, R., Mutagwaba, W., Mchwampaka, B., Wanga, G., Kahyarara, G. and Keller, C. (2001) 'Tanzania's precious mineral boom: Issues in mining and marketing'. Washington, DC: USAID.

Walsh, A. (2003) '"Hot money" and daring consumption in a northern Malagasy sapphire-mining town'. *American Ethnologist,* 30(2): 290–305.

4 Loosely woven love

Sexuality and wifestyles in gold-mining settlements[1]

Deborah Fahy Bryceson, Jesper Bosse Jønsson and Hannelore Verbrugge

Artisanal mining settlements have gained a reputation for being places of sexual amorality and the bane of nearby villages endorsing traditional moral standards. In several respects, this is not surprising: mining literature related to gold rush strikes worldwide, focusing on the gold digging activities of men, has often had the sub-theme of women's metaphorical gold-digging activities as prostitutes. Money-making is seen as the primary focus of men and women's aims, to the exclusion of marriage and family life. This chapter, based on qualitative interviews in 2009 with women living in artisanal gold mining settlements in southern Tanzania, interrogates the validity of this stereotype. Concentrating on social relations between men and women, we consider how sexual ties evolve from the perspective of women. In our analysis of the dynamics of monogamy, polygamy and promiscuity amidst rapid material change, we are alert to whether prostitution exists and deflects from bonds of caring, sharing and loving between the sexes.

Giddens (1992), writing on sexual intimacy in a capitalist context, defines an ideal 'pure' relationship as confluent love in which the individual man and woman mutually determine the conditions of their own association through respect and open communication. Our qualitative interview data provides the opportunity to gauge how far this ideal is from the reality of Tanzanian gold-mining settlements. We quote extensively from in-depth interviews with women from our survey mining settlement sites to reveal their motivations and expectations in conjugal relations. We begin with consideration of forms of marriage and sexual liaisons that were sanctioned in Tanzania's non-capitalist agrarian village communities. From there, we turn to how men and women meet each other in mining camps and, in the course of their daily lives as fortune-seekers, crystallize a new cultural frontier. Exploring the transition from sexual relations based on traditional family or lineage intervention to independent, often *ad hoc* coupling, leads to a consideration of 'wifestyles', an evolving spectrum of *de facto* conjugal relations that male miners and women have negotiated to secure material support, emotional security and sex from one another. In the conclusion, we review how occupational and cultural changes in artisanal mining sites across the country relate to marital ties in Tanzania generally.

Transforming sexuality

In Tanzania, sex is considered a fundamental, natural and pleasurable part of life that has the vital function of biological reproduction, producing children for the perpetuation of families, lineages and the nation-state. A generation ago, Bryceson and Vuorela (1984) characterized Tanzania as a high fertility culture moulded by its agrarian foundations where sex was highly valued for its child-begetting function ensuring the survival of lineages. Women's fertility was a central cultural concern. A woman's social identity as an adult was contingent on her achievement of motherhood. This chapter interrogates how sexual norms have been radically transformed in Tanzanian gold mining settlements.

Sex is almost invariably essentialized in the psyche of cultures worldwide, in denial of the culturally constructed form and content of sexual practices, values and human relationships (Caplan 1987). Sexual double standards are prevalent in many, if not most, cultures in one form or another. Victorian culture that imputed a strong sex drive to men as opposed to women represents one extreme. In East African cultures, the gender binary is more subdued but nonetheless in evidence. Nelson (1987), writing about Kenyan Kikuyu culture, observed the cultural belief that men's sex drive superseded that of women. While men viewed sex as a pleasurable, natural and healthy pursuit, it was acknowledged and condoned that women enjoyed sex but more stress was placed on the importance of female sex for procreation. Generally women were expected to exercise more restraint in sex.

As production relations alter in a society, reproductive and sexual relations are reconfigured (Bryceson and Vuorela 1984), a point reinforced by Giddens (1992) who argues that sex is freed from reproductive goals in many capitalist societies. Similarly, Diamond's (1998: 92) comparative review of human sexuality counters biological essentialism, demonstrating how changes in the material environment prompt new cultural constructions of sex derived from a highly adaptable and unique repertoire of human sexual behaviour that he refers to as a 'combination of marriage, co-parenting, and adulterous temptation'.

Diamond (1998) argues that people living at low levels of population density, are likely to have been inclined to a harem configuration in which dominant males monopolize sexual opportunities in the society at the expense of younger or weaker men. While this may be advantageous in small groups where hierarchical control provides corporate safety, as human communities grow in size, this reproductive strategy has the potential of becoming socially disruptive on the part of virile young men not given the opportunity to procreate. Monogamy is likely to become increasingly common.

However, the incidence of promiscuity is a possibility whether polygamy or monogamy prevails and indeed all three forms of sexuality can be coterminous to greater or lesser extents in any given community as our case study evidence indicates. Certainly, the transition from stable, low population density, decentralized non-capitalist agrarian societies to a concentrated artisanal mining population characterized by rapid turnover of highly mobile people in peak sexually active ages offers many temptations. Combined with the boom–bust atmosphere of miners working under stress for high stakes, gold mining sites exemplify extreme sexual enticement for men and women alike.

Sexual experimentation in Tanzanian mining areas has emerged against a historical backdrop of ritualized and symbolically controlled patrilineal, matrilineal and cognatic kinship systems (Mbilinyi 1988). More recently world religious influences, notably the polygamous practices of Islam and the monogamous strictures of Christianity, have played a role in evolving sexual relations. Now, as the impact of the global economy deepens and new forms of trade, investment and work relations spread, capitalist inter-personal relations are permeating sexual and family relations. The large-scale movement of men and women associated with mining is motivated primarily by a materialist quest for modernity aimed at gaining wealth and enjoying an improved standard of living rather than ensuring the continuation of lineages and agrarian ways of life or following religiously defined codes of behaviour. As the pursuit of capitalist modernity spreads, the association of sex with human reproduction weakens (Giddens 1992). Women feel less circumscribed about seeking sex for pleasure (Talle 1998).

Artisanal mining communities, with their makeshift settlements devoid of male elders' control, are very different from agrarian villages. Almost every resident is a migrant, hailing from a wide spectrum of home areas, making it unlikely that ritual life, if there were time for it, would or could be agreed upon in relation to marriage. Social controls on sexual fidelity are fluid, calling into question the nature of polygamous and monogamous practices. Promiscuity can thrive in these circumstances. This chapter sifts through field evidence from mining sites in southern Tanzania to ascertain women's attitudes towards changing sexual relations.

Polygamy, monogamy and secret sex

With over 100 tribal groups, Tanzania is ethnically endowed with a wide spectrum of marriage practices associated with different descent group structures. Unilineal descent dominates mainland Tanzania. Over the twentieth century, as population densities and the cash economy intensified, patrilineal practices have gradually and unobtrusively encroached on matrilineality (Moser 1987). Meanwhile, more overtly, conversion to Christian and Islamic beliefs that enshrine patriarchal principles took hold.

Cattle-keeping patrilineal groups, notably the Nyamwezi, Sukuma and Kuria, are well-known for their demanding bridewealth systems (Abrahams 1967; Fleisher 1999; Mhando 2011). Expensive bridewealth thresholds enforced by male elders have traditionally kept young men's marriage prospects at bay for a considerable time after their entry into adulthood. Elaborate rites of passage, as well as some form of bridewealth, structure the majority of Tanzania's lineage-based tribal groups.

Bridewealth, as a motivating force and pivot of local economies through time, has had a two-fold regulatory role: 1) inculcating female subservience and respect towards men and 2) providing a socially agreed contract of exchange that binds women in marriage (Lovett 1996). Bridewealth payments reflect the hierarchy of status and power within the community. Traditionally the prospective bride's worth was calculated on the basis of her behavioural demeanour as a dutiful wife, hard worker and above all fertile child-bearer. Such qualities in a woman were believed to contribute to the wealth and status of her husband.

It was possible for men to arrange engagement to an unborn child, with payment of a bridewealth deposit at birth, if it was a girl. Girls were married soon after puberty. This was related to the heavy premium placed on the girl's virginity, which could be checked by female elders on her wedding day (Wilson 1952). Unmarried women were frowned upon and deemed too disruptive to the moral order of the tribal community. Girls and women had no autonomy in determining when and whom they married. This was a decision of the elders of the prospective bride and groom's families. Once married, women were expected to be dutiful to their husbands and sanctioned by their husband's family and their own natal family to remain married. Divorce necessitated the return of bridewealth property by the woman's natal homestead to the husband's family. Such dealings brought shame and regret, leading to pressure on the woman to stay married.

In patrilineal groups, the paternity of children has generally been an issue vis-à-vis bridewealth payment. Similarly, in cases of discovery of a wife's infidelity, her husband would seek compensation from the male transgressor. Nonetheless, in most tribal communities, secret sex between lovers, married or unmarried, was not only known to happen but tacitly condoned, as long as the affair was pursued discretely. This gave young men a welcome chance for sexual encounters, usually through a *rendezvous* outside the village in secluded agricultural fields, woods or elsewhere (Caplan 1992, 2001). Illicit local liaisons tended to be kept undercover and were not a source of moral condemnation.

Meanwhile women who dared to leave their home areas and the protection of their lineage faced moral censure, labelled prostitutes (*malaya*) by virtue of their independence from male lineage control (Mbilinyi 1988; McCurdy 2001). Such unattached women posed a threat to the social order constructed by rural male patriarchs, whose power rested on control of women and younger men. The spread of Christianity compounded the social disdain that the prostitutes experienced, with Christianity's insistence on monogamous union casting independent women as potential home wreckers.

Miners' leisure: Drinking and flirting

Moving to the present, our artisanal mining survey sites are culturally set apart from surrounding rural villages, even though the two exist in close spatial proximity to one another. Our research methodology described in an endnote,[2] involved informal interviews with women across the age spectrum about their lives in Matundasi and nearby Itumbi mining camps. We quote extensively from these interviews to directly convey the women's agency, attitudes and sentiments.

Given the mobile and youthful demographic composition of the mining population, there is an absence of male elders for exerting moral pressure over sexual behaviour in the manner described above. The high turnover of migrants makes it impossible for everyone to be familiar with one another, let alone know every-one else's family backgrounds, thereby largely precluding community gossip from having a moderating influence on individuals' sexual behaviour. Some older members of the settlement cannot resist trying to compensate for the lack of coun-selling by speaking their mind about younger people's courtship activities, but there is a distinct impression that the two generations, who in the case of the women break down into 'older married women' and 'younger unmarried women', are speaking past each other.

Meeting and mating with the opposite sex is pragmatically facilitated in miners' daily lives by the existence of bars that serve as fuelling stations for fulfil-ment of people's basic needs for food and drink. Barmaids, mostly young women, nicknamed *dogo dogo*[3] (spring chicks) to signify how they represent successive waves of newly arrived young women, are employed or, more commonly, work for tips in these establishments.

Barmaids generally work as casualized labour. Very few receive a fixed salary or adhere to a work schedule. Instead upon their arrival in the settlement most approach the bar owners asking for the chance to work:

> There's a lot of staff circulation. The girls may stay a month or half a month, some of them are getting married, others are staying for a few weeks and then they retreat to another area. This happens because once a new barmaid is employed here, all customers want to go to the new one, so the old one switches to another area ... We just depend on introductions from people we know who come and say: 'this is my best friend and she is used to selling beers, please employ her' ... Trust is an issue. We have to put in writing how many crates the barmaid is taking each day to ensure she pays back the right amount of money. Many of them try to be honest but when they leave, some of them try to steal, in some cases, even my clothes. Most of the girls we hire are young. Once there was a newcomer of 40 years of age who used to be a barmaid in Mbeya. She wanted the job, but she looked the age of my mother so I refused.
>
> (Bar manager, aged 28, Itumbi, 8 September 2009)

The barmaids have various ploys for making money:

> The man orders and pays for 10 beers, but the barmaid will secretly return two to three beers to the beer seller so the seller will resell the beer and pay the proceeds to the girl. This is the way that the *dogo dogo* earn and some-times if the men become totally drunk, the girls take more of the beers and run away and sell the beers themselves. Sometimes they deliberately confuse the bill ... And sometimes they steal the money in the miners' pockets since miners are accustomed to putting all their earnings in their pocket, so that people can see that they are wealthy.
>
> (Bar manager, aged 33, Itumbi, 20 August 2009)

The boundaries between romantic dating, propositioning and sexual intimidation are continually blurred. Primarily in search of boyfriends, the girls expect to be treated with food, drinks and gifts from the men. Barmaids may ask for money for having sexual intercourse, but there is nothing fixed about such payments when they happen. The same amount of money may apply or extend to a whole night together. Negotiating signals on both sides tend to be ambiguous and contestable, but in areas where competition over the best girls is high and cash is flowing, payments may occasionally be as high as several hundred dollars.

> When a man with money enters a bar and buys a beer and offers it to a woman without saying anything, if the woman agrees to take the beer, he sees that as a sign of agreement that he can have sex with her. Sometimes it happens that one woman gets three beers from different men so this means that she has agreed to three liaisons. Now how is that going to be handled? That is why the women end up being beaten. I have seen many conflicts arising from women accepting offers of beer from different men.
> (Woman brewer, aged 32, Itumbi, 24 August 2009)

Arrangements to meet after the girl's shift require logistical manoeuvring since the bars are not brothels. In fact some bar owners have explicit rules banning men from the girls' rooms. Usually the men have places in mind where they can take or later meet with their selected sex partner.

> Usually men at first stay in rooms with more than one boy but because of wanting to have sex, they have tried to build their own huts and some of them are lending houses to each other. They are looking for young girls, because those are the ones without focused vision... It is very rare for boys to allow their girls to be used by other men.
> (Bar manager, aged 41, Itumbi, 21 August 2009)

Most young newcomers start their working lives as barmaids but those intent on getting beyond their good-time girl status consciously set boundaries on how they earn their money and steer their lives:

> The men flirt and some want sex or to attract one of us as a girlfriend. If you refuse, they have reason to be abusive. It is a very competitive environment and in terms of behaviour, there are no old men in Itumbi because all of them are very active, so even the old men are competing to get girlfriends. They compete with money. In Itumbi, if you have no money, you can't succeed so money speaks. There is a saying: 'no money, no honey.' Nonetheless in my case, fortunately, I can say no when one of them offers me money. It is easy to say no because my business provides me with something to eat every day. The key thing that makes many girls say yes is the need for food.
> (Bar manager, aged 26, 20 August 2009)

The girls' 'gold rush' tends to be short-lived and yields disappointing results. Many come from troubled backgrounds of family domestic abuse, dissension, violence or death, seeking personal autonomy and better life chances. They are responding to perceived opportunities while tending to ignore the obvious threat of HIV/AIDS. The reported HIV+ prevalence rate was 22 per cent in Matundasi in 2007.[4] Condom usage is not widespread. Men feel that it impinges on their sexual pleasure. Knowing they are running big risks and may be HIV positive, most people do not like to think – let alone talk – about the possibility of HIV infection.

> Letting people know your HIV status is taboo because it means that someone has been cheating. That is why people don't want to speak about it. Especially in these mining villages, appearance is everything, to not have a bad name. I don't know how to break this taboo.
>
> (Brewing and bar manager, aged 30, Itumbi, 23 August 2009)

Residents in the mining settlements identify, resent and rely on the presence of these continuing influxes of young girls. Many of the women came to the settlement through this channel. Now they are married and feel insecure about the presence of the newcomers vis-à-vis their menfolk. On the other hand, the girls are the axis of the catering and service trade. Their labour is needed and is profitable. This nonetheless does not stop many older members of the population complaining about the girls' lack of morality.

Wifestyles: Sexual partnering

Existing literature on sexual relationships in mining settlements and mineral rush periods gives prominence to the role of prostitutes in servicing men's sexual needs (Goldman 1981; Gray 2010). Whereas one might readily interpret the generous drinks tipping of barmaids by miners, men's gift-giving and erratic receipt of small payments for sexual services as prostitution, this would overlook the fact that the normal organizational features of professional prostitution are largely absent, notably: girls' occupational identity as prostitutes; brothel premises affording girls a room for sexual business; market pricing of the sexual act; organizational management by male pimps or female madams. Instead women insist that both having sex and their sex partners were their choice rather than a forced or practical necessity (Nelson 1987; White 1990; Talle 1998; De Boeck 1999; Desmond *et al.* 2005.[5] Sexual attraction and coy behaviour of 'boy meets girl' was the norm, with the man in particular concerned with the exclusivity, at least momentarily, of his claim for attention from the specific woman he had gifted.

Women and girls, focused on attracting men, depended on men's gifts of food and money for daily survival. This was the basis of daily social interaction rather than specialized prostitutes offering sex to men on an established fee basis. The bar owners, where the men and women met, were not in the habit of recruiting barmaids, nor was there evidence of any of them or others acting as madams or pimps, arranging and charging for the premises or situational context in which a prostitute would sell her services. Rather the sexual intercourse that ensued between barmaids and male customers took place in a wide range of *ad hoc* settings from miners' rented rooms, to girls' accommodation, at a friend's or in the bush. Most importantly, all of the girls interviewed either lived in hopes of finding a reliable man, or, in a minority of cases, eschewed sexual relations with men altogether.

The women's verbal observations about sexual relations reveal motivations as well as patterned strategies. We use the term 'wifestyles' to denote distinct sexual relational niches that women occupy vis-à-vis men that vary on the basis of emotional and economic ties to their sex partner as well as the degree of sexual exclusivity between the two individuals. Wifestyles reflect the collision of historically ingrained and innovative forms of sexual ties. Tribal life-cycle courting and marriage patterns of an ascriptive nature, under the direction of rural patriarchs, are progressively being dislodged by the cumulative effect of individuals' livelihood, lifestyle and sexual partnering decisions in response to new opportunities, risks and vulnerabilities (Hodgson 2001). The new sexuality does not arise solely from market commodification. The rising momentum of cultural and social experimentation embedded in the spread of capitalist values, work norms and leisure time pursuits, spurs new sexual preferences and associated emotional needs. Path-dependent sexual relationships unfold, be they promiscuous, polygamous or monogamous, which deeply impact on people's material welfare.

It should be noted that the term 'wife' is used very loosely in mining settlements. Very few people are formally married in traditional or religious terms. Relationships blur from sexual partner to boyfriend to husband, in the absence of demarcating rituals or public ceremonies. The following outlines five relational ties that allow for fluidity in one direction or another:

Good-time girls (dogo dogo)

Aged in their early teens through to mid-20s, many if not most girls entering as migrants find their way into an arena of sexual conquest that can lead to misadventure. One night stands abound. When the mines are producing gold, the men are in high spirits celebrating their success or at least optimistic expectations of success with the girls. The young women rely heavily on the free food, drinks, and gifts of fashionable clothing that come their way.

The girls' presence in the mining settlement is subject to continually high turnover. During the rainy season when there is little gold digging, many migrate elsewhere due to the seasonal lull in livelihood prospects. Others leave because of illness from the excesses of alcohol, an erratic diet, exposure to sexually transmitted diseases and conflictual interpersonal relations or abandonment by their newfound boyfriends.

The young boys are trying to attract or even harass the young girls. They inform each other of which woman is easy-going or not . . . they don't like to waste time . . . these young girls are having so many misadventures.

(Brewer, miner, and farmer, married to first husband for 13 years, aged 28, Itumbi, 22 August 2009)

While there is novelty, fun and adventure during the mining seasons, the young women nonetheless face many hazards. It is from these successive cohorts that miners find cohabiting partners. Newly formed couples may manage to stay together, get married and in rare cases establish longstanding conjugal relations. In this way, some newcomers eventually become the settlement's hard-working, respected matrons who bemoan the passions and pathos of their successors.

Cohabiting girlfriend-wives (hawara)

When compatibilities are discovered – be they social or sexual – cohabiting relationships tend to be motivated by social and economic convenience on the part of either partner or both. Sharing accommodation can save money and affords people many of the comforts of home, day-to-day cooperative interaction and sex. Girls are eager to find a man to live with, given their need for a sense of both material security and physical protection.[6] Genuine affection brings many of these couples together. Others' cohabitation may be prompted by the birth of a child, which the miner acknowledges as his. Their decision to live together is sometimes marked by an impromptu gathering of friends and well-wishers. But that is rare.

Most couples begin their cohabitation through happenstance barely cognizant of a joint social existence let alone considering how long they may live together. The passage of time may strengthen compatibility and interdependence of the couple. After about three to six months of being together, the couple are seen to have withstood the test of time and are generally considered married in *hawara* relationships that infer permanence and sexual faithfulness of the women towards her male partner (Talle 1998). However, the actual duration of the couple living together is frequently a matter of months not years. When one or the other partner vacates the shared premises with all of his or her material possessions, most are walking away from each other with total finality, tantamount to a clean-break divorce minus the need for any legal proceedings.

Life in Itumbi is not very good. My friend that I migrated with three months ago is now married to a certain boy here in Itumbi, but I have seen that some of the girls are getting married during the dry season, but during the rainy season, when there is very little gold being extracted, they are already getting divorced. Being married to a miner is a temporary thing. If they have no money, they are very polite. They are not after women or young girls. But when they start earning money, they start seeking to have a relationship.

(Unemployed, depends on boyfriends, aged 16, Itumbi, 21 August 2009)

Polygamous marriages

Despite the many cultural precedents for polygamy in Tanzania, traditional polygamy, as opposed to polygamous practices in mining localities, is fundamentally different. In the latter, almost everyone is a migrant with lack of knowledge of their spouse's family background. Not infrequently, women marry and only discover later that their husbands are polygamist. Furthermore, the high mobility of miners ordains that many have wives in distant places to which they remit considerable sums of money. Various breaches of trust and family welfare may arise.

> My husband's second wife was a newcomer. If they get information that miners are earning, they try to trap them. When I heard that my husband was married to another wife, I felt really bad because I didn't plan for such a life. I never expected this from him. Many people, especially the old and wise ones, who saw me in a sorrowful condition tried to advise me: 'you have two children. Now, with this special gift from God, if you decide to leave these children here with your husband' do you think that this second wife will care for your children? Or if he sends the children to his home area where you don't know anyone, do you think that it will be good for the children?' I realized that I had to stay. That is why I am always busy with running projects, which can provide me with something to support my children... Now, the second wife has left and I am happy. It is difficult for my husband to support a second wife because his mining is not going well. During the period of his second marriage, the pit was providing millions. He was giving millions to the second wife. For me, the maximum support I got was just US$ 31 (Tsh 50,000). Now, however, since the pit is not producing my husband is very attentive to me and many people are saying to him: 'now you see the importance of using the first wife, the second wife has run away and you are getting support from your first wife'. I think that maybe he has learnt a lesson... However, when my husband was away with his second wife, my health improved and I was relieved by not having to put up with his complaints and interference in my business. When he came back without money, it was again the same old problem he would demand: 'give us some money, because we are running out of capital to finance the gold pit'. That is why I am becoming financially weak. I'm supporting his gold pit. But am I going to get back my money or will all the money be taken again to the second wife? Once I think about this, I lose my desire for this marriage.
> (Bar manager, used clothes, maize trade, tailoring, married to second husband, aged 40, Itumbi, 25 August 2009)

> My boyfriend has a younger wife but he helps support me and my children. Sometimes, all the money he earns, if it is very little, goes to his wife because I feel that if he spends all the money here while his wife and children have nothing that is not right. Sometimes my boyfriend can stay six months

without earning. And I support him if he is here so that once he earns he helps me. So once I notice that the money is very little, I'm advising him to send money to his wife and if it is a big amount, he supports me.

(Bar manager and used clothes sales, widowed with longstanding married boyfriend, aged 39, Itumbi, 24 August, 2009)

Monogamous marriages-cum-business partnerships

Despite the highly mobile and sexualized environment in which residents of the mining settlements live – which militates for short-term, casualized sexual relations – out of the 32 interviewed women, there were seven who had marriages that endured for over 8 years and three for over 20 years. All except two were the interviewed women's first and only marriages. However, even in the two cases involving second husbands, the marriages were of an enduring nature. In one case it was apparent that the marriage was lodged on a firm religious belief in the sanctity of marriage. But the others were couples that operated with a joint economic trajectory of pooled income and property as a single welfare unit. The husbands' and wives' productive activities were characterized by a collaborative or complementary division of labour and a high incidence of joint investment and special arrangements for sending their children to good schools outside of the mine settlement. Economic trust underlined the monogamous marriages as illustrated in the following quotes.

Nowadays, life in mining and the miners themselves are changing. They have seen that women who are not involved in running any projects are not helpful to them when they are lacking money. So some of the men are supporting women who are running projects in order to get support when they become broke from not finding gold.

(Bar manager, alone, aged 26, Itumbi, 25 August 2009)

I met my husband when he was buying beers wholesale. He was running a small shop then. He is now running the biggest bar in Itumbi. At night people come to watch TV at his place and it is very busy. I deal with the money for the drinks, organizing the number of beers and crates. I also have a shop outside. We started living together in 2001. I had been assisting him up to that time. We are working together. My husband is dealing with mining also. Presently, I supervise all the home projects because my husband is dealing with mining, running ball mills and washing places. We have divided our workload duties. My husband owns a PML and a washing place. We earn around US$ 625 per month (Tsh. 1 million) from the bar and the washing place. We are not farming. Sometimes we have an argument but very few times and it doesn't take a long time before we agree again. We are afraid of disturbing our plan but in general, it is going well. Together we have planned our future. We will eventually retreat to the regional capital city because we have already bought a house, which needs maintenance only. We are planning to open a big shop there, as well as keeping the smaller shop here ... I know that the women in Itumbi are used to following any man who has a good life so I assume that there must be some women chasing my husband. We have a plan and it is still on-going. I don't know if he is spending extra money on other women, but for the money, which we have planned, everything is fine.

(Bar manager, shop, PML, mine washing, married monogamously for eight years, aged 28, Itumbi, 8 September 2009)

Single, independent women

In contrast to the above monogamous marriages where the women expressed satisfaction and happiness with their marriages, there was a very strong representation of women who were single out of necessity or choice with some deliberately avoiding close interdependent relationships with men. In Tanzania, historically it was unthinkable for a woman not to marry. The belief was that women were always protected by their fathers (or maternal uncles in the case of matrilineality) as children, by their husbands once married and by their sons if widowed. Traditionally, women gained social status from marriage and having children (Bryceson 1995). However, those who now choose to live alone, either through bitter experiences endured during previous marriages or fear of HIV/AIDS are relatively numerous. Some young unmarried women retain their autonomy from men with the intention of avoiding AIDS and/or building an independent economic base for themselves. Most independent women had been married or in relationships with boyfriends that had left them with children that they were raising largely on their own as explained in the following case studies:

When I came here, I had capital so I decided to buy a small house here and then I agreed with a certain man to stay with him. That man had a wife who died leaving three children. After staying with me for a few months, he decided to go and get his children so we had eight children in total – ten in the household. I noticed that my husband's mining was not paying. We stayed for a long time without money. It was a heavy load to take care of all these children. I decided to separate. That is why now I am alone supporting my five children in my own house. I already tried living with two husbands, but it is risky to have a mining husband. It is very rare for men in mining to have a humanitarian character. If I continue to cope with them I will die from AIDS. I regret that the life of my children is very tough but at least I am alive. If I die from HIV/AIDS, what type of life will the children have? Most men who mine are here in order to earn money, not to take care of someone. I have decided that I can have a relationship with some other men, maybe in the future but at present, I have to concentrate on finding capital because my daughter is very bright. If she gets educated, she will be able to have a job so that she can take care of the family.

(Bar manager, maize/banana trader, married twice now divorced, aged 33, Itumbi, 20 August 2009)

My first desire was to continue schooling but I failed to get that chance. And when I consider the five deaths of my elder brothers and sisters, I am afraid of taking boyfriends. In this life here, there is a continuous circle of exchanging men and women every day (laughing). The circle of life in mining is not good.

(Bar manager, alone, aged 26, Itumbi, 25 August 2009)

Anchor wives in home areas

Having studied male–female relationships within the mining settlements, we were nonetheless not in a position to interview an important wifestyle category, which functionally exists in the form of men's money remittances and visits away from the mines to women, notably wives or mistresses living in places geographically distanced from the site. Most miners' anchor wives are situated in their home areas. They are usually first wives of the miners that married following traditional tribal rites of their home communities concerning bridewealth payments. Such marriages do not always endure as miners migrate from one mine site to the next, but of those that do the man's social identity, emotional connections and economic property tend to be closely linked to his anchor wife. The anchor wife's continuing residence in the home area often serves to safeguard his claim to ancestral homeland and other inheritance property. Sukuma men, originating from distant areas near Lake Victoria, were the most numerous in our miners' survey, and were often polygamous with anchor wives resident in their home areas. The following commentary is from a woman observing her Sukuma husband's continuing links with his anchor wife.

I am free to do whatever business I like, selling fish or even buying gold as a broker. My husband is very flexible. I don't worry. He allows me to do business because it is the only way of earning income in the household. We share taking care of my grandchild. My husband is polygamous and has a first wife who stays in Mwanza. I am his second wife. My husband is good at taking care of my grandchild, but once I earn money, he may use some of it; I don't know anything about this money because he has to send the money to his first wife. He has six grown up sons and daughters so he has to provide some money for them. Sometimes he goes to Mwanza and sometimes he transfers the money. They don't come here. All his relatives are staying in Mwanza so once he earns something he goes there and then returns here. The first wife is in Mwanza where they built a house and it is his home area whereas here is just a working place. He came here with me for work. This kind of marriage is not very helpful or secure for me especially in the future since my husband is getting older and he has already stopped doing heavy-duty work. We have our own house but it is not improved or modern. I am just thinking that maybe, as the days are going on, there will be a time when my husband will stop working and maybe his children from Mwanza will come and take him back and then I will be here alone with my grandchild.

(Mine processing worker, married to polygamist, aged 57 years, Itumbi, 28 August 2009)

Wifestyles juxtaposed

Historically, Tanzanians, particularly youth and rural women, had very little scope for choosing their economic and social destiny in life. They grew up in agrarian tribal societies in which the division of labour by age and sex was ascribed. Life-cycle rituals celebrated changes in their social status. In the case of a girl, puberty rites marked the dawn of her status as a nubile woman of child-bearing age. Soon after, she would be married to a man in exchange for bridewealth that her family may have negotiated years before. Her designated role as a wife and mother within the structure of a patrilineal or matrilineal agrarian community was largely pre-ordained.

Our use of the term 'wifestyles' is intended to provoke debate on how intimate relations between men and women are altering in the twenty-first century, specifically in Tanzania's mining settlements. We reject the assumption that prostitution is the essence of such relations in Tanzania's mining settlements. Rather we find it more useful to see a complex interplay of competing sexual desires, emotional needs, social status, daily practicalities, and economic security objectives at play.

Various feminists have depicted marriage as prostitution, arguing that women's autonomy is exchanged for economic security (Goldman 1979; Friedan 1964; Greer 1971). Certainly the range of wifestyles is, in our view, underpinned not only by the human need for sex but also efforts to establish interdependent ties between the sexes. Furthermore, in some of these wifestyles, it appears that women as well as men have had voice in defining the nature of the relationship, along the lines of Gidden's (1992) concept of a 'pure' relationship. Tanzania's rural subsistence ethic is likely to have a strong influence. Rural societies sought egalitarian exchange ties, in the face of sporadic famine (Bryceson 1990). Similarly, the high-risk environment of a mining settlement, posing threats of economic failure, illness and physical insecurity, is likely to propel men and women alike to seek relationships of interdependence.

The above outlined wifestyles can be read along a gradient of time and emotional commitment. Economic exchange-cum-partnership is at stake with changing and usually dichotomous objectives on the part of men and women. Relations between men and good-time girls obviously represent the lowest level of time and emotional investment, with pleasurable abandon being one of the strongest attractions for men. Young women, on the other hand, are usually combining a quest for pleasure with the short-term goal of survival. Such encounters provide them with food, drink and sometimes clothing. Meanwhile, they are hoping to find the right man who can offer them economic security, which is all the more imperative if they have yet to construct a viable economic livelihood in the settlement.

Becoming a girlfriend or wife is a status that most girls hope to reach quickly. It is important to stress that it is not only women depending on men's income. Miners, given their erratic income-earning, fall back on girlfriend/wives' income-earning as well. Emotional and financial interdependence is mutual, with the possibility of either the man or the woman providing the major inflow of income.

Whatever the case, the income exchange is likely to be vital for continued habitation in the settlement. Nonetheless, live-in relationships often are of a short duration amounting to a few months, weeks or even days, before a couple part ways.

The latter three categories denote more mature relationships involving older women, usually with children. Raising children changes the dynamic of a relationship and tests the commitment of the man. The degree of a man's emotional and economic commitment is vital to child welfare and is influenced by the couple's spatial context, notably whether the couple physically live in the same house or at least the same settlement as opposed to living in different localities. Secondly, if the husband and wife's relationship is sexually exclusive, it appears that monogamy, whether it is adhered to or not, may give a woman more assurance of her husband's economic commitment to raising a family. By contrast, the anchor wife living away from the mining settlement in the husband's home area may be afforded material support from his extended family.

The existence of large numbers of independent women who avoid relationships with men and raise children on their own suggests that the interdependence of men and women through the formation of makeshift marital ties, however hard they are sought, often fail under the duress of life in the mining settlement. These cases, frequent as they are, must be counterpoised with the existence of the enduring monogamous business-partnership marriages, which may not be sexually exclusive but have proven to be solid units for raising children and running businesses that appear most likely to bring prosperity to the husband, wife and children as a family unit.

Nonetheless, enduring monogamous marriages are not the norm. Casual relationships and marriages are most common, a product of interpersonal flux based on emotional, economic and social circumstances rather than prostitution. The duress of gold market uncertainty and male miners' frequent migration to new gold rush sites may make it impossible for a marriage to solidify. Thus, wifestyles are mixed and matched through an individual's sexually active life. Polygamy, monogamy and promiscuity are all likely to play a role at one time or another in a woman's sexual life in the mining settlement. It is worth noting that this pattern, although less marked, has been observed to be increasingly common in Tanzania's urban areas as well, notably in Dar es Salaam (Talle 1998; Cloutier 2006).

Conclusion

Contrary to the popular belief that sexual relationships between men and women are 'natural' in the sense of being biologically given, this chapter documents how they are continually being socially and economically reconstructed through male and female negotiation in a period of rapid occupational change (Bryceson and Vuorela 1984; Giddens 1992; Diamond 1998). Demographic, cultural and labour patterns in Tanzania's mining towns differ fundamentally from that of rural areas. Both men and women are less concerned with female fertility and women's role in lineage perpetuation, mirroring the tendency towards sexuality freed from the imperative of reproduction under capitalism that Giddens (1992) identified. Women's status is aligned with sexual desirability and, in some cases, financial partnership, rather than childbearing.

Family formation is taking place in Tanzanian mining settlements, and the characterization of most women in mining towns as prostitutes is a misrepresentation. Women, young and middle-aged, endeavour to attract and then maintain the sexual interests and the financial support of men for the sake of material security. Men's aims are not dissimilar, but their polygamy practices and mobility, impart complexity and uncertainty in the process of Tanzanian mining family formation.

Men and women's negotiations over sexuality are inextricably entwined with concerns about residential arrangements, financial flows and child support in Tanzanian gold-mining settlement. The preceding verbatim quotes documenting women's experiences and views indicate that attainment of Gidden's 'pure' relationship of sexual and emotional equality between the sexes is very distant. Despite the general acknowledgement that sexuality is a realm of pleasure-seeking for men and women, women are on an unequal footing with men. Men have more leeway to be promiscuous given their high mobility and license to be polygamous. They often hide the sexual and family relations that they have had or are currently pursuing beyond the mining settlement. Women are far less likely to keep secrets about their family life and, as child-bearers and the main child-carers, they are often literally 'left with the baby' and children that are unsupported by the father/s.

Nonetheless, women in mining settlements tend to see themselves as liberated and modern. Having evaded bridewealth arrangements, they are no longer subject to male patriarchal control exerted by their rural elders and are able to exercise choice in marriage and sexual partnerships. In the mining settlement context, union of the conjugal couple may have a romantic edge, but the negotiations are essentially about securing material security, comfort and advance as a couple, with the question mark always hanging over whether the man is committed as much as the woman to the relationship. Purity of the relationship is best measured in terms of mutual commitment.

Men and women's migration to mining settlements to secure an improved lifestyle generates winners and losers. Men need gold strikes to succeed. In the case of women, the evolution of wifestyles documented in this chapter have become part of the fabric of mining communities, and profoundly affect their welfare circumstances. Co-habitational relations with men are highly unstable, particularly those experienced by young girls, girlfriends and polygamous wives. In the event of their material distress, there is no security fallback of the consensual village community or the welfare state enforcing male responsibility for family provisioning. In such a context, miners' wifestyle choices are critical for women and children's welfare. Not surprisingly, most women seek to achieve interdependency with men, despite the odds.

Notes

1   This chapter is based on the following article: D.F. Bryceson, Jønsson, J.B. and Verbrugge, H. (2013) 'Prostitution or partnership: Wifestyles in Tanzanian Artisanal gold-mining settlements'. *Journal of Modern African Studies* 51(1), 33–56.
2   Our gold mining settlement survey sites, Matundasi and Itumbi, located in Chunya, southwestern Tanzania are adjoining settlements 15 km apart with a combined population of 7,640 in 2007 (local government officials' most recent estimate). Thirty-two women in Itumbi (26) and Matundasi (6) were selected and interviewed by Hannelore Verbrugge with the assistance of John Wihallah in August–September 2009. A snow-balling technique was used to identify interviewees within an occupationally stratified sampling grid of the area's five major economic activities: i) alcohol sales (barmaids, restaurant bar managers, brewers), ii) trade (cloth, food), iii) mining, iv) services (pharmacists, hair stylists) and v) farming, across a full range of economically active ages (16 to 57 years). The grid ensured representation of a broad spectrum of experiences and opinions. The oral history interviews centred on the women's family background, migration, occupational change, conjugal relationships and children.
3   *Dogo dogo* literally means 'little ones' but in the context of successive waves of new incoming girls, it has taken on the connotation of 'spring chicks'.
4   This was recorded in nearby Matundasi mining settlement during a national testing campaign involving 760 residents: 168 were positive (52 males and 116 females).
5   White's (1990) meticulous study of prostitution in colonial Nairobi draws attention to the blurred line between wife and *malaya* prostitutes servicing male sexual and domestic needs.
6   Talle (1998) notes that single women felt a stronger need for physical protection in the mining settlements than urban towns in Tanzania.
7   Men get custody of the children under tribal customary law but currently, if legal and other authorities are involved, the custody arrangements are more tailored to circumstances that are deemed beneficial to the children.

References

Abrahams, R.G. (1967) *The Peoples of Greater Unyamwezi*: *Ethnographic Survey of Africa*. London: International African Institute.
Bryceson, D.F (1990) 'African women hoe cultivators: Speculative origins and current enigmas' in Bryceson, D.F. (ed.) *Women Wielding the Hoe: Lessons from Rural Africa for Feminist Theory and Development Practice*. Oxford: Berg Publishers, pp. 3–22.
Bryceson, D.F. (1995) 'Gender relations in rural Tanzania: Power politics or cultural consensus?' in Creighton, C. and Omari, C.K. (eds) *Gender, Family and Household in Tanzania*. Avebury: Ashgate, pp. 37–69.
Bryceson, D.F. and U. Vuorela (1984) 'Outside the domestic labor debate: Towards a theory of modes of human reproduction'. *Review of Radical Political Economics* 16(2/3), 137–66.
Caplan, P. (1987) 'Introduction', in Caplan, P. (ed.) *The Cultural Construction of Sexuality*, London: Tavistock Publications, pp. 1–30.
Caplan, P. (1992) 'Spirits and sex: A Swahili informant and his diary'. in Okely, J.M. and Callaway, H. (eds) *Anthropology and Autobiography*, London: Routledge, pp. 64–81.
Caplan, P. (2001) 'Monogamy, polygyny, or the single state? Changes in marriage patterns in a Tanzanian coastal village, 1965–94'. in Creighton, C. and Omari, C.K. (eds) *Gender, Family and Work in Tanzania*. Aldershot: Avebury, pp. 44–66.
Cloutier, L. (2006) *Income Differentials and Gender Inequality: Wives Earning More than Husbands in Dar es Salaam, Tanzania*. Dar es Salaam: Mkuki na Nyota Publishers.

De Boeck, F. (1999) 'Dogs breaking the leash': Globalization and shifting gender categories in the diamond traffic between Angola and DR Congo (1984–1997)' in Lame, D. and Zabus, C. (eds) *Changements au Feminin en Afrique Noire. Anthropologie et Littérature* (vol. I), Paris: Editions L'Harmattan.

Desmond, N., C.F. Allen, S. Clift, B. Justine, J. Mzugu, M.L. Plummer, D. Watson-Jones and Rose, D.A. (2005) 'A typology of groups at risk of HIV/STI in a gold mining town in north-western Tanzania'. *Social Science and Medicine* 60, 1739–49.

Diamond, J. (1998) *Why is Sex Fun? The Evolution of Human Sexuality*, London: Phoenix.

Fleisher, M.L. (1999) 'Cattle raiding and household demography among the Kuria of Tanzania'. *Africa* 69(2): 238–55.

Friedan, B. (1964) *The Feminine Mystique* (Mass Market edn), New York: Dell.

Giddens, A. (1992) *The Transformation of Intimacy: Love, Sex and Eroticism in Modern Societies*. Stanford, CA: Stanford University Press.

Goldman, E. (1979) *Red Emma Speaks: Selecting Writings and Speeches* (edited by A.K. Shulman, 2nd edn). Avebury: Ashgate Publishing Ltd.

Goldman, M.S. (1981) *Gold Diggers and Silver Miners: Prostitution and Social Life on the Comstock Lode*. Ann Arbor: University of Michigan Press.

Gray, C. (2010) *Gold Diggers: Striking it Rich in the Klondike*, Berkeley, CA: Counterpoint.

Greer, G. (1971) *The Female Eunuch*. New York: McGraw-Hill.

Hodgson, D.L. (2001) '"My daughter...belongs to the government now": Marriage, Maasai, and the Tanzanian state', in Hodgson, D.L. and McCurdy, S.A. (eds) *"Wicked" Women and the Reconfiguration of Gender in Africa*, Portsmouth NH: Heinemann; and Oxford: James Currey, pp. 149–67.

Lovett, M. (1996) '"She thinks she's like a man": Marriage and (de)constructing gender identity in colonial Buha, Western Tanzania, 1943–1960'. *Canadian Journal of African Studies* 30(1): 52–68.

Mbilinyi, M. (1988) 'Runaway wives in colonial Tanganyika: Forced labour and forced marriage in colonial Rungwe district 1919–1961'. *International Journal of Sociology of Law* 16(1), 1–29.

McCurdy, S.A. (2001) 'Urban threats: Manyema women, low fertility, and venereal diseases in Tanganyika, 1926–1936', in Hodgson, D.L. and McCurdy, S.A. (eds) *"Wicked" Women and the Reconfiguration of Gender in Africa*. Portsmouth NH: Heinemann; and Oxford: James Currey, pp. 212–33.

Mhando, N.E. (2011) *The Need for Wives and the Hunger for Children: Marriage, Gender and Livelihood among the Kuria of Tanzania*, PhD thesis, Goldsmiths, University of London.

Moser, R.P. (1987) 'Transformations of Southern Tanzanian marriages', in Parkin, D. and Nyamwaya, D. (eds), *Transformations of African Marriages*. Manchester: Manchester University Press, pp. 323–9.

Nelson, N. (1987) '"Selling her kiosk": Kikuyu notions of sexuality', in Caplan, P. (ed.), *The Cultural Construction of Sexuality*. London: Tavistock Publications, pp. 217–39.

Talle, A. (1998) 'Sex for leisure: Modernity among female bar workers in Tanzania' in Abram, S. and Waldren, J. (eds), *Anthropological Perspectives on Local Development: Knowledge and Sentiments in Conflict*. London: Routledge, pp. 26–54.

White, L. (1990) *The Comforts of Home: Prostitution in Colonial Nairobi*. Chicago: University of Chicago Press.

Wilson, M. (1952) *Good Company*. London: Oxford University Press.

5 The creativity of action

Property, kin and the social in African artisanal mining

Eleanor Fisher and Rosemarie Mwaipopo

Analyses of neo-liberal change in African mining tend to frame discussion through the lens of an overarching structural perspective. Far less attention has been paid to the way change is enacted within social relations in mining communities. To this end, our chapter considers how development in the Tanzanian mineral sector transforms people's relationships and stimulates new iterations of power and agency within local trajectories of development, focusing on the case of artisanal gold mining in Mgusu village in Geita region. The aim is to trace how neo-liberal change configures market rationality and property relations in ways that can fundamentally alter social relationships within the local community, occupational groups and families, raising both opportunities for wealth accumulation and the potential to entrench poverty. The creative action involved in these processes generates new associational ties and repertoires of practice, as miners respond to change and the need to protect their livelihoods.

We start with the simple observation that the acquisition of land for mining is often associated with personal conflict and socially disintegrative disputes over property between kin and residents within a community. Such disputes happen in the context of private property ownership of individual mining rights being a relatively new phenomenon. Under tribal customary law and communal ownership of land emerging from socialist policies of the post-Independence Tanzanian state, notions of private property were alien. Property rights that have been legislated in recent mining laws are often not known, understood or valued at the community level. Instead notions of moral rights to livelihood and *inter alia* physical survival generally prevail, providing the moral underpinnings of community cohesion.

That disputes over property are tied to conflict within the local community and between kin comes as no surprise (Hirsch 2010). What we endeavour to deconstruct here is how mineralization of the economy and private ownership of mineral rights within communities are generating a more complex social division of labour, which imparts altered meaning to family relations and miners' connections to one another, to external agencies, and to a locality through productive labour and residence. Mining associational work ties and private property have introduced a new dynamic in rural-cum-urban societies (Bryceson 2010).

Mining settlements are populated by large numbers of multi-ethnic migrants. Instead of tribal governance norms, miners become subject to national laws defining their access to the land, mining rights and the fruits of their labour, the pits. In the process of a mining settlement's growth, new associational ties of cooperation and competition arise, and conflicts are generated over land, access to minerals, and rights to engage in mine activities. Over the course of Tanzania's rapid mineralization, the state has contributed to these processes at both national and local levels by defining and only selectively implementing policies and laws identifying the rights and responsibilities of miners.

Policy discourses on artisanal and small-scale mining in Africa are infused with a neo-liberal language of individualism. In this view economic action is driven by the entrepreneurial, information-acquiring, property-owning, improving small-scale miner. Far less is written about the creative action and formation of collective social ties that are needed to pursue artisanal mining livelihoods. Policy discourses ignore how primitive accumulation arises from the privatization of assets through new property laws that advantage people who are aware of the 'new rules' and are in the right place at the right time to benefit.

These circumstances have the potential to generate complex conflicts between *de facto* rights, based on the practice of mining, and *de jure* rights, based on legal status. Furthermore there are new external actors, notably civil servants and politicians, who can be obstructive as well as instrumental to miners seeking to secure better access to mining wealth. Thus community dynamics become less consensually mediated as recourse to the law by different parties, threats of force, and manipulation of ties to powerful outsiders increasingly surface increasingly surface. Justifications invoked over these contestations all reveal social connections and forms of action that anchor neo-liberal artisanal mining within a particular time and place, exposing wider dynamics and political struggles over mineral resources and the market (Moore 1998).

This chapter uses processual ethnography (Moore 1987) to examine creative action on the part of a group of miners. We interrogate how economic change and associated power relations are manifest in miners' acts of dissent, accommodation and force through examination of diagnostic events that reveal the ongoing dynamics of artisanal mining in the wider context of Tanzania's mineralization (Rabinow, 2005). Central to our empirical investigation is the question of why artisanal gold miners choose to follow particular courses of action when seeking to make their living and how they defend a mining livelihood when challenged by legal impediments. Following on from this, we ask what their actions reveal about how alignments are created between neo-liberal rationalities, people's relationships and their inter-subjective identity as artisanal miners.[1]

Data has been compiled from empirical research conducted in 2004 and 2006 and archival research in 2008.[2] Primary data was elicited through in-depth interviews and focus group discussions with artisanal miners in Mgusu village, officials in the Geita district Administration and Geita District Mines Office, representatives of mining companies operating in Geita district, and officials from the Ministry of Energy and Minerals and the Ministry of Natural Resources and Tourism.

Framing creative action

Contemporary studies trace the many stakeholder conflicts that arise from how mining sector reform and neo-liberal development have failed to address the interests of artisanal miners and mining communities (Carstens and Hilson 2009; Hilson and Yakovleva 2007; Tschakert 2009). However, research is less clear about how neo-liberal rationalities are emboldened within the everyday spaces occupied by artisanal miners, including their relationships and inter-subjective understanding of what it means to be a miner.

Neo-liberalism, popularly understood as a market ideology that delimits the reach of the state, is underlined by stress on the centrality of the market and social action driven by the entrepreneurial and competitive individual (Harvey 2005). Some studies suggest that neo-liberalism in Africa incorporates modes of inter-vention and control that are indirect, acting on and through the interests of subjects and organizations (Ferguson 2006). However, rather than conceptualiz-ing neo-liberal institutions as simply imposing on people's subjectivity and actions, we place emphasis on the dynamic of local transformations generated by actors with different interests and resources.

Adopting this perspective, we draw on Joas's theory of creative action (Joas 1996), with its leanings on the philosophical tradition of American pragmatism, to critique notions of rational action prevalent in economic and social thinking. Joas argues that creativity can be conceived as a fundamental characteristic of action, rather than only one component alongside the 'rational' and 'normative'. Joas (1996: 145–95) proposes three assertions: first, 'situation', namely that thought and action are not separated but emerge in *situ*. Second, 'corporeality', in which human action references a body that exists in relationship to will but not in a hierarchy of the cognitive mind exerting strict control over the body. And third, 'sociality', that action and actors are inherently integrated within social groups. Our rationale for this approach is that it permits us to move away from ideas of rational action that underpin the prevailing neo-liberal ideology of 'the individu-alized and entrepreneurial artisanal miner'. We are also informed by Li's (2005: 27) Gramscian approach to power, which understands the practice of politics within 'constellations of power in particular times and places, and the over-determined, messy situations in which creativity arises'.

Trajectories of development in Tanzania

As described in the Introduction to this book, artisanal gold mining in Tanzania emerged as a widespread livelihood activity in the 1970s and 1980s, when large-scale gold mining was virtually non-existent. Artisanal mining initially benefited from liberalization policies of the late 1980s and early 1990s, with certain indi-viduals well-placed to capitalize through access to information and resources (Chachage 1995; Cooksey 2011). However, with the entry of large-scale mining interests over the last decade and a half, the opportunities that artisanal miners gained from economic liberalization are being increasingly challenged by land

and labour displacement and human rights abuses, all underpinned by a growing imbalance of power and relations of inequality.

Questions about the distribution of benefits from large-scale mining, the terms under which foreign companies operate, associations with corruption, and the negative consequences of mining operations on rural people, land and livelihood have been the subject of heated public debate within the Tanzanian parliament and media (Cooksey 2011; Curtis and Lissu 2008; Lange 2011). At the heart of these controversies are questions about social values and equalities, economic change, democratization, and relations of power, autonomy and ownership in the face of neo-liberal and globalized development (Shivji 2006; Chachage and Cassam 2010; Mbilinyi 2010). Despite heavy criticism, government has repeatedly protected the interests of large-scale foreign mining investors, overturning a past development orientation that sought to benefit the poor majority (Chapter 10).

Some have argued that institutional reforms introduced to facilitate foreign direct investment in mining internationally have reduced the capacity of the state to govern (Shivji 2006). However, framing change in terms of a simple state with-drawal as the tentacles of neo-liberalism are extended ignores the Tanzanian state's enduring political and social salience (Hodgson 2008). State institutions remain present, notwithstanding questions over nature and effectiveness.

Caplan (2007) asks how Tanzanians make sense of the transition from an avowedly socialist society to a neo-liberal one and the issues of power and inequality this engenders. She identifies a disjuncture between dominant discourses of progress and local perceptions of change, including poverty and powerlessness. In her view, globalization and liberalization present both threats and opportunities, with effects being spatially uneven and dependent on people's position in society. In the Tanzanian context, the question is how new opportuni-ties are grasped, constraints imposed, and inequalities experienced in relationships people hold with one another.

The rapid economic change that has coalesced around the mineral sector has stimulated and reflected wider processes of developmental transformation in relationships between the state, market and civil society. The novelty of the newly imposed property relations and the continuing proximity of community values centred on the priority of the moral right to pursue livelihoods to ensure material survival are critical to an understanding of how the legalisms of the neo-liberal context are not always over-determining. How these abstractions of legal and moral rights become manifest, being shaped by the relationships artisanal miners hold to one another and other relevant actors and the course of action that follows, is what we explore in our case study of artisanal mining in Mgusu village, framing the discussion according to the significance of creative action (Joas 1996).

Delineating the contours of a gold mining area

The development of mineral rights and state administration of forestry resources around present-day Mgusu village can be traced back to large-scale mining investment in British colonial times. State jurisdiction over natural resources and past mining company interests contextualize the legal parameters for contemporary disputes over property rights.

Gold was discovered in the region south of Lake Victoria during the German colonial period (1891–1919) (Chapter 1). Claims were pegged and registered, then later held, after the First World War, as ex-enemy property within 'excluded land'.[3] Gold mining in the 1920s, insofar as it existed, was carried out by immigrant prospectors of Boer, Russian and European origin.[4] Between 1931 and 1934 prospecting commenced in the southwest of the region, an area covering present-day Geita district where Mgusu village is located, in land viewed by British colonial officials as 'tsetse-infested' and 'largely uninhabited'.[5]

Prospectors' success southwest of Lake Victoria (near Mgusu) attracted the attention of Tanganyika Concessions Limited and in 1934 Kentan Gold Areas Limited was formed to develop these interests.[6] This was carried out by its subsidiaries, the Saragura Development Company Limited and the Geita Gold Mining Company Limited. Gold milling was centralized in Geita and started in December 1938. Land was surveyed and mapped; a total of 123 square miles were demarcated under a 'Special Exclusive Prospecting Licence', including the area around present-day Mgusu village.[7] Over 30 prospects were found and mining leases and claims taken out on these areas. Gold milling was centralized at Geita Gold Mine from 1938. The mine successfully expanded to become the largest in East Africa; however development was impeded by the Second World War.[8] Production later picked up but not to projected levels and in 1965 the mine was closed.[9]

Gold mining extended colonial control over natural resources in the region. Management of water sources and forests were a concern due to demand for water and timber exerted by Geita Gold Mining Company. In 1941 the Mine was granted a right to dam the Mabubi River, which flows through Mgusu.[10] In 1954 the Geita Gold Mine Forest Reserve (477 km^2) was gazetted, replacing a previous concession, to make provision for future mining needs through adequate reservation of unspoiled woodland. The Reserve enabled stack fuel to be obtained by the Mine free of royalty.[11] Gazetting the area was to have important future consequences for artisanal miners attracted to Mgusu because mining without a permit, use of timber, settlement, and agriculture were not permitted and remain illegal in a national forest reserve.

In presenting this archival material as a background to contemporary ethnography, we need to be aware of social relational 'forms of absence' as a basis for delineating tenure security and property rights (Luning 2010). Around Mgusu village, property rights related to a forest reserve and a large-scale gold mine were created historically. The tides of economy and history stopped the demand for timber and water from the locality, leaving land unoccupied and unused, with occasional artisanal miners paying little heed to the existing legal property rights for government reserved land as they went about earning their living.

Embedding sociality within the locality

Miners say Mgusu was started by *wachoji* (sing. *mchoji*) after the discovery of gold in the Saragura-Mgusu Hill area in 1987. In the local Sukuma language, *mchoji* means 'seeker', a person who is not propertied and goes anywhere to look for gold. People recall that a person nicknamed *Mzee Fisi* (Mr Hyena) struck gold in an old gold exploration trench from colonial times.[12]

As news of the discovery spread, thousands of people came to dig pits on Mgusu hill at the edge of Geita Forest Reserve. The Mabubi river running through the area was used for domestic water and gold processing, while wood from the forest was used as the pit 'timber' – the log fitted to the top of the pit to hoist ore – and for making sluice boxes to clean the ore.

Mining was organized according to a system in which a pit holder employed small teams of diggers (Chapter 3). The pit-holders were recognized within the mining community as having *de facto* rights to mine by virtue of having dug pits and organized labour; however they had no *de jure* rights according to Tanzanian law. Miners told officials they were 'only prospecting', with considerable fluidity of entry and exit of pit-holders and diggers from the locality depending on new artisanal gold discoveries across the region.

The activity of artisanal miners in Mgusu attracted the interest of Dar Tardine Tanzania (DTT)[13], a subsidiary of a Swiss company, which in 1987 gained a prospecting licence for parts of Mwanza region (now Geita region). This included a license for the Mgusu area. Alongside prospecting it deployed 'sub-contractors' to buy artisanal gold. For Mgusu, DTT sub-contracted one man as a gold buyer, an ex-government official who will hitherto be referred to as Mr X. Mr X and his wife also provided personal finance for the artisanal miners to develop their pits. The artisanal miners who obtained credit from Mr X were obliged to sell their gold to him. This market channel was endorsed by the Tanzanian state; the percentage of artisanal gold sold through this means from Mgusu is unclear.

In 1990, the government put a stop to DTT's mining activities. Following a parliamentary investigation, DTT was charged with fraud and gold smuggling (Mutagwaba *et al.* 1997). Soon after this, and in keeping with wider liberalization processes in which the Tanzanian government sought to formalize the illegal activities of artisanal miners, the Ministry of Energy and Minerals encouraged both artisanal miners and DTTs sub-contractors to apply for Prospecting Licences as a step towards making them legal operators with a Primary Mining License (PML). Present-day artisanal miners allege that Mr X asked his friend the District Commissioner to assist him to get a licence from the mines office in Dodoma. The artisanal miners subscribed $US 0.50 (Tsh 500) a pit to facilitate the application because they believed he was doing it on their behalf. On Mr X's return none of the miners checked the document due to unfamiliarity with the nature of legal documents. They went on working under the misplaced confidence that they were secure. As one miner explained 'people did not see the need to get a licence because what they wanted most was their daily income and therefore they were content with whatever process assured them of this' (Interview with B.O., May 2004).

The process of consolidating private ownership of the mines was completed in 1992 with registration of prospecting licences for two claims in the name of Mr X by the Geita Zone Mines Office. It was only sometime after completion that miners realized the claim titles were registered in Mr X's name and not to them as a group. As one remarked, 'this meant that we were now under him!' (Interview with M.K., June 2006). Some saw Mr X as outsmarting them by capitalizing on their ignorance (Kiswahili: *'ujinga wetu'*). After a period of dispute, they got Mr X to agree to their continued mining of their pits in exchange for Mr X receiving 30 per cent of the hard rock they mined. This was a private arrangement, not stipulated in mining law, but it was (and remains) a common practice across Tanzania in which a claim owner sub-leases pits to pit holders in return for an agreed percentage of the ore (Chapters 3 and 7).

The development of mineral claims in Mgusu and the subsequent dispute forms the first diagnostic event in our case study. Creative action on the part of artisanal miners, including movement across a territory, habitation and forms of sociality based on mining relations interfaces with the changing development context of liberalization and mineralization of the economy. Here a shift from *de facto* rights based on local agreement to *de jure* rights of individual property ownership is clear, as the Tanzanian government pursued a formalization policy for artisanal mineral claims. In the process ties of dependency were entrenched, limiting miners' choices and threatening their ability to mine the area, with constraints upon them reinforced by the need for credit to finance their mining operations. In effect, as government policy in the mineral sector became more liberalized, personal relationships, knowledge of specific gold rich localities, and existing ties of dependency became instrumental in shaping the circumstances under which certain individuals benefited from mineral formalization processes. It also contributed to inter-subjective identity formation in terms of consolidating a group of miners who asserted themselves as pit-owners, as opposed to claim-holders or various categories of diggers.

A village as situated development

Alongside the process of building sociality in Mgusu through mining and habitation, artisanal miners sought to gain official recognition of their settlement as a village. They began in the 1990s and were finally successful in 2006.

By 1989, Mgusu had the makings of a permanent settlement. Its population was substantial, fluctuating between 8,000 and 10,000 people (Chachage 1995; Kulindwa *et al.* 2003).[14] With population growth, critical livelihood issues arose. People's mining and gold processing needed to be supplemented by agriculture, which was not permissible in the surrounding forest reserve. Some defrayed an over-reliance on purchased food by renting farmland in neighbouring villages.

State officials were becoming tetchy about people living and mining in Mgusu due to encroachment on the national forest reserve. The District Natural Resources Office tried to prevent forest damage by reporting the miners to officials in the Ministry of Natural Resources and Tourism in Dar es Salaam.

Residents were antagonized by the arrest of three people who were given six-month jail terms for chopping down trees illegally. Their accounts emphasize the severity of this penalty, alleging that one woman became sick and died after serving her jail sentence. Eventually the Ministry of Natural Resources and Tourism and the Ministry of Energy and Minerals agreed a compromise arrangement in which fees and taxes would be charged for tree cutting and settlement.[15]

The dispute over settlement and resource use prompted the miners to campaign for the status of a legally registered village: village leaders were elected, an administrative office built, and the district administration was lobbied, including the Forestry section of the District Natural Resources office to try to de-gazette the reserve. Issues of political allegiance and power became salient at the time of the national presidential and parliamentary elections in the 1990s. Mgusu was the site of election rallies where promises were proffered about the future of the settlement in return for political support. In addition, the campaign for village registration was given impetus in 2000 by the development of the large-scale Geita Gold mine by AshantiGold and AngloGold.[16] Residents were displaced from areas around Geita town and artisanal miners ejected; being on a border of the large-scale concession, residents of Mgusu feared it was only a matter of time before they too were targeted.

This second diagnostic event in our case, the transformation of Mgusu into a registered village, demonstrates how creative action on the part of artisanal miners can gravitate towards new forms of sociality and situation through democratic political action as a resolution for their anomalous positionality vis-à-vis the local and national state and to gain livelihood security when threatened by large-scale mining interests.

Corporeality through death and kinship

Mr X, who owned prospecting licences for Mgusu, died suddenly in a road accident. Following his death, his younger brother, Mr Y, was appointed executor of his estate. This facilitated his take-over of his brother's Prospecting Licenses, registered in Mr Y's name in 1995. His intention to develop a mining operation became apparent to artisanal miners in Mgusu and caused outrage when officials from the Ministry of Energy and Minerals visited to check the area prior to issuing PMLs.

Mr Y formed the Kwanza Mining Company (a pseudonym) to exploit gold reserves in Mgusu in 1996. Kwanza Mining had licenses for 3.2 hectares – covering most of the pits and some residential areas. Creating a company formalized the claim holder's relationship of superiority over the artisanal miners, as affirmed in a daily record of their names in the Company's register when they worked in the Kwanza Mining pits. Nevertheless the financing arrangement remained the same with pit-owners giving Mr Y 30 per cent of their produce, while retaining 70 per cent to be distributed between themselves and their diggers. Mr Y did not support artisanal miners' credit needs for equipment or food as his brother had done. When necessary this role was provided by gold buyers and those with finance to invest.

Thereafter, without the knowledge of the Mgusu artisanal miners, Mr Y entered into an agreement with a foreign owned company, Open Coy Minerals Limited (a pseudonym), for exploration of four claims in the area. Open Coy expressed interest in drilling to assess gold reserves with a view to establishing a joint venture or to purchase the area outright. Concerned that their day-to-day access to the pits would be jeopardized, the miners reported Mr Y to the Ministry of Energy and Minerals. Feeling betrayed for a second time, they vowed to fight against his claim ownership. Some villagers apparently told Mr Y 'we will kill you' or threatened to throw acid at him, after which he avoided visits to Mgusu and left day-to-day operations to his managers (Interview with S.K., June 2006). In 1998, the miners filed a court case against Mr Y and his family.

These contestations illustrate the opposing positions actors in Mgusu hold towards resources and the ways in which the state was drawn upon to try to resolve the dispute and legitimize their demands for security of work and residence. The claim holder, Mr Y, justified his right to exclude miners from what had become his legal property. He argued that 'the miners' discontent was based on their demand for a share of the exploration costs paid by... [Open Coy]..., rather than for the right to own the claim' (Interview with Y.M., June 2006). The miners felt that they had resisted restrictions on their gold mining activities and any threat to future activity that emerged from Mr Y's arrangement with a foreign gold mining company. One miner said: 'although we hated Mr X for cheating us over the licence, Mr Y is even worse, because he has led the big investors to come here' (Interview with S.K., June 2006). In 1999–2000, Open Coy Minerals Ltd withdrew its offer without explanation, possibly uncomfortable with the legal dispute or discouraged by apparently low gold reserves.

This third diagnostic event, Mr X's death and his brother Mr Y's subsequent actions, adds a further twist to the dispute over mineral rights in Mgusu. The corporeality of Mr X's death is expressed not just through the materiality of dying but also through inheritance, as property is contentiously redistributed. This included the mineral claims and exacerbated the miners' livelihood insecurity thereafter when Mr Y tried to sell his claims to an international investor. As such creative action frames the way claims form both material and symbolic objects situated within social relationships. Mr Y's agreement with a foreign mining company had the potential to displace the artisanal miners from the gold pits entirely. Again the miners made appeals to the state to seek resolution to the dispute, although this resolution never arrived, as we describe below.

Renewing sociality to bury the conflict

The mine claim dispute in Mgusu became protracted. Stakes were and remain high: significant numbers of people are dependent on artisanal gold mining for a livelihood. In 2004 our research recorded 2,401 pits operated by 2,391 men and 10 women, employing 5 or more labourers daily. Significant levels of investment by pit-owners and gold buyers are also recorded, including guest houses in Geita town, cars and retail shops. Individual stories illustrate this: James, an elderly miner who arrived in 1988 planned to go 'back home' to Tarime to start a business venture with his brother. He said 'although my colleagues regard me as one of the unsuccessful miners, I have used my income to educate my children, two are enrolled as undergraduates at university and three have completed high school' (Interview with J.K., May 2004).

In 2000, the Commissioner for Mining visited to arbitrate in the Mgusu dispute and discussions were held with a 'Committee to Obtain Justice for Miners', composed of 19 Mgusu artisanal miners. The wider context to this meeting was that Geita Gold Mine was being developed and the national government sought an atmosphere conducive to large-scale mineral investment, putting pressure upon regional and district officials to resolve disputes with artisanal miners and local communities. Early in 2001, the Commissioner wrote to the Mwanza Regional Mines Officer instructing him to present the issue to the Geita District Commissioner and the Police Officer in Charge of the District. The Regional Mines Officer recommended that both sides should agree on a collaborative arrangement for owning the mines. However, Mr Y's advocate rejected the proposal.

A Memorandum of Complaint was filed by the miners at the Mineral Commission's Legal Section. In January 2002, the miners were informed that their complaint was rejected on the basis that the claim owner was not obliged by law to honour their demands. The Commissioner was non-committal, informing the miners that his office's recommendation was not an instruction, but a proposal for dispute resolution. This prompted the miners, representing 901 complainants, to file Civil Case No. 55 of 2002 in the High Court of Tanzania against the Kwanza Mining Company.

Whilst the conflict took a public turn, it also had a private face in the form of bad relations between Mr Y and his late brother's widow, Mrs X. For a long time she had accused him of reneging on responsibilities as executor of the estate. In an interview, she recalled how she and her late husband had to sacrifice a lot to prepare the pits in Mgusu for production. Having minimal starting capital, she had to cook for the miners and provide some of their requirements for the pits to be profitable.

Mrs X obtained what she saw as her children's 'rightful inheritance' when in 2003 the PMLs for Mgusu had to be renewed. Following the application for renewal, the District Commissioner for Geita asked Mr Y to denounce his claim to the estate because the late Mr X's children had reached adulthood. The children asked for the mineral claims to be placed in their mother's maiden name to dissociate the family from the case in court. From that point onwards, she gained 50 per cent of the shares from the mine, her sons received 15 per cent each and Mr Y was left with 20 per cent (Interview with Mrs X, June 2006).

At this point, having been successful in the inheritance dispute, Mrs X redefined her allegiances, deciding to cooperate with her brother-in-law. Travelling together to Dar es Salaam for the High Court hearing: 'people who knew us ... [the past relationship] ... were taken aback, commenting that Mrs X has taken the same seat with her in-law!' (Interview with Mrs X, June 2006). For the

X-Y family the outcome was positive: the High Court judge upheld the earlier ruling of the lower courts arguing that the artisanal miners had no right to the pits.

The fourth diagnostic event in our case brings to the fore how mineral claims can become both material and symbolic objects within a dispute between kin, and are drawn into the public sphere as state authorities are drawn upon to resolve the conflict. Here creative action is revealed in both the way the family negotiated a course within a particular culture of governance and personal connections to power holders to obtain resolution to the dispute, and in the associational ties built between a group of artisanal miners' as they sought to retain access to their pits through the law courts. In the process *de jure* rights over mineral deposits were consolidated in favour of the X-Y family.

Challenging miners' creative action

The year 2004 saw the entry of another medium-scale foreign-owned company to Mgusu, Atlanta Gold Limited (a pseudonym). The X-Y family entered into an agreement with Atlanta to conduct drilling exercises: According to Mrs X, 'Atlanta capitalized on the dispute with my brother-in-law and used it to convince me to allow them to conduct exploration activities . . . I was informed about the company wanting a joint venture for purposes of conducting an exploration for a period of 5 years' (Interview with Mrs X, June 2006). The company agreed to pay annual exploration fees and US$ 300,000 at the end of the venture. 'But they conned me . . . they wanted to purchase my shares . . . later I heard Atlanta wanted the total transfer of my rights' (Interview with Mrs X, June 2006). District officials encouraged the sale. According to Mrs X, they said 'we are tired of the endless controversies regarding that plot, it is best that you sell it' (Interview with Mrs X, June 2006). The X-Y family received a sum of US$ 35,000 with agreement that final payment would be made after the judgment of the court case. However, according to Mrs X, Atlanta did not honour this deal.

Following the court case, Atlanta decided to erect a fence to prevent access of the miners to their pits. A company geologist described how they planned to move the artisanal miners slowly, pit-by-pit to reduce conflict, and also to appease the district administration through a small re-afforestation programme (Interview with G.G., April 2004). In the event, the caterpillar brought to build the fence destroyed 15 artisanal pits, unleashing the miners' collective wrath.

The sale of the X-Y claims to Atlanta ushered in a new chapter for Mgusu, with the artisanal miners under threat of total exclusion by a foreign investor. The issue was taken up by the District's Member of Parliament, who presented it to government. At the time wider questions were being asked about the benefits of mining for Tanzanian citizens. The Deputy Minister for Energy and Minerals requested the Mwanza Regional Commissioner to instruct Atlanta to stop erecting the fence until an amicable agreement had been reached.

In April 2006 Mgusu finally gained its legal status as a registered village. Miners, thinking village registration would place them in a stronger bargaining position with Atlanta, decided to negotiate directly with the company rather than the X-Y family, based on the claim that they owned 70 per cent of the proceeds from the mines against the 30 per cent that the X–Y family earned, and 50 per cent of the revenue that the village government accrued came from the gold processing plants.

According to a mining leader: 'We said now there is no Kwanza Gold Mining Ltd, Atlanta will have to negotiate with us' (Interview with N.O., May 2006). They employed an advocate to take their case to the Tanzania Court of Appeal. This cost US$ 9,500 (Tsh10 million), paid through mining proceeds. Mining leaders proudly explained that the outstanding fee was just US$ 2,700 (Tsh 2.7 million). The case was lost but mining by Atlanta Gold Ltd has not commenced and the dispute remains unresolved, with artisanal mining continuing. According to company publicity, this is because of the militancy of the miners, although its focus on development of sites elsewhere in Tanzania has sidelined the Mgusu concession.

Our final diagnostic event saw the *de jure* transfer of rights over gold mining into the hands of a foreign mining company, directly threatening artisanal mining livelihoods. However, the demands of the Mgusu miners emerged through creative action involving democratic protest and legal action, deterring Atlanta Gold from proceeding with exploration and production. The success of the artisanal miners in at least forestalling their displacement was due in part to the district administration being responsive to the artisanal miners' appeals to have a moral right to continue with their mining livelihood, although it is also the case that the administration would have to deal with ensuing conflict from displacement, a state of affairs it sought to avoid. Significantly, however, is the fact that currently Atlanta Gold is focused on exploiting mineral deposits elsewhere in Tanzania.

Conclusion

Tracing struggles over access to land for artisanal mining and settlement in Mgusu reveals a microcosm of how wider change is taking place within Tanzania's process of mineralization. The ambiguity of property relations predated economic liberalization being rooted in colonial administrative decisions, but once mining sector liberalization occurred the contorted privatization of mineral rights resulted in the consolidation of *de jure* rights in the form of PMLs held by certain individuals, creating local inequalities of power and deepening relations of dependency connected to the threat of loss of artisanal miners' informal access to mining as *de facto* rights were challenged.

Once rights to the mineral resources had been formalized as private property in the 1990s they could be sold to an outside company, with the potential for the artisanal miners and pit-owners to be excluded, rather than simply dependent on the claim-holder. In this respect, inequalities that existed in the past became reinforced through a particular culture of governing, which included the personalized relations that underpin inequalities in access to power and resources. At the same time there were countervailing processes, in terms of the way miners gained settlement rights, appealed to the High Court, and received support from sections of government. The court case, in which the artisanal miners challenged their pit dispossession, is an interesting dimension. Although they did not win, this demonstration of artisanal miners' recourse to the law without the support of national or international advocacy organizations, is highly unusual in a national context where it is more common for miners to riot or to engage in apparently illegal activity.

The Mgusu artisanal gold mining community sought for many years, ultimately successfully, to have their settlement registered as a village. In the process they incorporated the lowest tier of government into their community, creating a formal channel to articulate their interests. One can set this against popular images of willy-nilly population movement in the pursuit of artisanal mining. In this respect, although new features emerge within the development process, established practices and governance arrangements do not disappear, being instead reworked in the contemporary period.

Seeking village registration of a settlement as a course of enabling democratic action may be obvious to those familiar with residence and governance processes in rural Tanzania and perhaps surprising to those who are not. But this is a key point; in another time and place, an entirely different course of action may have been followed to secure miners' moral rights to their livelihood pursuits. In contemporary Tanzania, village status acts as a vehicle to demand rights and to articulate relationships between a community and different parts of the political system. For artisanal miners in Mgusu, registering the village created the possibility of strengthening the case for political support from higher levels of government in claims over mineral resources and settlement.

In describing how artisanal miners have built a livelihood and fought for the right to pursue this livelihood, we have used Joas's theory of creative action to critique the view that miners' agency can be simply reduced to rational action embedded within an enabling neo-liberal context of mineral sector change. Situating conceptual ideas on creative action within a processual ethnography that takes into account sociality between artisanal miners and how power is enacted at the local level, has enabled us to see how wider trajectories of development shape democratic choices that miners make despite the many constraints they face.

We have elaborated on how creativity is socially interactive, as artisanal miners move across a territory to situate themselves within a locality. In the process the roots of dispute are formed as they claim reserved land that historically has been under state jurisdiction. As the mining settlement grows, and individuals are successful at finding gold, creativity emerges not just in relation to past experience but also to the particular social and physical environment. Within this process, corporeality is found within mineral claims as both symbolic and material objects, with death bringing into question relationships between kin that are materialized through the distribution of property and subsequent dispute. In the process, past experience is reworked and a contemporary development situation is created; testimony to this is the way the village was formed.

Articulating change through the lens of creative action permits us to see how the neo-liberal market becomes embodied within people's agency, power relations and inter-subjective identity as miners. Within all these processes however it is clear that the enactment of neo-liberal market rationalities and changes in property ownership create both opportunities for wealth acquisition and the entrenchment of profound inequalities.

Notes

1   Inter-subjectivity refers to experience being generated through social interaction and embodied within people's identities, rather than being individual and fixed.
2   We are grateful for research funding from the Department of International Development (2004); Wageningen University (2006); and the Leverhulme Trust (2008).
3   'Annual report of land, surveys and mines department, Part IV' (1922); Hockin Papers, Rhodes House Archives (RHA), Oxford: Mss.Afr.5.1281 (1).
4   Oates, F. (1939) 'Record of a safari in the Lake Province', RHA, Oxford: MSc.Afr.s.603.
5   Hockin, V.T. (1952) 'A brief history of mining in Tanganyika', Hockin Papers RHA, Oxford: Mss.Afr.5.1281 (1).
6   Hockin ibid.
7   Carter, G.S. (1959) 'Exploration of Geita and N.E. Extension Mines', Appendix 1, Geological Survey of Tanganyika, Tanzania Mineral Archives (TMA), Dodoma. MssGSC/7/RGH/1[C.136A].
8   Tanganyika Department of Mines (1953) 'Prospecting in Tanganyika', Hockin Papers, RHA, Oxford: Mss.Afr.5.1281 (1).
9   Landcastle, R. (1963) 'A review of the mining industry', Hockin Papers, ibid.
10 Letters, Geita Gold Mining Area, Tanzania National Archives (TNA), Acc.215, File 1230.
11 Provincial Commissioner's Annual Report, Lake Province (1955: 55). Government Printer: Dar es Salaam.
12 For details of the trench, Nanyaro, K. (1979) 'Report on mineral exploration of the Bulyanhulu gold prospect with a review of other gold occurrences in Kahama, Geita and Biharamulo districts', TMA: C.2154.
13 Also referred to as Dar Tardine al Umma Ltd.
14 Population numbers declined substantially but are now rising. According to village records in May 2004 there were 989 households with a total of 4,437 people and in June 2006 there were 1,428 households and a total population of 5,756 people.
15 The new regulations were: (i) every gold miner in possession of an area (pit) should fence it; (ii) every miner should account for and pay revenue/tax for every tree used at the Geita Natural Resources offices; (iii) all abandoned pits should be refilled; and, (iv) every Mgusu resident should pay Tsh 2,500 a day to the District Natural Resources and Tourism office to compensate for illegal settlement in a forest reserve.
16 In 1996 AshantiGold acquired mining rights to the area occupied by Geita Gold Mine in colonial times. In 2000 it entered a partnership with AngloGold for the development of Geita Gold Mine, becoming one of the largest open caste gold mines in Africa. In 2004 they merged to become AngloGold Ashanti.

References

Bryceson, D.F. (2010) 'Between moral economy and civil society: Durkheim revisited', in Bryceson, D.F. *How Africa Works: Occupational Change, Identity and Morality.*

Rugby: Practical Action Publishing. pp. 265–87.

Caplan, P. (2007) 'Between socialism and neo-liberalism: Mafia island, Tanzania, 1965–2004'. *Review of African Political Economy* 34(114): 679–94.

Carstens, J. and Hilson, G. (2009) 'Mining, grievance and conflict in rural Tanzania'. *International Development Planning Review* 31(3): 301–26.

Chachage, C. and Cassam, A. (eds) (2010) *Africa's Liberation: The Legacy of Nyerere*, Oxford: Pambazuka Press.

Chachage, S.L.C. (1995) 'The meek shall inherit the earth but not the mining rights: The mining industry and accumulation in Tanzania', in Gibbon, P. (ed.) *Liberalised Development in Tanzania*. Uppsala, Sweden: Nordiska Afrikainstitutet.

Cooksey, B. (2011) 'The investment and business environment for gold exploration and mining in Tanzania: Africa, power and politics programme'. [ODI. Background Paper 3]. Available from www.institutions-africa.org/publications/country/tanzania (accessed 5 October 2011).

Curtis, M. and Lissu, T. (2008) 'A golden opportunity? How Tanzania is failing to benefit from gold mining'. Dar es Salaam: Christian Council of Tanzania (CCT), National Council of Muslims in Tanzania (BAKWATA) and Tanzania Episcopal Conference.

Ferguson, J. (2006) *Global Shadows: Africa in the Neoliberal World Order.* Durham, NC, and London: Duke University Press.

Harvey, D. (2005) *A Brief History of Neo-liberalism*. Oxford: Oxford University Press.

Hilson, G. and Yakovleva, N. (2007) 'Strained relations: A critical analysis of the mining conflict in Prestea, Ghana'. *Political Geography* 26: 98–119.

Hirsch, E. (2010) 'Property and persons: New forms and contests in the era of neoliberalism'. *Annual Review of Anthropology* 39: 347–60.

Hodgson, D.L. (2008) 'Cosmopolitics, neoliberalism, and the state: The indigenous rights movement in Africa', in Werbner, P. (ed.) *Anthropology and the New Cosmopolitanism: Rooted, Feminist and Vernacular Perspectives*. Oxford and New York: Berg. pp. 215–32.

Joas, H. (1996) *The Creativity of Action*. Cambridge: Polity Press.

Kulindwa, K., Mashindano, O., Shechambo, F. and Sosovele, H. (2003) *Mining for Sustainable Development in Tanzania*. Dar es Salaam: Dar es Salaam University Press.

Lange, S. (2011) 'Gold and governance: Legal injustices and lost opportunities in Tanzania'. *African Affairs* 110/439: 233–52.

Li, T.M. (2005) *The Will to Improve: Governmentality, Development, and the Practice of Politics*. Durham, NC, and London: Duke University Press.

Luning, S. (2010) 'Beyond the pale of property: Gold miners meddling with mountains in Burkina Faso'. in Panella, C. (ed.) *Worlds of Debts: Interdisciplinary Perspectives on Gold Mining in West Africa*. Amsterdam: Rozenberg, pp. 26–49.

Mbilinyi, M. [Zarro, A.] (2010) 'Society for International Development Forum Interview with Marjorie Mbilinyi'. 7 June 2010. Available from www.sidint.net/interview-with-marjorie-mbilinyi-models-priorities-pressures-of-women-today-in-africa/ (accessed 30 May 2011).

Moore, S.F. (1987) 'Explaining the present: Theoretical dilemmas in processual ethnography'. *American Ethnologist* 14(4): 727–36.

Moore, S.F. (1998) 'Changing African land tenure: Reflections on the incapacities of the state'. *European Journal of Development Research* 10(2): 33–49.

Mutagwaba, W., Mwaipopo-Ako, R. and Mlaki, A.L. (1997) 'The impact of technology on poverty alleviation: The case of artisanal mining in Tanzania' [Research Report No 97.2]. Dar es Salaam, Tanzania: Inter Press Tanzania Ltd.

Rabinow, P. (2005) 'Midst anthropology's problems'. in Ong, A. and Collier, S. (eds) *Global Assemblages: Technology, Politics and Ethics as Anthropological Problems.* Oxford: Blackwell. pp. 40–52.

Shivji, I.G. (2006) 'Let the People Speak: Tanzania Down the Road to Neoliberalism'. Dakar: CODESRIA.

Tschakert, P. (2009) 'Digging deep for justice: A radical re-imagination of the artisanal gold mining sector in Ghana'. *Antipode* 41(4): 706–40.

6 Beyond belief

Mining, magic and murder in Sukumaland[1]

Deborah Fahy Bryceson, Jesper Bosse Jønsson and Richard Sherrington

Since the oil crisis of the late 1970s, peasant farming has been eroding under the influence of stringent structural adjustment cutbacks and the labour-displacing effects of market liberalization policies. Processes of capitalist accumulation and impoverishment now permeate Tanzania's rural areas. A country, fostered under an inclusive *ujamaa* philosophy of African socialism with the stated aim of a relatively egalitarian division of the fruits of independence, is now experiencing a fundamental upheaval of its moral economy (Bryceson 2010). Within mining settlements, new hierarchies of status and authority are emerging in conjunction with the surge in artisanal mining (Bryceson and Jønsson 2010). Relational ties within mining and between mining communities and surrounding rural settlements are being embroidered around a new division of labour and its erratic, but sometimes highly lucrative, material rewards.

This chapter focuses on a disturbing wave of murders of albinos linked to miners' efforts to secure charms for luck and protection against danger while mining in the late 2000s. The international press shrouded the killings in an aura of traditional superstition, overlooking the contextual circumstances, which were at odds with this interpretation. In fact, Tanzania's artisanal mining boom was and is firmly embedded in global commodity and wage labour markets and capitalist profit-optimization strategies. From late 2007 through 2010, close to 50 albino murders were reported. Most of the deaths occurred in Sukumaland, located in northwest Tanzania, the epicentre of Tanzanian mining activities and homeland of the Sukuma people, the country's largest ethno-linguistic group, renowned in Tanzanian popular culture for their witchcraft beliefs, healing, and divination skills. The Tanzanian government were quick to react in blaming local healers and warning them that they must immediately stop the practice, but the delivery of justice[2] through the nation's law courts was slow. This chapter concentrates on the context within which the murders took place.

Artisanal miners' ambitions comprise our starting point for understanding the tragic victimization of albinos in Tanzania. We interrogate the agency of those involved directly and indirectly in the murders: the miners, some of whom seek albino charms, the healers (*waganga*), some of whom prescribe and sell the charms, and the albino murder victims.

Value-laden economic change

The study of the relationship between commodification, the occult and body parts in Tanzania was initiated with Sanders' (2001a) insightful analysis of rumours of human skin trading in southwest Tanzania during the late 1990s. Sanders linked a surge in occult practices and idioms across the country to the pressures and opportunities people faced following the imposition of the economic liberalization policies of the World Bank and IMF. Ubiquitous commodification permeated Tanzania through the encouragement of mobile trade, commodity and labour markets, and liberalized media coverage. Socially embedded inter-personal ties and economic exchange relationships increasingly gave way to the faceless exchanges of the money-mediated capitalist economy.

In the realm of African witchcraft and healing practices more generally, the literature abounds with documentation of how responsive witchcraft and healing patterns are adapted to the changing social and economic order (Colson 2000; Luedke and West 2006; Mesaki 2009). The sudden as well as gradual cumulative influx of large numbers of migrant miners at several strike sites has catalyzed some annoyance, resentment and envy in the surrounding Sukuma villages over the past two decades. Cultural and generational divides between the residents of the mining camps and local villagers are readily apparent in a collision of incongruent consumption preferences and social values, interpreted as a rising challenge to the extant rural authority structures. Social change propelled by the rapid mineralization of the economy has fomented new forms of social division between those who eagerly embrace the fluid materialism of an unknown future associated with mining, against those who retain a foothold in the disintegrating agrarian world once dominated by kin, clan and ethnic loyalties, who are defensive about that known world and their ebbing power to control what is happening to it. Both groups are Tanzanian, but we argue that they represent different sub-cultures, much as teenagers in many countries espouse radically different values from their parents, despite sharing their nationality and social background (Hodkinson and Deike 2007; Roszak 1996 [1965]). In Tanzania, the values of the two sub-cultures have coalesced around occupational distinctions of agro-pastoralist and miner, mixed with age differences. Miners tend to be younger than the traditionally trained Sukuma *waganga*. These differences place the two sub-cultural groups in contrasting conjunctural positions vis-a-vis the material prospects arising from mining activities. A possible edgy outcome is new-found well-being and enjoyment for those embracing mining values, while others rooted in the village agrarian order are susceptible to disappointment and envy.

However, the miners and the *waganga* have potential mutual trading interests, capable of drawing them into interaction with one another if and when the gap between their differing cosmologies and values can be bridged. The reflexive construction of a fetish provides the bridge for the transfer of money and power between them and their contrasting worldviews. Miners seeking luck and protection make lucrative payments to *waganga* who are accorded recognition for their power in the realm of the supernatural. Through market forces of supply and demand, in effect, they have mutually created the albino fetish. There are sufficient shared material concerns on the part of the *waganga* and spiritual belief on the part of the miners to motivate them to engage in exchange. But the question remains why the lives of albinos are tragically sacrificed in the process.

The expansion of commodification associated with mineral production now includes a market in body parts for the production of lucky charms. The commodification of body parts metaphorically dramatizes the tension between varying metrics of power and wealth of rural agrarian and mining pursuits. We explore how cultural creativity has generated this travesty of human exchange, by examining the agency of different categories of actors in the fetishized exchange.

Tanzanian artisanal miners: promises and pressures of success

What characterizes artisanal mining, probably more so than most other livelihoods in Tanzania, is the high level of potential earnings counterweighed by the unpredictability of mining outcomes, uncertainty of income, and personal risk. Besides the many adversities and limited investment capital, miners do not know the exact location, size, and accessibility of the mineral occurrences, and the accountability of partners. They therefore engage in various risk-minimizing and cost-sharing practices in order to ensure success and/or a long-term existence within the sector (Jønsson and Fold 2009).

Across Tanzania's mining zones many believe that most activities of the living are shaped or affected by unseen forces of (an)other spirit world, consisting of the ancestors (*mzimu*), God (*Mungu*), witchcraft (*uchawi*), and evil spirits (*mashetani*). They also believe that fortune and mineral discovery, and the power to be given or deprived of life, are within the ambit of the invisible world. Like their rural predecessors who sought rain and good harvest by propitiating ancestors, many Tanzanian miners expend a great deal of effort in attempts to assuage or seek favour from the world beyond their own. Although there are several ways to engage with the other realm with a view to reducing, harnessing, or controlling one of its resident's powers or intentions, perhaps the most common and readily accessible, is through divination and the use of medicines (*dawa*). *Dawa* is a term that can be attributed to numerous artefacts including the concoctions of local 'healers' (*waganga*), witchdoctor/sorcerers (*wachawi*), wizards (*waanga*), home-made herbal remedies (*miti shamba*, literally 'farm trees'), amulets (*hirizi*), and modern medicines (*dawa ya kisasa*).

While there are incalculable types of *dawa*, the uses that they are put to may, following Cory's (1949) analysis of Sukuma medicines, be divided into four classes: i) protective medicines to safeguard against evil influences; ii) assertive medicines to make people successful in various walks of social life; iii) creative medicines to produce fertility in humans, animals and fields; and iv) aggressive medicines for homicide and bewitching persons and objects. To a large extent, how morally tenable a medicine is (within a particular locale) depends on the context and the aim, but in general, *dawa* that is used to harm or to generate wealth and status is considered immoral and associated with witchcraft.

In part, this immorality derives from the widely held belief that if people want something that is highly desirable and difficult to acquire or achieve, they must forego something that is equally precious and desirable to themselves or others. In Tanzania, it is with this understanding that people who find sudden wealth are suspected by onlookers of engaging in nefarious dealings with the occult. Rumours associated with this belief include individuals selling their children or other kin to sorcerers in exchange for wealth-creating medicines; or paying sorcerers to create zombies out of the recently dead to assist in income generating labour activities such as harvesting fields stealthily at night, or to make themselves invisible so that they might conduct property theft. This tit-for-tat exchange however is believed to be ambiguous when it comes to commodification and modernity (Sanders 2009). There is perplexing uncertainty as to whether the accumulation of modern goods has been attained at the expense of others.

When quizzed about the origins of the efficacy of medicine, practising *waganga* and miners with some knowledge of *uganga* attested that the power of medicine is often unknown but taken as true because it is derived from the spirits with whom the *waganga* have direct contact. Others choose to believe that the traditional agrarian way of life has a different *modus operandi* as opposed to more modern walks of life like mining. Miners with this frame of mind may dismiss the spirit world as inconsequential to their mining outcomes. There are gradations of belief on the part of miners, and some firmly trust in the power of the *waganga* to predict when and where a mineral strike will take place and are keen to consult *waganga*, as illustrated in the following case:

Miners see luck as an entity that can be procured or transferred to them through the intercession of the *waganga* dispensing *dawa*. The expectation of the miner is that the *mganga* will harness their spiritual powers to make them lucky ('to make their star shine', *kusafisha nyota*). The miner must follow the conditions and rules laid down by the *mganga* aimed at removing curses or protecting against witchcraft and wizardry. Instructions are given on the right conditions in which the client must take the *dawa*, in a way analogous to how a patient seeks health through Western medical treatment.

The eagerness to believe in the power of *uganga* to facilitate mineral discovery has to be understood in the context of the extremely harsh economic conditions that have prevailed in Tanzania, exacerbated by the seeming inexplicable and unfair way in which some miners prosper and others do not. *Waganga* divination narratives and promises of success through ritual performance feed the imaginations of those who desire wealth.

Despite these weighty moral issues, scepticism about *waganga*'s effectiveness and utility persists in many miners' minds. Respectable *waganga* are not generally assumed to be profiteering. Their prices depend on the nature of the service rendered. *Waganga* are reported to be understanding if miners cannot pay immediately, but in such cases the miner must pay a symbolic amount followed by further payment once he can afford it. Others see the *waganga*'s charges as too high or are loath to accept some of the healers' insistence on behavioural change or other actions, which impinge on their lifestyle or lead to adverse repercussions.

As one informant stated, if a *mganga* asks for a lot of money before he treats you or if the price is high you know he is a conman (*tapeli*).

Sukuma *waganga*

The Sukuma have been long known in Tanzania for their skills as healers. Sukuma knowledge of *uganga* is admired and often remarked upon as the cause of the economic success of artisanal miners' who seek their services (Tanner 1956a, 1956b; Sanders 2001b).

Sukuma *waganga* traditionally received rigorous training and rituals to gain their credentials as healers (Stroeken 2001). It is incumbent on the initiated to put their healing knowledge into practice, which could be likened to a western-trained doctor's allegiance to the Hippocratic Oath. The principles of Sukuma healing rest on the extraction of the energy force from the natural habitat combined with *shingila*, the medium through which the force is transferred to the patient, which is perceived as 'a "penetrator" from the human world that makes healing power meaningful and effective' (ibid.: 294).

In practice, there is not necessarily a clear line between the *mganga* (healer) and *mchawi* (sorcerer). The diviners link the two through visions and efforts to create a desired future outcome. Through a diviner's exploration of a client's past relationships and current motivations, the client's frustrations or aims are contextualized and comprehended, before the *mganga* makes suggestions for altering existing circumstances and relational ties to achieve the desired outcome. The transition of the *mganga* from healer to dealer in the occult arises from the range of spiritual powers that extends from healing individual ailments and smoothing social disruption to bending the future in favour of the individual at the expense of someone else.

In the 1970s, Nyerere's implementation of a villagization programme, which concentrated settlement in villages, destabilized Sukumaland. The unease of living in closer proximity to one's neighbours led to a cultural, rather than a political, outburst. Stroeken (2001) argues that this was expressed in the rising incidence of witchcraft accusations. Previously, most witches were identified amongst kin within the confines of the homestead compound, but accusations of witchcraft began to spread to residents of the village at large (Abrahams 1981; Mesaki 1994).

Mesaki's (1994, 2009) insightful research on Sukuma witchcraft patterns over the last three decades documents that 3,693 people were killed in witchcraft-related incidents in Tanzania between 1970 and 1984. Sixty-four per cent of the deaths occurred in Sukumaland, with women being the prime targets of the witch killings (85% of 2,347 killings). From 1997 through 1999, the victimization of older women was even more pronounced. They constituted 91 per cent of the 185 witch suspects who were killed (Mesaki 2009: 79). Elderly women found themselves in an increasingly vulnerable position as younger family members migrated from the homestead leaving them without adequate familial support.

One of the most pronounced destabilizing forces in the countryside is now the economic decline of peasant agriculture and the surge in artisanal mining (Bryceson *et al.* 2012). Sukuma homesteads are being depleted of youthful labour at the same time as large numbers of migrants are arriving, spurred by the area's numerous mineral strikes. The livelihood restructuring away from agro-pastoralist activities and social values deflects from the Sukuma's conservative homestead-based, decentralized settlements resting on patriarchal authority. A key indicator of this shift in social values is the rise in property crime and the inability of local law enforcers to act.

These changes are now undermining the authority of local male elders. The Sukuma social values and forms encouraged work achievement over ascription, but such achievement was defined within a Sukuma-inflected agro-pastoralist way of life. As youth have started seeking income in non-agricultural pursuits, elders have continued to farm, upholding the work ethic and communal sentiments (Madulu 1998). The agrarian work ethic traditionally inclined rural people to disapprove of material wealth that did not result from the sweat of one's brow. Swahili-speaking town-dwellers, fishermen and miners, who are seen as dependent on trade and 'lucky finds', are criticized for their 'unearned' wealth (Wijsen and Tanner 2002). Their greater purchasing power has been a potential source of envy.

As shops filled with consumer goods under Tanzania's economic liberalization during the 1990s, elders expected young men to continue to practice traditional Sukuma frugality, shunning luxuries like corrugated iron roofs and motorbikes in favour of virtuously investing in cattle for brideprice payment (Madulu 1998). But with the growing momentum of mining and Lake Victoria fishing in the region, elders have lost their controlling grip on the local economy, and watch young men spending lavishly on alcohol, women and entertainment, modern housing and motorbikes (Jønsson and Bryceson 2009).

The mining boom accentuates the comparative rootlessness of people, reflected in large-scale male and female migration to mineral strike sites. Historically, very few rural people were acquainted with mining as a livelihood strategy. When mineral strikes started occurring in the 1980s, mining became the shortcut to wealth, far more attractive than agriculture or petty trade. However, all the unknowns of mining cause a mixture of high expectations of wealth, uncertainty, perplexity and fear. Why have some people found wealth within a very short period, while others prospect and mine for years without success? These questions spur miners to seek the divination skills and medicines of *waganga*.

Given that so many miners are migrants new to the mining site area, they tend to rely on word of mouth from those already treated to identify a good *mganga*. In other cases, miners travel considerable distances to find the right *mganga*. But there is also a new breed of *waganga* who is readily at hand, advertising their talents in the bars that miners frequent at night (Jangu 2010; Stroeken 2001, 2010). Lacking the requisite traditional training for becoming *bona fide* Sukuma *waganga*, these are entrepreneurial *waganga* looking for gullible miners, who share a similar outlook as miners in terms of their quest for cash. In effect, they are straddled between miners' and *waganga*'s subcultures. Mesaki (2009: 83) observes that professional standards started declining during the 1990s, drawing attention to a division of labour between 'diviners' who identify witches and 'paid thugs' who dispose of them, often in the spirit of doing so for the public good since witches are deemed to be a threat to the community generally.

The albino fetish

The Tanzania Albino Society (TAS) estimates there are approximately 8,000 albinos in the country. What is striking about the current wave of albino murders is that researchers who have studied Sukumaland have yet to cite any precedent in traditional beliefs and practices for the targeting of albinos. Historically there has been no special symbolism, nor any traditional practices to suggest that albinos would become implicated in such rituals.[3] Worldwide, albinism is rare in human populations, but in East Africa, its incidence is considerably higher.[4] Human albinism is associated with the carrier's susceptibility to skin cancer and blindness through exposure to the sun. While many albinos lead active work lives, others have tended to be sheltered in the home, set apart from the rest of the agrarian population, giving them a reclusive, often invalid status in the household and community where work in the open air is the norm.

A hushed practice of mercy killing at birth is rumoured to be the fate of many albino infants, linked to the anticipation of their perceived physical vulnerability and inability to pull their weight in local farming efforts. In Tanzania, albinos are frequently referred to as *zeruzeru,* which is believed by some to derive from the English word zero and by others as an archaic term for ghost-like creatures, which is likely to relate to their lack of skin pigmentation as well as the denial of the albino's personhood, reflected in the frequent absence of any burial markings when they die.

Prevailing evidence suggests that the current albino fetish is a recent innovation rather than a tradition in Tanzanian *waganga* circles. Tanzanian miners have various views on how and why *waganga* started recommending albino body parts as lucky charms to improve their mining efforts. Those interviewed treated the topic gingerly and were usually at pains to personally disassociate themselves from the practice. One miner, suspicious of the *waganga*'s intent, saw the use of the albino fetish as a means: '... to deceive people because these *waganga* believe that the *zeruzeru* aren't missed in the community. They believe that they are not useful people and if they die they are not lost' (Simon S. aged 48, Maganzo, 6 June 2009).

One sceptical miner pointed to the analogy between finding rare gold and using rare albino charms when asked about the significance of albino bones: 'I really don't know. Perhaps because they are so few. ... Using albino body parts is just plain harmful' (Peter B. aged 39, Matundasi, 19 May 2009). Others denied that there was anything magical about albino body parts or the presence of albinos: 'It is complete stupidity and doesn't have any meaning; anything we have *zeruzeru* also have' (Johannas C. aged 39, Idukilo, 5 June 2009). 'It's just nonsense. They don't bring success. I know completely because a long time ago I worked with albinos in mining and so I asked myself, why weren't diamonds produced at the pit where we worked?' (Simon S. aged 48, Maganzo, 6 June 2009).

A Sukuma *mganga* discounted the power of the albino fetish and suggested the culpability of gangs searching for albinos:

> We Sukuma do not have a culture of killing people. Our duty is just to be *waganga* using substances extracted from the trees and plants . . . The government's moves to constrain *waganga* are very justified because some *waganga* have been causing the death of albinos. That is both wrong and non-functional. Body parts of wild animals may work, but not human body parts. Lions, elephants, etc. are known to have strong powers but the use of albino body parts won't help miners succeed. Maybe some *waganga* think it helps, but there are also some *waganga* who do it for the money and are deceiving people.
>
> (Emmanuel M. 48 years, Matundasi, 19 May 2009)

In the late 2000s, local discussion of miners' and *wagangas*' intended means and ends, as opposed to the tragic outcomes of their actions and the inevitable views on the apportionment of blame, is riddled with disgust, fear and vested interest. The materialist profit-seeking rationality of all the agents directly involved, be they miners, *waganga* or the assassins, was underlined by deep-seated beliefs in the power of charms. The albino fetish was a mental construct requiring the abduction, murder and dismembering of albinos for their body parts. The bones were commonly pulverized and either buried in the mine pit, often in the belief that they would turn into gold or gemstones, or alternatively applied on the body during bathing or carried on the body in various forms of amulets for protection or increased luck.

Newspaper reports indicate that most of the murdered albinos were between the ages of 10 and 30. They met their death at the hands of male gangs of assailants,[5] either barging into homes and killing and dismembering (sometimes in full view of the victim's family), or alternatively through abduction. Given the sheltered lives of albinos, a local person, not infrequently an extended family member, was likely to be involved who knew the habits, movements and needs of the targeted albino, and led the victim to a secluded location on the basis of familiarity and trust, where other members of the gang were on hand for the murder and dismembering. The way in which the victim was killed varied, some being subjected to brutal butchering attacks, others preceded by drowning or strangulation, but almost all included body dismemberment with a machete.[6]

Waganga sold the fetish to miners for very large sums of money.[7] The *waganga* prescribing, the gangs abducting albinos, and the miners paying for and using the albino fetish were all implicated, but the accusations and arrests were overwhelmingly levelled at the gangs engaged in the actual murder. At the close of 2008, out of 90 arrests only eight were *waganga*.[8] There were only hazy outlines of the agency involved in the inexorable creation of an albino fetish. As protagonists, the *waganga* and miners, representing old and new orders, seemingly converged in their beliefs, motivations and ambitions. Literature on African witchcraft and modernity revealed an interplay between rich and poor and the spirit and material worlds that was relevant to understanding the nature of the albino fetish and its destruction of human life.

The physical appearance and perceived vulnerability of most albinos makes them enigmatic and an easy target for those who believe that human sacrifice is a requisite step towards the aggrandizement of wealth and power. Miners were endeavouring to enhance their wealth, while *waganga* and their accomplice assassins sought immediate profit at the high end of the market, servicing miners who were cash-rich relative to themselves and most rural dwellers. *Waganga*'s societal role was associated with a conservative patriarchal rural order that was losing its authority as wealth-begetting miners were seen to be conspicuously consuming and attracting the attention of local women. However, in the exchange, there was likely to be a net transfer of power and wealth to the *waganga*, from miners who needed not only luck but also protection against physical threats to their well-being. By playing on miners' insecurities and selling the albino fetish to them, *waganga* gained wealth and reinvigorated their power and status in the countryside.

The albino fetish exchange may have helped in effect to level the status of the exchange partners. The fetishized albinos were helplessly caught in between. The fact that miners sought the *waganga*'s skills to facilitate their mining returns validates the *waganga*'s still potent cultural power. By selling albino charms, *waganga* immediately gained wealth and status in consonance with the neoliberal commodification process. This trade-off originated in the devaluation of albinos' personhood in the traditional rural order. Paradoxically, albinos experienced revaluation and were vested with wealth-bestowing powers akin to a deity. The albino fetish became an expensive charm because it was perceived as harnessing spirits that were far more powerful than any plant or animal charm that *waganga* could otherwise offer. In so doing, the traditional belief that individual wealth was bought at the cost of human life was fulfilled: *waganga*, assassins and miners, who were party to the fetish exchange, sacrificed the albino victim in their pursuit of personal gain.

Emotively charged, the albino fetish bridged the gulf between the miners and *waganga*, serving both agents' aspirations for wealth and power. However, the actual creation of the albino fetish remains a murky area. Who specifically instigated it? It is unlikely that anyone will ever be able to trace this. Who propagated it? Unidentified *waganga*, be they *bona fide* traditionally trained or commercial upstarts or both, have ubiquitously vested albino body parts with special powers under competitive pressure to gain an edge in the lucky charm market.

Only a handful of miners, convinced of the power of the albino fetish, could spark rumours with an outreach capable of launching a new ritual fashion, which would then be sustained on the basis of miners' curiosity, competitiveness and cash outlays. But, it is important to stress that many miners rejected the fashion on rational grounds, or condemned it from a humanist position. As for the *waganga*, it was impossible to establish whether the fetish-initiating and prescribing *waganga* were restricted to the commercially motivated con-man fringe of practitioners. Court proceedings, which focused primarily on the contract killers, did not reveal the layered complexity of the *waganga*'s supply of the albino fetish.

The albino fetish seems to be taking a somewhat similar course to the Sukuma witch killings, whereby diviners targeted old women well beyond their productive and reproductive prime as witches. Culturally ostracized and not accorded a social identity, albinos occupy a void in which they are seen as receptacles for the spirit world, or in the words of Stroeken (2008: 156) a fetishized 'token emptied of intrinsic meaning, purified from cultural norms and brought down to the coincidence of convention'. In fetish creation, they are dehumanized and deified. The Comaroffs (Comaroff and Comaroff 1993) draw attention to how the human body and emotions are consumed in witchcraft, unveiling changing power relations and values. Witchcraft is more than a metaphor for social change; acting out social change, and often shaping it. As global mineral market chains expand in the region, the illusive wealth-bestowing powers of the market become concentrated in human bodies that were previously devalued, while mineral deposits previously ignored become the central pivot of the local and national economy.

The succession of brutal murders of albinos in Sukumaland inflicted a reign of terror on them and their families. Fear of abduction prevented many young albinos from attending local primary schools.[9] Most albinos hid in the confines of their home, knowing that even there they were not safe. The Tanzanian government provided sheltered accommodation for some during this crisis. For the most part albinos lost their freedom of movement and lived in fear for their lives (Red Cross 2009).

Murder with impunity?

The tragedy of the albinos' predicament in Tanzania has been compounded by the outrage of the victims' families and a concerned national and international public, who witnessed a lack of judicial response to the growing number of albino murders for a year and a half from the time the murders began. Mesaki (2009) recounts a similar situation with respect to the cumulative murder of witches in Sukumaland during the 1970s and early 1980s. The 2,347 witch-related deaths were followed by 1,662 arrests, but only 7 cases had been prosecuted and ended in convictions by 1988. He observes that court proceedings were greatly impeded by lack of substantive evidence. The murderers tended not to be local but had been led to their victim by locals, sometimes family members. Those giving evidence were therefore not familiar with the 'hit and run' assassins and afraid of pointing to those locally involved for fear of reprisals.

While the international and national press sensationalized the albino murders as primitive killings fuelled by greed and poverty, it is important to distinguish these murders from historical patterns of Sukuma *uganga* practices and suspected witch killings. Differences are evident in a then and now comparison of the exchange between the miner and the *mganga*. First, Sukuma *waganga* were traditionally consulted for a retrospective interpretation of events or social interaction; their main role was to remedy affliction of one or another types, notably to cure illness, reverse misfortune, and restore the status quo of well-being. Now, miners are asking *waganga*s to facilitate their future mining success.

Second, illness was formerly explained in terms of the community in which the individual lived. Emphasis was placed on identifying what misalignment had taken place in the individual's social relationships in his/her family and local setting. Now, social inter-relationships between the miner and his family and neighbours are not so much at issue. Mining clients may seek help to prevent discord between mining colleagues, but they are primarily imploring *waganga* to provide the instrumental means to achieve their material profit-seeking goals. The *waganga* are more pharmacists than psychologists, on hand to dispense the most effective medication to enable the individual to succeed.[10] Gangs of paid assassins with local accomplices murdering albinos do so without reference to or concern for the resolution of local inter-relationships; they are also engaged in a profit-making service.

Third, the social ideal amongst Sukuma was traditionally one of egalitarian consumption. This nonetheless took place amidst the accumulation of cattle and wives by patriarchal patrons who regulated homestead production and controlled social relations. *Waganga* facilitated social rule enforcement and maintenance of the decentralized power nodes of the patriarchal homestead heads, generating awareness, respect, awe and fear in the regulatory powers of the spirit world that they mediated. But this power base has now been seriously eroded as Tanzanian agriculture has declined and mining has surged. The albino fetish has unobtrusively become a means to redress the local power imbalance through trade in a fetishized commodity vested with value reflecting the convergence of interests of the old and new order. Now *waganga* are on a charm offensive, projecting themselves as the medium through which material success can be gained. They trade in neo-traditional modernity at the expense of the safety, welfare and human life of local albinos. In the creation of the albino fetish, albinos have paradoxically been both dehumanized and deified.

Evans-Pritchard's (1937) classic work on witchcraft among the Azande of Sudan stresses that witchcraft and magic were utilized to explain *why* rather than *how* things happened. Now, given the current craving for magic with favourable future outcomes, we see *waganga* taking on a new role of facilitating individual material success rather than social harmony and understanding. The albino fetish has creatively emerged from exchange between agents representing two very different value systems: that of a localized patriarchal, agro-pastoralist community with its power source vested in male elders, and that of comparatively young miners in new settlements tied to global value chains. At a symbolic level, the albino fetish represents the perpetuation of collective human-centred valuation, in conformity with Tanzanian *waganga* traditional practices, but through fetish commodification, *waganga* and miners realize value through the dehumanization of the conduit of value, the albino. In other words, the result is a travesty of human-centred valuation: albinos' lives are sacrificed for the individual monetary gain of miners, *waganga*, and their assassin accomplices.

Wijsen (2008) argues that the Sukuma have historically been a far too pragmatic people to let religious rituals and magic beliefs get in the way of their daily livelihood pursuits and material objectives. This accords with our assessment that the albino fetish does not represent deeply rooted traditional spiritual beliefs. Albino body parts are a newly fashioned commodity rooted in accelerating capitalist competition, dramatizing the existence of pockets of opportunistic wealth accumulation amidst proliferating poverty.

The interface between miners and *waganga* has created a fetish around which miner, *mganga* and assassin all have material gain rationalized in a symbolic world of scarcity in which albinos and minerals are intimately linked. The production of the fetish through the act of murder is integral to the process of seemingly limitless commodification embedded in the logic of capitalism. The albino fetish promises wealth and success, very similar to the logic and promise of the global market, whereby liberalized competitive markets are seen as optimizers of the world's wealth and welfare in all places, for all functions, at all times. The human costs involved in market operations are always discounted against economic efficiency and successful wealth generation of individuals and capitalist firms. The global market is in effect a mega fetish, engaging people in exchange from a multitude of cultures, all under the belief of net gain for everyone. There are seemingly never any losers. Those that cannot compete should simply go elsewhere, find some other place to live and work, or disappear like the *zeruzeru*.

Despite these correlations, there is a difference between Tanzanian miners' albino fetish and the global market fetish of neo-liberalism. Albino deaths are tragic and seen as such in Tanzania. By contrast, while the Western liberal world condemns the albino deaths as barbarism, ideological blindness to the implications of the global market fetish in the developing world prevails. Global capitalism has an enveloping logic that can undermine livelihoods, destabilize local rural economies, and distort the humanism of longstanding agrarian cultures and exchange relationships within families, communities and nation-states worldwide, with scant regard for the welfare outcome of those adversely affected.

Tanzanian miners and *waganga* trading partners represent different subcultures within a national culture undergoing rapid and radical transformation. Miners of the neo-liberal global order and *waganga* of the rural agrarian order are polarized on the basis of occupation, generation, and above all their positionality vis-à-vis global neo-liberal market opportunities.

In conclusion, it is important to stress that many miners are indifferent to, scorn or condemn the use of albino body parts, at the same time as fascination with the fetish now extends beyond the arena of Tanzanian miners to other occupational walks of life and neighbouring countries, propelled by people eager for material success. It is grossly simplistic to assume that the albino fetish simply reflects primitive beliefs that can be eradicated through education. Nor can it be regarded solely as a response to a capitalist profit motive that can be addressed by curbing exploitative practices or supporting the poor. The albino fetish arises from the logics of two incongruent social orders, which have collided with one another. The fetish has bridged the divide generating a symbolic *modus operandi* between the old agrarian order and a new coalescing mining-centred power bloc in Sukumaland. In the quest for mutually beneficial exchange and material rewards, miners and *waganga* have simultaneously marginalized, dehumanized, objectified and deified albinos, many of whom are among the rural society's most vulnerable members.

Notes

1   Derived from the following article: Bryceson, D.F., Jønsson, J.B. and Sherrington, R. (2010) 'Miners' magic: Artisanal mining, the albino fetish and murder in Tanzania', *Journal of Modern African Studies* 48(3): 353–82
2   In May and June 2009, court cases were instigated in Shinyanga, Mwanza and Tabora, along with a trial in Burundi where eleven suspects were charged with twelve albino murders and the transport of body parts to Tanzania (*Daily News*, 5 May 2009, 7 June 2009; *Radio Nederland Wereldomroep*, 20 May 2009).
3   Personal communications, Koen Stroeken, 14 March 2009; Ray Abrahams, 12 June 2009. A more general debate within the Tanzania Studies Association (January 2009) about the position of albinos in Tanzanian society did not reveal a precedent for albino murders. Dr. Jeff Luande, Tanzania's foremost expert on skin cancer who has been treating albinos for decades, commented that the killings seemed to 'come from nowhere' (Red Cross 2009: 13).
4   Genetic mutations associated with the population forming the Bantu migration from west to southern Africa over 3,000 years ago increased the average likelihood of albinism at birth from 1:20,000 to 1:3,000 in East Africa (King and Summers 2005), inferring that the albino population in Tanzania, a country with a population of 45 million would be 15,000, which is 7,000 more than the TAS estimate of 8,000.
5   The gangs themselves are said to use 'I don't understand' (*sielewi*) charms, which seem to desensitize them to their actions.
6   Confirmed by Hon. MP Al-Shaimaa Kwegyir who visited several of the victims' families (interview, 16 March 2010).
7   Tanzanian police placed the market value of a complete albino body at US$ 75,000 (Red Cross 2009, confirmed by Hon. Al-Shaimaa Kwegyir, who has tried to convince the media to avoid mentioning the price, as it could result in escalated killings). US$ 2,000 for albino bones was the price quoted by one *mganga* in a video made in 2009 by BBC journalist Vicky Ntetema when she posed as a potential client (*BBC News*, http://news.bbc.co.uk/go/pr/fr/-/a/hl/world/africa/7523796.stm). On 3 February 2010, two men were arrested in Kagera Region in possession of two albino body parts, which they tried to sell for Tsh 600,000 (US$ 375 (*Daily News*, 6 February 2010).
8   *Daily News*, 2 November 2008.
9   Tanzanian schools for the disabled in Mwanza region had a large cluster (103) of albino boarding students seeking safety there (Red Cross 2009).
10 See Stroeken (2010) for a detailed study of the Sukuma *waganga*'s therapeutic roles.

References

Abrahams, R. (1981) *The Nyamwezi Today: A Tanzanian People in the 1970s*. Cambridge: Cambridge University Press.

Bryceson, D.F. (2010) 'Africa at work: Transforming occupational identity and morality'. in D.F. Bryceson (ed.) *How Africa Works: Occupational Change, Identity and Morality*. London: Practical Action Publishing. pp. 3–28.

Bryceson, D.F. and Jønsson, J.B. (2010) 'Gold digging careers in rural East Africa: Small-scale miners' livelihood choices'. *World Development* 38(3): 379–92.

Bryceson, D.F., Jønsson, J.B., Kinabo, C. and Shand, M. (2012) 'Unearthing treasure and trouble: Mining as an impetus to urbanisation in Tanzania'. *Journal of Contemporary African Studies* 30(4): 631–49.

Colson, E. (2000) 'The father as witch', *Africa* 70(3): 333–58.

Comaroff, J. and Comaroff, J. (1993) *Modernity and Its Malcontents: Ritual and Power in Postcolonial Africa*. Chicago, IL: University of Chicago Press.

Cory, H. (1949). 'The ingredients of magic medicines', *Africa* 19 (1): 13–32.

Evans-Pritchard, E.E. (1937) *Witchcraft, Magic and Oracles amongst the Azande People*. Oxford: Oxford University Press.

Hodkinson, P. and Deike, W. (eds) (2007) *Youth Cultures: Scenes, Subcultures and Tribes*. New York: Routledge.

Jangu, M. (2010) 'Environmental change and transformation of health care services: Contextualizing, consuming and producing traditional healing in Mwanza, Tanzania'. Conference on Engaging Anthropology in Development, Ouagadougou, Burkina Faso, January.

Jønsson, J.B. and Bryceson, D.F. (2009) 'Rushing for gold: Mobility and small-scale mining in East Africa'. *Development and Change* 40(2): 249–79.

Jønsson, J.B. and Fold, N. (2009) 'Handling uncertainty: Policy and organizational practices in Tanzania's small-scale gold mining sector'. *Natural Resources Forum* 33(3): 211–20.

King, R.A. and Summers, C.G. (2005) 'Albinism and Hermansky-Pudlak syndrome', *Management of Genetic Syndromes*. doi: 10.1002/0471695998.mgs005.

Luedke, L. and West, H. (eds) (2006) *Borders and Healers: Brokering Therapeutic Resources in Southeast Africa*. Bloomington, IN: Indiana University Press.

Madulu, N.F. (1998) 'Changing lifestyles in farming societies of Sukumaland', [Deagrarianisation and Rural Employment Programme Working Paper]. Leiden, The Netherlands: Afrika-Studiecentrum.

Mesaki, S. (1994) 'Witch-killing in Sukumaland'. in Abrahams, R. (ed.) *Witchcraft in Contemporary Tanzania*. Cambridge: Cambridge African Monographs. pp. 47–60.

Mesaki, S. (2009) 'The tragedy of ageing: Witch killings and poor governance among the Sukuma', in Haram, L. and Yamba, C.B. (eds) *Dealing with Uncertainty in Contemporary African Lives*. Stockholm: Nordiska Afrikainstitutet. pp. 72–90.

Red Cross (2009) *Through Albino Eyes: The Plight of Albino People in Africa's Great Lakes Region and a Red Cross Response*. Geneva: International Federation of Red Cross and Red Crescent Societies.

Roszak, T. (1996 [1965]) *The Making of a Counter Culture: Reflections on the Technocratic Society and its Youthful Opposition*. Berkeley, CA: University of California Press.

Sanders, T. (2001a) 'Save our skins: Structural adjustment, morality and the occult in Tanzania'. in Moore, H. and Sanders, T. (eds) *Magical Interpretations, Magical Realities*. London: Routledge. pp. 160–83.

Sanders, T. (2001b) 'Territorial and magical migrations in Tanzania', in De Bruijn, M. van Dijk, R. and Foeken, D. (eds) *Mobile Africa: Changing Patterns of Movement in Africa and Beyond*. Leiden, The Netherlands: Brill. pp. 27–46.

Sanders, T. (2009) 'Invisible hands and visible goods: Revealed and concealed economies in millennial Tanzania'. in Haram, L. and Yamba, C.B. (eds) *Dealing with Uncertainty in Contemporary African Lives*. Stockholm: Nordiska Afrikainstitutet. pp. 91–117.

Stroeken, K. (2001) 'Defy the gaze: *Exodelics* for the bewitched in Sukumaland and beyond', *Dialectical Anthropology* 26(3–4): 285–309.

Stroeken, K. (2008) 'Believed belief: Science/religion versus Sukuma magic'. *Social Analysis* 52(1): 144–65.

Stroeken, K. (2010) *Moral Power: The Magic of Witchcraft*. New York: Berghahn Books.

Tanner, R.E.S. (1956a) 'The sorcerer in Northern Sukumaland, Tanganyika'. *Southwestern Journal of Anthropology* 12: 437–43.

Tanner, R.E.S. (1956b) 'An introduction to the spirit beings of the Northern Basukuma'. *Anthropological Quarterly* 29: 69–81.

Wijsen, F.J.S. (2008) 'Beyond Ujamaa: African religion and societal evil', in Doorn-Harder, P. and Minnema, L. (eds) *Coping with Evil in Religion and Culture*. Amsterdam: Editions Rodopi V.V. pp. 169–84.

Wijsen, F.J.S. and Tanner, R.E. (2002) *I Am Just a Sukuma: Globalization and Identity Construction in Northwest Tanzania*. Amsterdam: Editions Rodopi B.V.

Part II

Mining communities, organizational constructs and policy

7 Dealing with ambiguity

Policy and practice among artisanal gold miners

Jesper Bosse Jønsson and Niels Fold

In 1992, the World Bank published its Strategy for African Mining arguing that the endorsement of reformed mining codes[1] could transform the underperforming African mining sector into a driver of economic recovery. The new mining codes that followed in many African countries expanded the opportunities for commercial, particularly foreign, mining companies and led to substantial rises in exploration and mining investments (Campbell 2004, 2009). In addition, the existence of artisanal mining and its importance for poverty reduction have gradually been recognized, which has resulted in efforts to legalize, formalize, and regulate the sector. Funds from the World Bank were allocated to draft new artisanal mining codes in a number of African countries with the stated aim of building human and institutional capacity in order to implement the legislation and address the sector's associated problems (World Bank 1992, 2004).

In tandem with the recognition of its importance, the artisanal mining sector has received increasing attention from the international donor community (Hilson 2005, 2007). Evidence suggests, however, that the impacts of the artisanal mining support programmes have been limited, mainly due to the failure of top-down support approaches to adequately involve beneficiaries, the limited capacity within government institutions, and the lack of knowledge about artisanal miners' livelihoods (Banchirigah 2006; Hilson 2007). Hence, Hilson (2005) strongly advocates more baseline studies within artisanal mining settlements to provide information on the number, age, origin, ethnicity, and educational background of miners.

In addition there is a strong need for a better understanding of the operational activities within artisanal mining. This is necessary not only to increase the efficiency of development projects aimed at improving living and working conditions in mining settlements but also to develop and adapt the regulatory mechanisms to long-enduring practices. If basic practices differ substantially from official prescriptions of the mining codes over an extended period of time this indicates that certain elements of the regulatory framework may need to be reconsidered. Moreover, this chapter stresses the need for understanding variations of organizational practices among artisanal mining settlements, how they have evolved and consolidated, and why they may differ significantly between settlements. Only by incorporating common practices as well as variations in some of the crucial organizational components is it possible to design robust and resilient changes to the regulatory artisanal mining framework.

Considering the large body of literature on artisanal mining in Tanzania, research providing insight into the organization of artisanal gold mining activities is limited (Chachage 1995; Kulindwa *et al.* 2003; Mwaipopo *et al.* 2004; Fisher 2007, 2008). Moreover, these studies are based on research in settlements around the Lake Victoria Gold Fields, in particular Geita District, although gold is extracted by artisanal miners in at least 15 of mainland Tanzania's 25 regions. Focusing on the organizational dynamics of the Matundasi and Londoni gold sites, which are two lesser-known artisanal gold mining settlements, this chapter contributes to knowledge on Tanzania and indeed the African artisanal gold mining sector more generally.

The chapter begins with an account of the codes pertaining to artisanal mining in Tanzania, contrasting them with basic organizational practices in artisanal mining prevalent in the country. Subsequently, three pertinent operational components that vary in form and management practices between the two study sites are examined: dealing with licence acquisition, accessing working capital and sharing output. These components are considered vital for the proper manoeuvring of local artisanal mining operators, and the reasons for the variations are essential to understand for policy makers and development practitioners. Finally, we discuss the relevance of the findings for policy and development interventions targeting the artisanal gold mining sector in Tanzania.

Tanzania's regulatory framework for artisanal mining

The 1979 Mining Act provided Tanzanians with the opportunity to engage in mining activities through prospecting rights in areas designated for prospecting and mining for minerals that did not require large expenditures and specialized equipment and to post claims within these areas. Thus, the act implicitly permitted artisanal mining activities. This was followed by the Small Scale Mining Policy Paper of 1983, which encouraged citizens to supplement their incomes by participating in mining activities (Chachage 1995). Still, it was not until 1990, after the monopoly of the State Mining Company had ended that the mining and selling of gold was liberalized completely (Phillips *et al.* 2001). From then on, artisanal miners were encouraged to acquire claims (Lange 2006).

The 1979 Mining Act was replaced with the 1998 Mining Act, which provided for the presence and development of an artisanal mining sector and prescribed co-existence between artisanal and large-scale mining. The Mineral Policy of 1997, mainly a statement of intent, prescribed the development and formalization of the artisanal mining sector in order to facilitate sustainable development. It endorsed provision of extension services, improved tenure rights, clearer marketing channels for minerals, and access to credit and training (Tanzania 1997).

The Mining Act of 1998 and the subsequent Mining Regulations of 1999 provided artisanal miners with the opportunity to acquire Primary Prospecting Licences (PPLs) and PMLs. A PPL was granted for a period of one year, could be renewed, and authorized the owner to prospect for minerals within one of Tanzania's eight mining zones, provided that the selected prospecting area had not been occupied by other mineral right holders. A PML was granted for five years and gave the owner the right to exploit an area of up to ten hectares. It conferred on the holder the exclusive rights, subject to compliance with safety and environmental regulations, to carry out mining activities in the area. Whereas large mining investors were required to conduct environmental impact assessments and produce environmental management plans, PML owners only needed to adhere to a set of basic social and environmental regulations. These were intended to prevent child labour, health and safety hazards, and environmental degradation (Tanzania 1998, 1999).

From the time the 1998 Mining Act was endorsed in 1999, an unprecedented debate on the mining sector in Tanzania began. It focused on the legislation, the presence of large-scale mining, the role of artisanal mining, and mining's contribution to the country's efforts to reduce poverty. Newspaper headlines from the past decade give an idea of the criticism the government and large-scale mining companies faced: 'The paradox of Tanzania's mineral wealth'; 'Mining firms violate union laws...'; 'Mining not benefiting Tanzania...'; 'Protect rights of small-scale miners, says Bishop...'; 'State wants shares in mining firms'; 'Cheyo blasts Karamagi; Who is the minister working for, the people of Tanzania or the mining companies?'; 'Mining: Why communities get less'; 'Gold plunder exposed'.[2] The debate increased and intensified and eventually led to the passing of a new Mineral Policy in 2009 and a new Mining Act in 2010.

The Mineral Policy of 2009, again a mere statement of intent, promoted increased integration between the mining sector and other sectors of the economy in order to improve mining's contribution to the national economy. The policy also prescribes the development and increased formalization of the artisanal[3] mining sector in order to facilitate sustainable development, specifically stating that the government will 'develop and implement programmes to transform and upgrade small-scale mining into organised and modernised mining... and cooperate with stakeholders to facilitate small-scale miners to access market for minerals, geological information, technical and financial services' (Tanzania 2009: 17).

With regards to artisanal mining, the Mining Act of 2010 constitutes only a limited number of significant changes from the 1998 Mining Act. The 2010 Mining Act defines a PML as 'a licence for small scale mining operations, whose capital investment is less than US$ 100,000 or its equivalent in Tanzanian shillings' (Tanzania 2010a). A PML is acquired subject to payment of application and preparation fees of US$ 6 (Tanzania shilling [Tsh] 10,000) each plus an annual rent of US$ 6 (Tsh 10,000) per hectare, which is a minor change from the 1998 act, where licence holders had to pay an annual rent of US$60 (Tsh. 100,000) for the PML irrespective of size (to a maximum of ten hectares). It is granted for seven years, which is two years more than in the 1998 Act. The new mining act has a maximum of 20 PMLs or 200 hectares per PML holder. The assistant commissioners of minerals seated in each of Tanzania's eight mining zones have the mandate to sign PMLs, which may speed up the processing time of a PML application, as the 1998 Mining Act had the Commissioner of Minerals based in Dar es Salaam as the sole signatory. Once granted, a PML can be mortgaged, renewed or transferred to another holder, including foreign firms. The PML owner is responsible for the entire mining operation taking place on his claim (Tanzania 2010a, 2010b).

One of the few major changes in the 2010 Mining Regulations is the fact that artisanal miners are now required to submit to the Zonal Mines Officer, within four months from the date of the granting of the PML, an Environmental Protection Plan (EPP) together with an 'environmental investigation' and 'social study report', while prior to the new legislation they simply needed to adhere to a set of very basic social and environmental regulations. According to the Mining Regulations, PML holders are required to conduct 'baseline environmental investigation and social study with regard to human settlement, burial sites, cultural heritage sites, water, vegetation, animals and soil, and submit a report regarding the outcome of the investigation and Environmental Protection Plan to mitigate the environmental effects to be caused by mining operations in the licensed area' (Tanzania 2010b: 4).

Although the issue of designating areas specifically for artisanal mining purposes was mentioned in the 1998 Mining Act, it is given closer attention in the new act, with guidelines for implementation (Tanzania 2010a). PPLs have been abolished in the new act, as it was claimed that many artisanal miners used the PPL to mine instead of prospecting. In addition, the royalties on metals are up from three to four per cent, and calculated on gross revenue instead of on 'net back-value'. With regard to gemstones, the royalties will be 1 per cent for cut stones and 5 per cent for uncut stones. Another of the more significant changes in the new act also concerns gemstones: foreigners will not be able to hold gemstone-mining licences without agreeing to a minority stake partnership with Tanzanian citizens.

Organizational practices in Tanzania's artisanal gold mining sector

The artisanal mining sector, however, is far from as homogeneous or as neatly structured as anticipated in the legislative and regulatory framework. Therefore it is necessary to pay attention to the distinct economic and functional differentiation amongst miners (Chachage 1995; Kulindwa *et al.* 2003; Mwaipopo *et al.* 2004). Despite occasional shifts over time in individuals' positions, a hierarchical organization exists between owners of mining licences, pit holders, and mine workers.[4] These relationships are outlined below.

Mine workers' initial entry into the artisanal mining sector does not involve significant barriers. However, sustaining a career within artisanal mining involves enduring a number of hazards and uncertainties of livelihood failure and occupational risks (Phillips *et al.* 2001; Mwaipopo *et al.* 2004). Overall, the capabilities of persistent miners improve as they become increasingly experienced and skilled, and expand their networks within the mining community. Hence, artisanal gold miners have an opportunity for professionalized career advancement depending on their apprenticeship, dedication, readiness to move, and networking skills (Chapters 2 and 3). Of the 41 pit holders and PML owners interviewed in this study, 36 had started as mine workers and had worked their way up to where they were during the interviews. Only four had started as pit holders, two of whom were widows of former pit holders taking over the operations of their late husbands; one was a silent partner in a pit. The one respondent who had started as a PML owner had inherited the claim from his father.

Entry into the more operational sides of artisanal mining requires interpersonal skills to negotiate effective social and managerial relationships. According to regulations, PML owners are responsible for mining activities conducted on their claim, i.e. for hiring and paying labour, organizing the mining, and endorsing safety and environmental regulations (Kulindwa *et al.* 2003; Mwaipopo *et al.* 2004). This, however, rarely transpires. Most PML owners are not engaged in actual mining activities, but instead lease out the mineral access to pit holders who organize the mining activities. Sub-leasing of pits contradicts the mining legislation, and formal contractual obligations between the PML owners, pit holders and workers are exceptionally rare; hence their relations may be terminated without notice. The secure position of PML owners' vis-à-vis pit holders and mine workers with no legal recognition often generates tension (see also Fisher 2007, 2008).

However, as also revealed in this study, the distinction between the three functional groupings (PML owner, pit holder and worker) is not always clear and individuals tend to shift categories over time and space. Sometimes PML owners mine in their own concession areas and they may run parallel activities in several places depending on the number of acquired PMLs. They may also start up activities as pit holders on the mining areas of other PML owners. PML owners and pit holders may even join a group of mine workers in another location to earn cash with the purpose of accumulating sufficient means to start up or sustain mining operations. Both PML owners and pit holders enter into PML applications and pit partnerships with others in order to spread their investments and minimize risks of losses. This seemingly chaotic pattern of relationships is a consequence of the unpredictability of artisanal mining in terms of existence and accessibility of deposits, occurrence of technical problems, and accountability of partners.

The production process for hard rock mining consists of constructing galleries, blasting gold-bearing reefs, and hoisting rocks to the surface, as well as transportation, crushing, grinding, and washing of ore, and amalgamation. This production cycle is locally referred to as a 'shift', which generally extends a pit vertically or horizontally by a few metres. It typically takes between a few days and four weeks depending on the hardness of the rock and, in particular, the available technology. Of major importance for the mining operation is the pit holder's management of labour during and between the shifts. The decision to end a shift is typically determined by safety precautions, the need for money for continuous running costs, and the time that workers can stay motivated. However, some of the more organized pit holders plan the production target, in terms of number of bags or sacks expected from a shift and break when the number – for example 100 bags – is reached. The exact time to end the shift is decided by the pit holder in consultation with the PML owner.

Within a shift the production process encompasses a number of managerial requirements of the pit holder such as procurement (or renting) of machinery (e.g. compressors, drilling equipment, generators and water pumps) and simple equipment (e.g. hammers, chisels, pick axes, shovels, buckets, washing pans, and rope). In addition, other means of production such as timber to support pits, explosives for blasting, and diesel for machinery must be procured. Due to huge differences in mining conditions and technical requirements at each site, there is a considerable variation in the expenses of a shift ranging between below US$ 60 (Tsh 100,000) and several million shillings. Major PML owners have their own means of gold extraction and ore processing. However, most miners pay subcontractors for their processing services. Finally, pit holders have to identify and hire foremen and watchmen. Whereas these organizational tasks are basically similar in artisanal gold mining operations across Tanzania (Chachage 1995; Kulindwa *et al.* 2003; Mwaipopo *et al.* 2004), marked differences occur in PML acquisition, access to working capital and output sharing as exemplified by the cases of Londoni and Matundasi.

Licence acquisition

Except for the rare occasions where an area may be allocated for artisanal mining purposes, the 2010 Mining Act (as did the 1998 Mining Act) dictates 'first come, first served' procedures regarding licence acquisition. However, although gold discoveries are often made by artisanal miners or local people, the restricted capacity of mining authorities to disseminate legislative information on how to acquire licences to artisanal miners in a timely manner favours large-scale and junior mining companies as well as well-connected, typically urban-based, speculators. These have in-depth knowledge of the legislation and secure licences in mineral-rich areas before the vast majority of artisanal miners know of the opportunity. Furthermore, they may have been buying up the PMLs of artisanal miners, in some cases instigating the eviction of hundreds of artisanal miners. Moody (2007: 54) argues that the mining codes in Tanzania have allowed foreign companies 'to usurp land previously worked by thousands of small-scale miners, thereby jeopardizing their locally based economies'. The future livelihood of artisanal mining in Tanzania is thus uncertain amidst commercial mining interests.

The designation of mineral-rich land to artisanal mining purposes mentioned in various official documents (e.g. Tanzania 1998, 2010a) has only been implemented on rare occasions. This illustrates how a lack of resources impedes the institutional capacity of the mining authorities (Phillips *et al.* 2001; Mwaipopo *et al.* 2004), and the vested interests and power of the large-scale mining companies (Emel and Huber 2008). Despite these general trends, there are variations in the ways that PMLs have been obtained in Londoni and Matundasi.

When gold was discovered in Londoni, a foreign junior company was interested in securing a Prospecting Licence (PL) to the area.[5] As a consequence, artisanal miners' initial PML applications were rejected. The ones who had already put up pegs for their requested claims subsequently lobbied to get the area designated for artisanal mining. After a long and opaque negotiation process involving the Regional Commissioner, the Minister of Energy and Minerals, the Commissioner for Minerals, and especially the local Member of Parliament, the government decided to allocate an area of approximately 10 square kilometres for artisanal mining. Thus, on May 1, 2005, six months before the national elections, the acting Commissioner for Minerals came to Londoni to issue the first 72 PMLs. This is likely to have contributed to the popularity, in and around Londoni, of the ruling party and the local Member of Parliament, who was re-elected at the elections. In the period between 2006 and 2008 many of the mining camps emerging around the high-producing PMLs were flagging Chama Cha Mapinduzi banners thus stressing their, at least momentarily, allegiance to the ruling party. In early 2007, there were 215 PMLs in Londoni.[6] According to respondents and informants, a tendency to include government officials from district level and upwards or their relatives as partners in PMLs has emerged as a means to facilitate the acquisition process.

The 21 PML owners and pit holders interviewed together owned, individually or in partnerships, 77 PMLs (of which only a small number were being exploited) and had applied for an additional 178. Thus, Londoni artisanal miners aspire to accumulate PMLs in partnership with others, instead of one or a few PMLs each, in order to reduce risk and enhance the likelihood of a profitable resale or rich gold discovery. The possibility of selling PMLs to junior companies[7] led artisanal miners in Londoni to apply for PMLs on land allocated to local residents for agriculture and housing. In late 2006, this had resulted in 30 formal complaints from Londoni villagers to Manyoni District officials. However, both the 1998 and the 2010 Mining Acts overrule the 1999 Village Land Act and whereas mining issues are dealt with at the zonal or ministry level, land issues are primarily managed at the village and district levels. Generally, formally operating miners have the law on their side in land disputes and if a case ends up in court, the compensations paid to farmers are limited. In Londoni (and elsewhere), some land-use conflicts have been resolved, as PML applicants have included farmers as PML co-applicants.[8]

In contrast to Londoni, as of 2008, only nine PMLs have been issued in Matundasi, as nearly all remaining land was held as PLs by junior companies. This significantly constrained prospective and entrepreneurial artisanal miners' possibilities for acquiring PMLs and essentially excludes them from engaging in formal mining activities in Matundasi. To compensate, governmental mining officials, prior to the abolishment of PPLs, accepted that artisanal miners mined the unused areas held by the junior companies subject to acquisition of PPLs or payment of an annual PML fee for which official government receipts were issued. If the licence holder commenced prospecting activities, however, the artisanal miner would be evicted.[9] Such PML owners/applicants are recognized by the community as the rightful claim holders. Land-use conflicts like the ones experienced in Londoni between migrant miners and sedentary farmers are rare in Matundasi. As most residents have come to Matundasi because of the gold, and thus usually prioritize gold extraction, conflicts are typically settled quickly through compensation to the landholder in the form of a share of the gold extracted from the area.[10] Hence, due to the particular historical formation of Matundasi where no pre-mining agricultural tradition prevailed, counter claims on land use have been internalized in the local economic dynamics.

Access to working capital

In some cases, pit holders are able to finance the operations from their own funds. At other times, running costs are paid or laid out by local investors from within or outside the mining site, e.g. PML owners or local businessmen and women. Often, however, credit in the form of short-term informal loans is obtained from local brokers to finance all or parts of the operations provided the brokers are convinced of the pit holders' capabilities to strike gold and subsequently sell to the broker, sometimes for a price slightly under the settlement's spot price.

Informal loans are of vital importance for artisanal mining operators, who face difficulties in obtaining formal loans (Spiegel 2011). None of the respondents had received loans from formal credit institutions, which, moreover, have interest rates of 15–20 per cent. According to Spiegel (2011: 8) '[h]igh interest rates at banks, lack of subsidies (which could reduce rates) and inflexible repayment options have often been noted as barriers to credit access in rural contexts in Tanzania'.

Each artisanal gold mining settlement of a certain size has its gold brokers, who are entitled to trade minerals within Tanzania provided they have a broker licence, issued by the assistant commissioners, for minerals. Whereas some brokers have licences, many do not, which was also the conclusion of Phillips *et al.* (2001) in their study of the market access of artisanal miners in Tanzania. Brokers often finance a network of buyers who travel to remote mining areas to purchase gold. The gold brokers typically sell the gold to urban-based dealers, mainly in the city of Dar es Salaam, who are licenced to trade and export minerals.[11] The majority of the gold dealers in Dar es Salaam are Indian goldsmiths, whose significance is indicated by the fact that the normal unit of measurement within Tanzanian artisanal gold mining is the traditional Indian weight unit of *tola*, equivalent to 11.7 grams.

There are five main brokers in Londoni, of whom only one owns a broker licence. Additionally, there are around 30 small buyers supplementing their income from mining by buying small quantities of gold and selling to the brokers. Eighty-seven per cent of the Londoni respondents have received informal loans from local brokers, varying from three to as many as 50 loans for one PML owner and with amounts ranging between US$ 125 (Tsh 200,000) and US$ 1,250 (Tsh two million). Borrowers have to sell their gold to the broker and are paid up to US$ 1.25 (Tsh 2,000) less per gram than the current price in Londoni as interest, depending on the broker's knowledge of and relation to the borrowers. On average, respondents were paid US$ 0.86 (Tsh 1,375) less per gram than the prevalent gold price. With the then gold price of US$ 13 (Tsh 21,000) per gram of gold in Londoni (March 2007), this is equivalent to an interest rate of 6.5 per cent.

Also in Matundasi, only one of the five main brokers possesses a licence. The two biggest brokers provide artisanal miners with loans. Forty-seven per cent of Matundasi respondents have received informal loans from local brokers, varying from one to 20 loans and with amounts ranging between US$ 190 (Tsh 300,000) and US$ 1,875 (Tsh three million). Respondents mostly had to sell their gold to the broker and all but two received the prevailing spot price. Thus, on average, they were paid US$ 0.08 (Tsh 125) less per gram than the prevalent gold price. With the then gold price of US$ 13 (Tsh 21,000) per gram of gold in Matundasi (March 2007), this is equivalent to an interest rate of less than one per cent.[12]

Output sharing

Mine workers are not paid salaries, but instead receive a share of the output. Usually, there is a verbal or tacit agreement between pit holders and workers that the latter will stay with the pit holder under the conditions laid down before the start of the shift subject to consensus on fair working conditions, i.e. coverage of the workers' costs (food, medicine, basic health services and pocket money). In addition, the pit holder has to observe certain standards of managerial treatment of the workers, such as respect of individual idiosyncrasies, and a reasonable number of breaks during the working day. If these conditions are not fulfilled, workers may leave and look for work with alternative pit holders, again entering a 'stable labour market' during the next shift. Observers (e.g. Kulindwa *et al.* 2003) have argued that the system of non-paying of salaries is exploitative, only benefiting PML owners and/or pit holders. Still, spontaneous reactions from mine workers at the study sites indicate that many would not change the insecurity of output sharing with a fixed monthly salary: high hopes of a rich strike providing substantial amounts of money are common.

However, the sharing of output from artisanal gold mining takes on various forms depending on the local practice, labour availability and skills, reef richness, and the bargaining strength of workers, pit holders and PML owners. Most of the early arrivals in Londoni came from settlements located around Lake Victoria to the northwest of Londoni, known for their longstanding gold discoveries and high number of artisanal miners. They brought with them a sharing system applied throughout most artisanal mining settlements of northwestern Tanzania. In this system, the PML owner usually takes 30 per cent of the output and the rest is divided between the pit holder (40 per cent) and the workers (30 per cent). The different shares are usually measured in number of bags of ore prior to process-ing. Mine workers divide their 30 per cent according to elaborate systems whereby, for instance, the drillers receive more than the hoisters. Employees such as watchmen and foremen as well as people occupied with various specialized tasks such as blasting and electrical drilling are typically paid a certain number of bags of ore per shift.

Ore(s) with estimated similar gold content are placed in bags and divided according to the agreed shares. Each group takes responsibility for the ore, making sure it is processed and the gold is extracted and sold to local brokers. Up through the 1980s, a system of sharing ore instead of gold or cash emerged in most artisanal gold mining settlements around Lake Victoria, as many hard rock operations became formalized and increasingly extensive. Miners argue that sharing ore instead of gold eases the sharing process and makes it more transparent. It prevents PML owners from adding to their share and gives miners the freedom to sell their gold to whomever they want. Moreover, some miners' strong belief in personal luck and/or an appeal to magic make the process of selecting the right bags an appreciated event, as some of the miners believe their engagement in a variety of religious practices, e.g. sacrificing, seeking advice from priests and diviners, and using charms, will positively affect their share.

The nature and type of output sharing varies amongst the various concessions with regard to issues such as who pays the watchmen, whether mine workers are paid their share before or after the pit holder has deducted his expenses, and whether or not PML owners make use of the infamous *dharura* a so-called emergency fee collected at the discretion of the PML owner, often in the form of a number of bags of ore. This happens especially if the PML owner is out of money, the pit holder has struck a rich deposit, or a major accident has occurred within the PML. In Londoni, respondents reported monthly operational expenses between US$ 350–4,700 (Tsh 560,000–7,500,000) and gold outputs ranging between 25 grams and as much as 1.5 kilos in the biggest PML during the peak of the gold rush.

In Matundasi, the system of sharing ore existed until around the new millennium. However, according to experienced respondents, people were getting different outputs after gold extraction. Whereas one would get US$ 6.25 (Tsh 10,000) for a bag, another would be getting Tsh 100,000 from the same 'shift'. As a result, PML owners, concerned about losing money, insisted on another system. Thus, today the PML owner manages the gold and pays the pit holders and workers their shares. This has led to allegations of the PML owners cheating by secretly increasing their share. In contrast to Londoni, PML owners in Matundasi get some of their earnings by insisting on buying all the gold extracted within their claims and distributed to pit holders and mine workers as their share, at a price 20–30 per cent below the settlement's spot price. Locally, this is known as the claim's price. Beyond this, output sharing in Matundasi is far more heterogeneous than in Londoni, with almost every claim having its own arrangement. The existing systems within hard rock mining can be classified into four main types.

i.   The PML owner pays running costs, while pit holders do all the mining themselves until they reach the gold-bearing reef. Subsequently, mine workers are invited in to take over the work, which is organized by the pit holders. Hereafter, the three groups share equally, but pit holders and workers have to sell to the PML owner at the claim's price.

ii.   Pit holders fund and run the operation and share the proceeds on a fifty-fifty basis with mine workers. They sell gold to the PML owner at the claim's price.

iii. PML owners employ miners whom they pay between US$ 4 (Tsh 7,000) and US$ 25 (Tsh 40,000) per metre of digging depending on the depth and the hardness of the soil/rock. When the reef has been mined and the gold extracted, proceeds are shared equally between workers and the PML owner, who pays running costs and buys all gold at the claim's price.

iv.   The PML owner pays the running costs. When the miners' strike gold, the costs are deducted, after which the mine workers share the gold and sell it to the PML owner at the claim's price.

Types iii) and iv) are characterized by an absence of pit holders. This often means that the PML owner functions as the pit holder due probably to the low grade nature of the deposit and a related reluctance on the part of pit holders to embark on mining operations on the claim. Alternatively, the mine workers function as the pit holders. In most Matundasi operations, drillers and hoisters each take half of the workers' share. As there are more hoisters than drillers, the latter get a higher share per person. Watchmen and foremen are paid the equivalent of a certain quantity of ore per 'shift'. In Matundasi, respondents reported monthly operational expenses between US$ 47 (Tsh 75,000) and US$ 1,560 (Tsh 2,500,000) and gold outputs ranging between 0 and 300 grams.

Policy implications

As has been demonstrated in this chapter, Tanzanian mining legislation differs considerably from the practices of artisanal gold mining. The prescriptions of the Mineral Policies (1997 and 2009) are not implemented and the mining regulations from 1998 and 2010 were and are only partially followed. Instead, alternative and local systems of organization and governance have evolved within artisanal mining settlements. However, if the development potential of artisanal gold mining is to materialize, mining regulations need to be adjusted in order to support the sector and enhance a socioeconomically sustainable working environment. Among other things, there is a need to adopt and formalize certain forms of practice in the institutional framework. These regulatory changes need to be sensitive towards variations in local contexts such as different types of deposits, the age of settlements and the organization of mining activities. From our examination of different organizational practices, four issues seem to warrant further elaboration in a policy perspective.

First, mineral-rich land with available prospecting and mining licences has been significantly limited, thus constraining artisanal miners' possibilities of acquiring PMLs. Nothing indicates that the mining legislation has led to any kind of procedural consolidation of traditional artisanal mining areas – the mandate of the Minister of Energy and Minerals to designate areas entirely for artisanal mining purposes has only rarely been applied; Londoni being one of the few exceptions. Evidence from Londoni and Matundasi illustrates the different possibilities for artisanal miners to secure mining rights pressured by the strong presence of junior companies. In Londoni, timely lobbying and political influence have ensured the designation of a large area for artisanal mining. In Matundasi, an 'informal formalization' has taken place with the government's mining officials silently accepting artisanal mining claims (in the form of an official government receipt for a PML application) at areas already acquired, but not used, by junior companies. However, this seemingly peaceful and pragmatic reconciliation of the mining legislation with the local moral economy of customary law is an unstable construct. If miners are told to leave they would most likely resist and question the rightful ownership of the mining rights. Conflicts are imminent and the informal formalization would only last to a certain degree, as it will be threatened and eventually collapse subject to the active arrival of junior and/or large-scale mining companies.

The result of the first come, first served policy's indirect favouring of large-scale and junior prospecting and mining companies could be addressed by designating a larger number of areas for artisanal mining. The mining authorities in cooperation with external donor institutions could conduct geological surveys in order to identify areas suitable for artisanal mining, i.e. rich but limited close-to-surface deposits. Speculation by junior companies and urban-based speculators holding licences and hoping for a profitable resale could be addressed by insisting on upholding the minimum amount of annual prospecting expenses. This would likely result in a large number of licence relinquishments, which could open up for the designation of artisanal mining areas. Obviously, such initiatives would have to be followed up by timely information dissemination on available areas and licences targeting artisanal miners.

Second, artisanal mining entrepreneurs with limited investment funds and inadequate knowledge of available deposits have for decades shared expenses and proceeds. Different sharing practices are recognized within artisanal mining settlements but they all situate pit holders – essentially the artisanal mining operators – in a vulnerable position. PML owners running their operations according to legislative prescriptions are extremely rare (Mwaipopo *et al.* 2004; Fisher 2008), indicating the inappropriateness of the legislation in its current form and the need for amendments to formalize the position of pit holders. Presently, if a PML owner chooses to sell a PML, the pit holders (and mine workers) are likely to be evicted; formalizing the sub-leasing of PMLs while at the same time affirming a number of basic rights and responsibilities to pit holder would substantially reduce risks related to pit holders' insecure tenure. Formalization of the positions of pit holders would in such cases ensure that due compensation is paid to them, factoring in the considerable expenses involved with pit construction.

Third, the provision of credit opportunities for artisanal miners prescribed in the mineral policies (1997 and 2009) has not manifested itself broadly in the artisanal gold mining community.[13] Interest rates within informal loan systems involving local brokers are not directly comparable with those set by banks and formal micro finance institutions as investments in social networks are required in order to gain access to brokers' loans. Nevertheless, the brokers' loans represent viable and attractive credit alternatives, with informal interest rates well below what is offered by banks and formal micro finance institutions, although the terms of the loans vary depending on the relations between brokers and borrowers. Loan conditions in Matundasi are more favourable than in Londoni most likely because: i) Matundasi is a mature settlement where miners and brokers are closely related, have stronger networks, and hence higher mutual trust; and ii) brokers from the nearby town of Chunya compete for the gold. Through the loans, the Matundasi brokers guarantee their right to buy the gold. Hence, support efforts to provide artisanal miners with credit either to embark on alternative livelihood trajectories or to optimize mining operations need to consider available loan opportunities within artisanal gold mining settlements. Provisioning of loans starting from US$ 1,875 (Tsh 3 million) and upwards may be reasonable for the procurement of key equipment such as compressors, water pumps, generators, and electrical winches. However, efforts to provide small loans of, for instance, US$ 300 (Tsh 500,000) with interest rates of 15–20 per cent are likely to be futile given the amounts and conditions already available within artisanal mining settlements.

Finally, many variations of mine workers' remuneration and benefits from sharing systems exist as reflected in the sharing systems in the 'rush' settlement of Londoni and the 'mature' settlement of Matundasi. These were partly a result of different traditions among the majority of present operators and partly a result of the limited number of claims in Matundasi. With the so-called claim's price, the systems in Matundasi appear more exploitative, most likely because claim owners can get away with it. If there were more PMLs and richer deposits relative to the number of workers, the sharing conditions would, to a larger degree, favour mine workers. Hence, the bargaining position of workers improves with the number of accessible gold deposits and the number of pits relative to the number of workers. When a local practice for output sharing has developed it seems to transform into common production conditions subject to sudden change in times of low production or mineral finds elsewhere.

Are low fixed salaries desirable under these labour market conditions? Mine workers claim they would rather have larger shares than fixed salaries.[14] Jønsson and Bryceson (2009) estimated average monthly earnings of gold miners in Londoni and Matundasi to be US$ 118 (Tsh 188,000), excluding provisions of food, medicine and pocket money. Although workers may experience long periods without payment, this still illustrates the rationale of the miners' statements, as average earnings in mining exceed most rural incomes. This is also supported by survey data from Geita district, which demonstrates that incomes for gold mining households are higher than national averages (Fisher *et al.* 2009). In addition, while the position of mine workers may be perceived as exploitative, they possess a certain level of power, as they can leave whenever they want and in some cases may rise to become pit holders or PML owners on the site or elsewhere. As a result, they are often well treated and their idiosyncrasies, e.g. smoking of marijuana, large intake of local brew, using abusive language, etc.

accepted by operators. More than anything else, they are valued for their ability to mine. Given the fact that salaries are extremely difficult to monitor and enforce in artisanal mining settlements, we do not see an urgent need to institutionalize workers' remuneration. Rather, the position of mine workers could be improved by formalizing their position as shareholders with a share equivalent to, for instance, 30 per cent (or more), which they could divide amongst themselves.

Conclusion

There is a tendency in African artisanal mining for differences between legislation and practice to force the majority of artisanal miners to operate informally, hindering an optimal development of the sector. By accepting the existence of practices that do not correspond to the prevailing regulation and adjusting the regulatory mechanisms accordingly, entrepreneurial risks could be reduced and mine workers' employment could be stabilized over a reasonable period. More knowledge of variations in organizational practices would ensure a higher level of resilience of the institutional framework for artisanal mining. The variations are linked to the nature and accessibility of deposits and local socioeconomic particularities, e.g. the division of labour tends to be higher in rush area settlements where miners specialize and allocate their resources to the most profitable activities and use sub-contractors for more marginal ones. Whether or not it is possible to generalize over different phases in a cycle of mining settlement dynamics – including sub-cycles linked to rich discoveries – is an interesting issue but more research is needed. In any case, a flexible approach is required to improve access to financial and technological support for the artisanal mining sector. The high mobility of miners demonstrates their adaptability to different local practices and as a corollary their ability to manoeuvre under different (informal) institutional settings.

A further strengthening and consolidation of artisanal mining would be an important means for governments in renegotiations with large-scale companies over mining conditions in the national territory. One or two decades ago, many African governments were desperate to obtain foreign exchange through the export of gold and other minerals, and mining concessions were offered on exceptionally favourable conditions. Large-scale mining companies, backed by multilateral and bilateral donors, were quick to enter the scene as neo-liberal policies swept away state-owned companies or institutions with control over mining output. However, as recent events in Tanzania indicate (the 2010 Mining Act and its preceding debate); state institutions are taking an increasing interest in reconquering some control over the country's mineral riches. A strong domestic artisanal mining sector would surely strengthen democratizing tendencies within artisanal mining vis-à-vis the national mining sector and the bargaining power of African governments in their quest for a fairer share of the proceeds from national resources.

Notes

1   A mining code 'is the combination of statute law, regulations and agreements which govern the allocation, tenure and operation of mining rights' (World Bank 1992: 21).
2   From: *Business Times*, 26 July–1 August 2002; *The African*, 17 January 2003; *Business Times*, 21–27 March 2003; *The Guardian*, 20 May 2003; *Daily News*, 11 July 2006; *Sunday Citizen*, 11 February 2007; *The Citizen*, 10 December 2007; *The Citizen*, 5 March 2008.
3   Named small-scale in the policy.
4   To study these categories of artisanal miners, semi-structured interviews were held with 41 owners of Primary Mining Licences (PMLs) and pit holders (21 from Londoni and 18 from Matundasi) initially identified through snowball sampling. They were interviewed progressively over the three periods of September–November 2006 (30 respondents), March 2007 (17 respondents), and February 2008 (16 respondents). Depending on their availability, respondents were interviewed once (26 respondents), twice (seven respondents), or three times (eight respondents). The first interview guide was divided into sections on respondents' background, institutional aspects of artisanal mining, organization of the mining operation, access to land, credit, service provision and appropriate technology, and mercury consumption and recycling. The two following rounds of interviews were follow-ups focused on relations between the functional groupings of PML owners, pit holders and mine workers, systems of output sharing, and the production cycles of artisanal mining. In addition, eight gold buyers (four in each settlement) and a number of informants from local and central government and large-scale mining companies were interviewed. See Chapter 2 for more background on our survey methodology.
5   Informants disagree on whether or not the junior company had already obtained the licence.
6   Personal communication, Mr. Aly Samaje, Head of the Licences Unit, Ministry of Energy and Minerals, 2 April 2007.
7   This has already happened in Londoni with many PML owners selling their claims to junior companies.
8   Personal communication, District Administrative Secretary, Manyoni District, 13 September 2006 and Londoni Village Chairperson, 15 September 2006.
9   Personal communication, Chunya District Resident Mines Officer, 13 November 2006 and 5 February 2008, and South Western Zonal Mines Officer, 9 November 2006.
10 Personal communication, Mr. Isaac Haileltha Mwandumbia, Matundasi Village Executive Officer, 3 February 2012.
11 Successful PML owners and, to a lesser degree, pit holders, occasionally take the journey themselves if they have enough gold to make it profitable. PML owners are lawfully permitted to trade and export minerals (Tanzania 2010a).
12 These aspects of the brokers' financial activities are considered confidential and data are therefore difficult to obtain. However, two of the brokers (one from each settlement) provided some information. They both estimated their monthly loans to approximately US$ 6,235 (Tsh10 million). The Londoni broker buys gold for between about $US 6,000 and 9,000 (Tsh10–15 million) monthly, equivalent to around 500 grams of gold, and sells it once a month in Dar es Salaam, earning around US$ 500 (Tsh 800,000) per trip.
13 Recent developments with the establishment of Savings and Credit Cooperatives (SACCOS) among artisanal miners in Geita District and an announcement by Tanzania Investment Bank about plans to support a microfinance loan facility to artisanal miners in cooperation with the Tanzanian government (*The Guardian* 25 June 2011) may change this. However, interviews made by Spiegel (2011) with Tanzanian bank officials, showed that a high degree of scepticism and reservation towards the

artisanal mining sector still prevails, mainly as a result of the difficulty of assessing the actual mineral richness, and thus value, of a PML.

14   In this case fixed salaries refers to low rural salaries typically paid to people with little or no education, and not the minimum wage of the mineral sector set at US$ 220 (Tsh 350,000), which are primarily intended to cover the large-scale mining sector.

References

Banchirigah, S. M. (2006) 'How have reforms fuelled the expansion of artisanal mining? Evidence from sub-Saharan Africa'. *Resources Policy*, 31(3): 165–71.

Campbell, B. (ed.) (2004) *Regulating Mining in Africa: For Whose Benefits?* Uppsala, Sweden: Nordic Africa Institute.

Campbell, B. (ed.) (2009) *Mining in Africa: Regulation and Development.* Norwich: Pluto Press.

Chachage, C.S.L. (1995) 'The meek shall inherit the earth but not the mining rights: Mining and accumulation in Tanzania', in Gibbon, P. (ed.), *Liberalised Development in Tanzania.* Uppsala, Sweden: Institute for African Studies. pp. 37–108.

Emel, J. and Huber, M.T. (2008) 'A risky business: Mining, rent and the neoliberalization of risk', *Geoforum*, 39(3): 1393–407.

Fisher, E. (2007) 'Occupying the margins: Labour integration and social exclusion in artisanal mining in Tanzania', *Development and Change* 38(4): 735–60.

Fisher, E. (2008) 'Artisanal gold mining at the margins of mineral resource governance: A case from Tanzania'. *Development Southern Africa* 25(2): 199–213.

Fisher, E., Mwaipopo, R., Mutagwaba, W., Nyange, D. and Yaron, G. (2009) 'The ladder that sends us to wealth: Artisanal mining and poverty reduction in Tanzania'. *Resources Policy* 34(1): 1–7

Hilson, G. (2005) 'Strengthening artisanal mining research and policy through baseline census activities'. *Natural Resources Forum* 29(2): 144–53.

Hilson, G. (2007) 'What is wrong with the global support facility for small-scale mining?', *Progress in Development Studies* 7(3): 235–49.

Jønsson, J.B. and Bryceson, D.F. (2009) 'Rushing for gold: Mobility and small-scale mining in East Africa', *Development and Change* 40(2): 249–79.

Kulindwa, K., Mashindano, O., Shechambo, F. and Sosovele, H. (2003) *Mining for Sustainable Development in Tanzania.* Dar es Salaam: Dar es Salaam University Press.

Lange, S. (2006) *Benefit Streams from Mining in Tanzania: Case Studies from Geita and Mererani.* Bergen, Norway: Chr. Michelsen Institute.

Moody, R. (2007) *Rocks and Hard Places: The Globalization of Mining.* Malta: Zed Books Ltd.

Mwaipopo R., Mutagwaba, W., Nyanga, D. and Fisher, E. (2004) *Increasing the Contribution of Artisanal and Small-Scale Mining to Poverty Reduction in Tanzania.* London: Department for International Development.

Phillips L. C., Semboja, H., Shukla, G. P., Sezinga, R., Mutagwaba, W., Mchwampaka, B., Wanga, G., Kahyarara, G. and Keller, C. (2001) *Tanzania's Precious Mineral Boom: Issues in Mining and Marketing.* Washington DC: USAID.

Spiegel, S.J. (2011) 'Microfinance services, poverty and artisanal mineworkers in Africa: In search of measures for empowering vulnerable groups', *Journal of International Development* 24(4): 485–517.

Tanzania, United Republic of (1997) *Mineral Policy of Tanzania* [Ministry of Energy and Minerals]. Dar es Salaam: Government Printer.

Tanzania, United Republic of (1998) *The Mining Act* [Ministry of Energy and Minerals]. Dar es Salaam: Government Printer.

Tanzania, United Republic of (1999) *The Mining Regulations* [Ministry of Energy and Minerals]. Dar es Salaam: Government Printer.

Tanzania, United Republic of (2009) *The Mineral Policy of Tanzania* [Ministry of Energy and Minerals]. Dar es Salaam: Government Printer.

Tanzania, United Republic of (2010a) *The Mining Act* [Ministry of Energy and Minerals. Dar es Salaam: Government Printer.

Tanzania, United Republic of (2010b) *The Mining Regulations* [Ministry of Energy and Minerals]. Dar es Salaam: Government Printer.

World Bank (1992) 'Strategy for African mining', [World Bank Technical Paper No. 181, Africa Technical Department Series, Mining Unit, Industry and Energy Division]. Washington DC: World Bank.

World Bank (2004) 'Striking a better balance – The World Bank Group and extractive industries: The final report of the extractive industries review'. Washington DC: World Bank.

8 An ethical turn in African mining

Voluntary regulation through fair trade[1]

Eleanor Fisher and John Childs

In recent decades there has been an ethical turn in expectations of how African mineral production and trade should be conducted. Good labour conditions, the absence of conflict and mining's potential for securing economic, social and environmental benefits are being demanded in the jewellery trade. As a consequence the quality of precious and semi-precious metals and gemstones is now being judged on their ethical credentials in addition to their aesthetic and mineral qualities. Mineral production for industrial manufacture, particularly in the electronics industry, is also coming under scrutiny. Adding value through ethics is closely associated with the use of voluntary (non-state) regulation.[2] This includes standards and associated certification and labels, which have been adopted by the minerals and metals sector in efforts to ensure improvements in the social and environmental conditions of production and to enable access to the profitable and expanding global 'ethical market'. In this chapter, we focus on ethical trading schemes that incorporate voluntary regulation, by using artisanal gold mining in Tanzania and the sale of gold through international fair trade markets as an exemplar to consider the development dynamics that emerge from ethical schemes.

Important stimuli for the rise of ethical issues in African mining include: advocacy on 'conflict' diamonds and minerals (Seay 2012); action against terrorism and alleged links to the gemstone trade (Schroeder 2010); threat to corporate reputation related to the negative social and environmental impacts of mining (MCEP 2006); and, consumer demand for ethically produced and environmentally sustainable jewellery. Each bring traceability and accountability to the fore (Blore and Smillie 2011). Beyond this come the goals of sustainability and poverty reduction in the development of the mineral sector, with ethical value chains seen as a means to achieve these ends. These objectives have led to a plethora of ethical initiatives. For example in gold mining alone, a 2010 report traces seven schemes (Cardiff 2010: I); while minerals from the Democratic Republic of Congo (DRC) are subject to at least six schemes (BRC 2010; MCEP 2006: 17–21). With so many interests and objectives at stake, the rubric of 'the ethical' in African mining is wide-ranging and contested.

Fair trade[3] is amongst various ethical schemes linked to African artisanal mining (Childs 2008; Hilson 2007). It has historically sought social justice for marginalized small-scale producers in developing countries by addressing the terms of international trade. Being explicitly redistributive in orientation and seeking to socially regulate global markets, contemporary fair trade has a broad mandate that includes livelihood transformation, policy representation, empowerment, and participatory governance arrangements. Given fair trade's focus on empowering marginalized producers by transforming their livelihoods through the market, it has the potential to recast the image of artisanal miners from lawless trouble-makers impeding development to hard-working artisanal producers whose trade contributes to economic development and social justice.

Adding value through ethics may enable artisanal miners to reap the livelihood benefits that flow from access to new markets and may contribute to local development processes, both materially within mining communities and through empowerment and democratization. Whether this potential can be realized is a major issue: an alternative is that existing patterns of power and inequality will be reproduced in entry and participation requirements for fair trade, in effect excluding particular types of artisanal miner. Most vulnerable are those with the weakest asset base, allowing for development benefits to be captured by particular interest groups through a distortion of the semiotics of 'fairness' (Childs 2008; Fraser *et al.* 2013; Marston 2013). This leads us to ask what the likely consequences are for artisanal miners when ethical value chains are introduced into the mineral trade: does fair trade have the potential to create new inclusive opportunities for market-led development transformation or will it reinforce established patterns of power and inequality with potentially detrimental and unintended consequences for artisanal producers?

To answer these questions we provide a background to the use of voluntary regulation for ethical trade, drawing on information from the agri-food sector, and give an overview of the emergence of ethical trade schemes within African mining. We then turn to the case of a fair trade intervention in Tanzanian gold markets. A project to promote Tanzanian gold production for the international fair trade market started in September 2012, based on the Fairtrade International (FLO)/Alliance for Responsible Mining (ARM) 'Fairtrade and Fairmined' Standard for gold. We consider that evidence from existing research can be a basis for learning about the opportunities and pitfalls of linking African artisanal gold miners to ethical markets. Our case is based on primary data from 40 life histories of artisanal gold miners in the sites of Nyarugusu, Ruamgasa and Ushirombo in north-western Tanzania. An in-depth understanding of the organization of artisanal gold mining in the region is also informed by previously published research (Childs 2008; Fisher 2007, 2008; Fisher *et al.* 2009).

Regulation through standards in Africa

Standard setting is closely related to quality assurance based on certification and accreditation, with consumer guarantees displayed through the use of labels. In the context of African mining, differentiating products according to ethical value can give access to new markets, and ethical standards and quality assurance can provide a mechanism for risk management. Standards associated with fair trade are also linked to social movement valorization challenging dominant market values (Tallontire 2006).

Standards are rules that identify the course of action that those who adopt them should follow, whether it is about being, doing or having something (Brunsson and Jacobsson 2000). The state has historically been the main promulgator of standards for regulation, with the action of public bodies equated with rules backed by legal sanctions. However with the growth of voluntary regulation, standards operate as a social contract in which the state provides indirect guarantees to agreements developed by non-state actors (Giovannucci and Ponte 2005). Rather than being simple technical concerns, it is argued that standards simultaneously reflect and transform social relationships and power dynamics (Hatanaka *et al.* 2005). Focusing on African artisanal mining, the questions then become who constructs ethical standards, how and why? And, significantly, what role do artisanal miners themselves play in these processes?

Emphasis is often placed on the power of standards to govern conduct at a distance. However an important issue is how local actors, interests and values shape the effect of standards on processes of socioeconomic transformation (Viteri and Arce 2013). The success of fair trade initiatives focused on African artisanal mining will largely depend on how ethical standards and associated certification are integrated with existing forms of artisanal organization. The economic realities, power dynamics and social relationships that constitute artisanal miners' lives and livelihoods have to be taken into account. A great deal will depend on how the design of a fair trading scheme builds upon peoples' experiences of present work practices and past development initiatives.

In the last two decades in African mining there has been a shift from the role of government as owner of mining operations to administrator and regulator for private industry. Processes of liberalization and globalization have arguably contributed to an opening up of the mining field to governance based on voluntary regulation, with networks of actors coalescing around African mineral sector development, as reflected in a language of 'broad-based partnerships' and 'multi-stakeholder participation'. Inevitably these networks generate knowledge and power outside the nation state, including through voluntary regulation (cf. Carnoy and Castells 2001).

Ethical trading initiatives enter into this institutional landscape with a focus on how mineral and metal products are produced and delivered through standards within the value chain. Table 8.1 provides examples of initiatives that are referred to in the text below.

Ethical standards initiatives

Notions of industry ethics have long roots in the jewellery trade, particularly in the United States (US) (JVC 2013). Historically alternative trade organizations have also linked artisanal production to ethical trade from developing countries (Litrell and Dickson 1999). However, the anti-apartheid movement and a 1988

Table 8.1 Ethical standards, guidance and legislation for African mining

	Standards, including mandatory legislation and non-mandatory guidance
	Public
Large-scale and artisanal	Minerals: US federal **Dodd-Frank Wall Street Reform and Consumer Protection Act** (2010). Supply chain due diligence for companies using products from the DRC; reporting to US Securities and Exchange Commission. www.sec.gov/about/laws/wallstreetreform-cpa.pdf
Large-scale and artisanal	Minerals: **OECD Due Diligence Guidance for Responsible Supply Chains of Minerals from Conflict-Affected and High-Risk Areas** (2010). EC/OECD member government guidance on supply chain management informing other standards; non-legally binding. www.oecd.org/investment/guidelinesformultinationalenterprises/46740847.pdf
Large-scale and artisanal	Minerals from Democratic Republic of Congo: **United Nations Guidelines on Due Diligence** (2010). Company self-certification of supply chains with third party audit. www.un.org/News/dh/infocus/drc/Consolidated_guidelines.pdf
	Private
Large-scale and artisanal	Tanzanite: **Tucson Tanzanite Protocol** (2002). US, Tanzanian, Indian industry associations, Government of Tanzania. Tracking of Tanzanite trading chain; industry self-certification. www.jckonline.com/article/294407-The_Tucson_Tanzanite_Protocols.php
Large-scale	Minerals, gas, material oil: **Extractive Industries Transparency Initiative** (2003) and **EITI ++** (2008) Government self-reporting, EITI compliance ensured through third-party validation; oversight by multi-stakeholder group. http://eiti.org/
Large-scale and artisanal	Tantalum, tin, tungsten, gold: **Conflict-Free Smelter Assessment Programme** (2010). Led by industry association [Electronic Industry Citizen Coalition and Global e-Sustainability Initiative]; self-assessment, third-party audit. http://www.conflictfreesmelter.org
Large-scale and artisanal	Tin: **International Tin Supply Chain Initiative** (2010). Led by industry association [International Tin Research Institute], third party risk assessment and audit. www.itri.co.uk
Large-scale and artisanal	Cassiterite (tin), coltan (colombo-tantalite), wolframite (tungsten) and gold: **International Conference on the Great Lakes Region (ICGLR) Certification Mechanism** for Conflict-prone minerals (2011). Industry responsibility; procedures designed by 11 governments of the Great Lakes Region plus multilateral and bilateral donors; civil society as 'watchdog'. www.pacweb.org/Documents/icglr/PAC_Report_on_ICGLR_RCM-03-2011-eng.pdf
Large-scale and artisanal	Diamonds, gold and platinum metals: **Responsible Jewellery Council Chain-of-Custody Standard** (2012). Led by industry body [RJC], third party audit. www.responsiblejewellery.com/files/RJCStandardCoCJun11.pdf

Table 8.1 continued

	Standards, including mandatory legislation and non-mandatory guidance
	Voluntary
Large-scale	Gold: **'Apartheid-free' gold** (1990). TWIN UK and the World Gold Commission. Ethical assurance based on trust within alternative trade networks + symbol and certificate (TWIN 1990).
Large-scale and artisanal	Tanzanite: **Tucson Tanzanite Protocol** (2002). US industry associations, Government of Tanzania, Tanzanian industry associations. Tracking of Tanzanite trading chain; industry self-certification.
Large-scale and artisanal	Rough diamonds: **Kimberley Process Certification Scheme** (2002). Government self-certification of supply chain supported by national regulations; oversight by KP signatories. www.kimberleyprocess.com
Large-scale and artisanal	Minerals: German Federal Institute for Geosciences and Natural Resources (BRG)/Governments of Democratic Republic of Congo and Rwanda (2009). **Standards for Certified Trading Chains** in ASM, AS producers/government/German bilateral aid, government audit. www.bgr.bund.de/EN/Themen/_rohstoffe/CTC/Home/CTC_node_en.html
Artisanal	Gold and associated precious metals: **Alliance for Responsible Mining Standard Zero** (2006). Civil society-led, multi-stakeholder group, independent certification by FLO-Cert. http://www.communitymining.org/index.php/en/standard-zero/development
Artisanal	Gold and associated precious metals: **Fairtrade and Fairmined Gold** (2011). Led by civil society in association with industry and governments, with third party certification; oversight by Alliance for Responsible Mining/Fairtrade International. www.fairgold.org/
Artisanal	Diamonds: **Development Diamonds Standards™** (DDS) certification scheme by Development Diamonds Initiative (under development). Led by civil society in association with industry and governments www.ddiglobal.org/dds/
Artisanal	**Conflict-Free Gold Standard** (2012). Self-assessment; chain-of-custody tracing; public reporting; oversight by World Gold Council. www.gold.org/about_gold/sustainability/conflict_free_standard/

Source: Authors. All websites accessed 1 November 2012

campaign to boycott gold produced in South Africa brought the issue of ethical mining in Africa to the fore: In 1990 UK Twin Trading and the World Gold Commission joined forces to produce wedding rings from 'clean', 'apartheid-free' gold, each stamped with an 'Anti-apartheid symbol' and provided with a certificate (TWIN 1990: 4).[4]

After the dismantling of apartheid, the ethics of mining in Africa remained an international concern due to connections between mining and conflict. This was fuelled by loss of US consumer confidence in the jewellery trade following the

9/11 terrorist attacks on the US World Trade Centre in 2001 (MacFarlane *et al.* 2003). International campaigns against mining and conflict that have fed into the creation of private and voluntary standards for artisanal mining include: the Oxfam/Earthworks-led No Dirty Gold campaign, the International Council for Metals and Mining, Mining Certification Evaluation Project, and CAFOD's Unearth Justice, Counting the Cost of Gold campaign (Cardiff 2010; CAFOD 2006). Attention initially focused on 'conflict diamonds' but a rise in the price of minerals such as tantalum and gold in the late 1990s played into awareness about 'conflict minerals', as armed groups in different African countries recognized they could fund their militarism.

Two schemes emerged in the early 2000s to certify absence of conflict and human rights abuses in gemstone production and trade:

First, the Kimberley Process Certification Scheme (KPCS) for rough diamonds, which has led the way for private and voluntary standards upholding ethical practices in the African mining sector. The KPCS was ratified by 52 governments in 2002 with support from the United Nations, the US congress and the European Union (Macfarlane *et al.* 2003).

Second, the Tucson Tanzanite Protocol (TTP), which is much narrower, being a traceability scheme for Tanzanite produced in Tanzania led by the Tanzanian government and Tanzanian, Indian and US-based industry associations. The TTP emerged as a response to alleged links between the Tanzanite trade and funding for Al Qaeda (Schroeder 2010).

The KPCS and TTP illustrate how artisanal and large-scale production and trade in minerals are linked to a politics of ethical consumption, connecting mineral value chains to international campaigns on human rights, environmental sustainability, corruption, and governance. Both initiatives connected NGO campaigning to industry action and multi-lateral leadership to establish conventions and protocols on African Mining; recently these conventions have included the OECD Due Diligence Guidance for Responsible Supply Chains of Minerals from Conflict-Affected and High-Risk Areas (OECD 2010), the UN resolutions on the DRC (UN 2009, with subsequent updates), and the 2013 UN-led legally binding international treaty to curb mercury pollution, with implications for artisanal gold mining in Africa.

The KPCS places onus on governments in diamond producing countries to self-certify the absence of conflict in the value chain backed by national regulations. A similar model of government self-reporting is integral to the 2003 Extractive Industries Transparency Initiative (EITI) for large-scale mining. Both initiatives assume that there are functioning government institutions to support the certification process and regulate ethical value chains. For the KPCS this is heavily criticized (Blore and Smillie 2011; Global Witness 2008). More recent schemes, including the 2009 Standards for Certified Trading Chains in ASM, the 2010 Conflict-Free Gold Standard, and the 2011 International Conference of the Great Lakes Region (ICGLR) Regional Initiative against the illegal exploitation of Natural Resources (RINR) Certificate, recognize how profoundly challenging traceability is in contexts where state regulation is weak or non-existent. Greater onus is now placed on mining industry action and third party auditing, with umbrella industry associations and civil society in a watchdog role (Blore and Smillie 2011).

Complicating this picture is a unique mandatory public regulation with repercussions for African artisanal mineral extraction: the United States federal Dodd-Frank Wall Street Reform and Consumer Protection Act (2010) Sections 1502 and 1504, whose objective is to ensure due diligence for companies with commercial activities in foreign countries (US Congress 2010). Section 1502 of the Dodd Franks Act emerged from a US-based advocacy campaign to end conflict in Africa. Publically traded companies are required to reveal sourcing of minerals from the DRC and regional neighbours, a controversial move in the US with, it has been argued, devastating consequences for African artisanal miners (Seay 2012).

Parallel with the rise of traceability schemes and responsible sourcing initiatives targeting minerals from conflict affected areas, has been a growth in ethical initiatives with a broader development orientation. These include the EITI++, which emerged in 2008 to encourage value chain management for sustainable development and poverty reduction in large-scale mining, and the forthcoming Diamond Development Standard started by the Diamond Development Initiative, which is focused on poverty reduction in artisanal mining and seen as a compliment to the KPCS.

It is, however, the entry of the Fairtrade and Fairmined Standard for Gold and Associated Precious Metals ('The Fairtrade and Fairmined Standard') that, according to the principles and aims of the fair trade movement, suggests the greatest potential for voluntary regulation to be used to stimulate the market in ways that support the interests of artisanal miners. Contemporary fair trade entered into metal markets with the *Oro Verde* (green gold) project in Latin America and the 2006 Alliance for Responsible Mining (ARM) Standard Zero for fair trade gold and associated silver and platinum. This created a prototype for the Fairtrade and Fairmined Standard from artisanal and small-scale mining that was launched by Fairtrade International (FLO) and ARM in 2010.

It is claimed that the Fairtrade and Fairmined Standard is the first independently certified international standard for artisanal gold production, intended 'to bring the opportunity for artisanal and small-scale miners to become certified and for consumers and ethical jewellers to support responsible Artisanal and Small-scale Mining gold production' (Hruschka and Echavarría 2011: 23). In line with wider Fairtrade™ standards, it incorporates components for social, economic, and environmental development plus labour conditions, and a development and capacity building supplement for 'Small-Scale Miners' Organizations' (FLO/ARM 2010). One notable feature of the Standard is that it extends the well-established FLO Fairtrade™ system into a new product area, unlike most of the standards cited in Table 8.1, which were developed specifically for the mining sector.

Standard Zero and the Fairtrade and Fairmined Standard are not the only ethical initiatives in artisanal mining that are referred to as fair trade; these initiatives can be grouped into three categories:

First, mineral production that is the subject of voluntary standards and independent certification and verified through a product label. In European markets these standards are dominated by Fairtrade International and its member organizations. This includes products bearing the Fairtrade™ label showing certification according to the Fairtrade and Fairmined Standard, e.g. sold by CRED Jewellery (www.credjewellery.com/).

Second, organizations (i.e. whole supply chains/brands) certified as fair trade according to voluntary standards and independent certification, principally by the World Fair Trade Organization and/or the British Association of Fair Trade Shops. Because the value chain is 100 per cent certified, some within the movement see this as the 'purest' form of fair trade (Davenport and Low 2012). This includes jewellery sold by Traidcraft (www.traidcraftshop.co.uk).

Third, metal and gemstone suppliers or jewellery makers/sellers who self-certify their products or companies as fair trade linked to a feature such as chain of custody documentation. Due to the use of private standards and self-certification and because these companies may not be part of either the WFTO or FLO systems, whether they are 'fair trade' is contentious (see Tallontire 2006).

Differentiation within the fair trade movement emerges from complex politics over principles, legitimacy and ideological direction. This has led to different 'strands' of fair trade, which contribute to an important feature within the wider contemporary ethical landscape in terms of a proliferation of often competing standards. One implication is that it can be hard for producers, consumers and other actors to understand the characteristics of a particular standard and to distinguish between different standards, as our case study below will illustrate (see also Fisher and Sheppard 2013; Giovannucci and Ponte 2005).

We have provided an overview of the entry of ethical trade schemes into African mineral production and the use of private and voluntary standards. Voluntary regulation raises the question of how ethical trade has entered the artisanal mining arena, intersecting with existing forms of labour organization, market relations, and governance processes in the construction of ethical value chains. Thus we turn to consider how the fair trade movement has engaged with artisanal gold production and trade in Tanzania.

'Fairtrade and Fairmined'/'Fair trade' gold in Tanzania

By buying Fairtrade and Fairmined gold you are making a difference to the lives of small scale artisan miners and their communities.

(www.fairtrade.org.uk/gold/ [accessed 21 November 2012])

The Fairtrade and Fairmined Standard has stimulated moves into African artisanal mining with the intention of improving the lives of increasing numbers of gold miners and expanding global Fairtrade™ certified gold supplies (Fairtrade Foundation 2010). Northern Tanzania has been identified as a location for the development of a Fairtrade™ and Fairmined project to market gold according to Fairtrade™ standards and certification. In this region, existing artisanal mining contributes to (Fisher *et al.* 2009) and urban development (Bryceson *et al.* 2012).

The Fairtrade and Fairmined project will build on forms of artisanal gold mining based on the use of hand tools and portable machines, with labour organized according to a system in which a claim-owner with a Primary Mining Licence (PML) employs workers or, more typically, sub-contracts areas of land to pit-holders and diggers (Chapter 3; Fisher 2007). Other people are involved in the processing and service sectors. Processed gold can be traded through licenced centres but is more commonly sold to informal gold buyers known in Kiswahili as *makota* (unscrupulous traders). In addition to buying gold, the *makota* provide credit for mine running costs and investment in mining equipment, acting as *de facto* sponsors to a pit-holder and group of diggers in exchange for the rights to purchase their gold. These are the middlemen that FLO/ARM seeks to cut out of gold trading transactions (Hruschka and Echavarría 2011).

In September 2012 the project to certify 'small-scale gold miners' in Eastern Africa was initiated by Solidaridad in the Netherlands, working with ARM and Fairtrade Africa, a network member of FLO, with US$ 1.3 million from Comic Relief (Fairtrade Africa 2012). Working to develop eight gold-mining cooperatives across Tanzania, Kenya, and Uganda, the plan is that they will become Fairtrade™ certified (by FLO-Cert) in three years (ibid.). It is too soon to assess the project's development impacts, however, this initiative follows the establishment in 2007 of a gold refinery in Mwanza and four 'Fair Trade Gold Centres' by a private company, African Precious Metals Ltd (UNEP 2011). This is financed by the Federal Bank of the Middle East and licenced by the Government of Tanzania (Jomo 2007; Lazaro 2007). The FLO/ARM/Solidaridad initiative will introduce a voluntary standard i.e. the Fairtrade and Fairmined Standard, while African Precious Metals Ltd uses a private standard (which FLO would argue is not fair trade). Interview data below captures miners' perceptions of fair trade based on their engagement with African Precious Metals Ltd, raising issues pertinent for the Fairtrade and Fairmined project.

African Precious Metals Ltd and the makota: Contesting fairness

A 'fair price' is central to Fairtrade™. For agri-food products such as coffee, Fairtrade International sets the Fairtrade Minimum Price to cover the 'Costs of Sustainable Production'. For gold the price is set differently, based on 95 per cent of the London Bullion Market Association (LBMA) fixing with a premium to reward compliance and deliver benefits (10 per cent of the LBMA fixing or 15 per cent for non-chemical extraction) (FLO/ARM 2010: 36).

The promise of a 'fair price' also forms the centrepiece of African Precious Metals Ltd's outreach work in Geita and Mwanza Regions. However, interviews with artisanal miners suggest that a fair price does not necessarily equate with a particular market channel; for miners with a relationship to a specific *makota*, the price and indeed production, is determined by the need for credit and the obligations this brings (cf. Banchirigah 2008: 35). This contractual aspect of the *makota*/miner relationship invokes competing discourses of content and discontent, being seen as both financial assistance and an unfair practice.

A representative of a mining cooperative in Ushirombo thinks the *makota* engage in unfair practices:

> Initially we sold to the *makota*, who would support us with the condition that we would then sell to them. However, we do it in line with the law and taxes so we now work with African Precious Metals Ltd. The *makota* buy the gold at an unreasonable price and they try to con you.
>
> (F.K., Ushirombo, 24 June 2009)

His account is, however, an exceptional view. Records indicate that African Precious Metals' intervention had the effect of increasing the price that the *makota* offered for gold at 5–10 per cent higher than the world market price. Therefore for many miners, 'fairness' results from selling to the *makota* and getting the best price available, as one reflected:

> I know there is a bank in Ruamgasa . . . [i.e. an African Precious Metals Ltd trading centre] . . . but I'll always go for the best price. And in my experience, it is the makota that offer the best prices. This, to me, is fair.
>
> (J.R., Ruamgasa, 18 June 2009)

Nevertheless, the price offered by the *makota* is problematic: Miners accept it because they need credit even if they are suspicious that the weighing scales have been tampered with. As one buyer expressed:

> I am aware of the bank, African Precious Metals Ltd in Ushirombo. I don't feel particularly threatened by it because their prices are no better than mine and what's more they don't provide loans to the miners like I do. Some people do sell their gold there, like members of the local cooperative, because they don't need advances on a day-to-day basis. The bank gets its money from them. Having said that, I still get the same amount of miners coming to me as I did before the Bank arrived.
>
> (C.L., Ushirombo, 27 June 2009)

In the case of African Precious Metals Ltd, some respondents saw the 'fair' price as a marketing strategy that was untrustworthy and duplicitous. A former disillusioned miner emphasized the gap between rhetoric and his experience by pointing to the large signs on the walls of fair trade trading centres stating 'FAIR TRADE' and observed:

> The writing on the wall is writing, it can shine with fancy paint but essentially it is there to lure. It is there to bring people in.
>
> (S.N., Nyarugusu, 9 June 2009)

For both artisanal miners and employees of African Precious Metals Ltd, the idea that transparency was integral to 'fair trade' gold was prevalent. However, they were not able to agree about what this meant. The company advertised itself to miners as providing 'fair' and 'scientifically proven' chemical methods for assaying the gold for purity and provenance alongside checking its weight. This modality of fairness was a source of pride for all four managers of the Fair Trade Gold Centres, demonstrating their company's commitment to providing a new market opportunity for artisanal miners. As the manager at the Ruamgasa Fair Trade Gold Centre asserted:

> When you say 'fair', you are talking about being open. The client can view this and know that the purity, testing and smelting of the gold is done right before their eyes. This is fair. Some other dealers use scales that are fixed. Our scales are checked by the Tanzanian Bureau.
>
> (G.A., Ruamgasa, 19 June 2009)

Despite the company's emphasis on the transparency of their methods, there was widespread reluctance amongst miners to believe the results from the chemical-based processing. Miners' either claimed not to understand how the measuring process worked or simply stated a preference for the hand-held scales used by the *makota* despite allegations that the scales were fixed and inaccurate. In these 'practices of negotiation' (Arce and Fisher 2003: 75) we see counter narratives being generated around the introduction of new ways of measuring and assessing the quality of gold. At the same time, abstract ideas of 'fairness' are being refracted through the knowledge and practices of miners and other actors within fair trade value chains.

Such practices of negotiation over quality attributes for fair trade gold are not confined to producers and traders in Tanzania. Following a FLO/ARM (2012) consultation over the Fairtrade and Fairmined Standard, a dispute erupted in social media over product composition and the acceptability of mass balancing for Fairtrade™ certified gold (Valerio 2012). Mass balancing, the mixing of product supplies from different sources, is widespread within commodity value chains and has permitted fair trade markets to expand. Some within the fair trade movement defend mass balancing by arguing that producers still get 100 per cent of the benefits from their products sales (FLO/ARM 2012). However, an open letter of 140 'responsible' jewellers to FLO/ARM argues that mass balancing of gold calls into question their ability to 'bring pure, traceable Fairtrade and Fairmined gold to a vibrant market' (Valerio 2012). For UK consumers and consumer watchdogs, the issue of mass balancing risks undermining the credibility of the Fairtrade Mark as a trusted consumer guarantee (BBC 2013). Indeed, within the fair trade movement this practice is ideologically controversial.

Formalization and entry requirements for Fairtrade and Fairmined gold certification

Artisanal mining in northern Tanzania, as elsewhere, has been the subject of repeated interventions focusing on formalizing the sector as a basis for good governance, technical improvement and market support. These interventions become part of the experience through which artisanal miners approach new projects. As the Treasurer of the Mwanza Regional Mining Association expressed:

> Always we are seeing new people from outside coming in and offering new ideas about how we should mine; we had Meremeta, we had the Bank of Tanzania, and you can see now in the village we have African Precious Metals Ltd. But the thing that people really want to know, when you ask me what I think about Fairtrade™ gold, is how is this going to be different? All those people that I mentioned failed to bring change to our lives. Why should this 'Fairtrade™ gold' be any different to them? Of course, I am open minded but I think there is still a sense when we see a new initiative like the one you mentioned (the Fairtrade and Fairmined project) coming in, there is still a sense of 'here we go again'.
>
> (G.H., Nyarugusu, 8 June 2009)

Organizations promoting the Fairtrade and Fairmined Standard have the ambition of gaining 5 per cent of the gold jewellery market over the next 15 years (Fairtrade Foundation 2010). However, to achieve this growth significant hurdles have to be overcome, notably the premise that Fairtrade™ certification is dependent on the formalization of artisanal mining (ARM 2011; Barreto 2011). As FLO/ARM (2010: 4) state, the 'overall objective of this STANDARD is to promote formalisation of the ASM sector' with a vision of 'a formalised, organised and profitable activity that is technologically efficient, socially and environmentally responsible; the sector's development takes place within a framework of good governance, legality, participation...'.

This places serious limitations upon the number of potential participants in the scheme given that the majority of artisanal miners in Tanzania and elsewhere in Sub-Saharan African countries operate without a licence. It also aligns the Fairtrade and Fairmined Standard with Tanzanian government policies intended to give artisanal miners legal and transferable titles to mineral claims. However, this is not straightforward. Fisher and colleagues (Fisher 2007, 2008; Fisher *et al.* 2009) have argued that Tanzanian formalization policies stimulate contradictory processes: A small number of artisanal miners have become integrated with state institutions and legal processes, while others, the vast majority, are excluded or incorporated on adverse terms that exacerbate insecurity through a practice of sub-leasing (Chapter 5). Recent figures highlight the inequity of this process: In Tanzania 3,932 artisanal miners of all mineral types hold a PML (MEM 2010), a figure that includes a high number of inactive claims, against an estimated 685,000 artisanal miners in total (in 2012).[5]

In effect, in Tanzania the need for a PML will constitute a significant entry barrier to artisanal miners gaining access to the FLO/ARM Fairtrade system for all but the minority of legal claim owners. These are the people most likely to have the time, financial resources, social connections and power for involvement in Fairtrade™ certification. For others who cannot meet entry and participation requirements these processes are likely to be exclusionary, an issue pertinent to Fairtrade™ certification of agri-food products elsewhere (Arce 2009; Dolan 2010; Fraser *et al.* 2013; Luetchford 2008; Marston 2013).

Conclusion

In this chapter we have raised the question of whether voluntary regulation through fair trade can create new inclusive opportunities for development transformation in artisanal gold mining. We have also proposed that ethical standards have the potential to reshape governance rationalities and political economies but that how this occurs will depend on local dynamics in the organization of artisanal mining and mining communities, as well as the approach to development taken by ethical initiatives.

The way ethical trade has so far entered African mineral production, both large-scale and artisanal, has taken a reductionist and instrumental approach to development (cf. Edward and Tallontire 2009). Emphasizing transparency and traceability in the value chain, ethical activities and responsibility are defined managerially by standard-setting organizations aligned with national governments and industry. Traceability and compliance are obtained through chain-of-custody documentation, while the choice to incorporate voluntary or private standards is driven by reputation, shareholder value, and desire to incorporate ethical qualities into the brand-name. This approach is too far removed from the circumstances of Tanzania's artisanal miners who do not have a corporate reputation or shareholder value to defend. A fixation upon transparency in relation to ethical trade carries the danger of diverting attention from the socioeconomic problems that define the artisanal mining sector (cf. Bracking 2009; Hilson forthcoming). Our case of fair trade gold markets in Tanzania suggests that so far the fair trade movement and market's entry into artisanal mining errs towards the instrumental and pragmatic, focusing on traceability in the value chain rather than empowering producers to use the market for economic gain and social development.

Fair trade markets are not necessarily understood by producers as 'fairer' (Fisher 1997; Lyon 2006; Marston 2013; Tallontire 2000). Those working within the Fairtrade International system would argue that African Precious Metals Ltd's gold transactions are indeed not 'fair' i.e. Fairtrade™ certified. Nevertheless, this experience reveals important stumbling blocks that the Fairtrade and Fairmined project in East Africa will have to surmount to succeed.

The unintended consequence of the Fairtrade and Fairmined project aligning itself with national policies centred on formalization of artisanal miners is that it is likely to exclude the vast majority of artisanal miners and focus on successful claim owners who are the formalized holders of a PML. This is an unequal and highly politicized policy context: it is likely to present artisanal miners with a 'top-down' development intervention, rather than challenging the status quo in ways that involve artisanal miners in a more radical rethinking of how the market can be used to support the interests of marginalized producers.

In addition to the issue of formalization, international value chains for fair trade will need to enable miners to access credit and other forms of capacity building support in return for sales of their gold in ways that overturn the role of *makota* within the artisanal gold trade. This will necessitate challenging local power relations and ties of dependence. Given current proposals (Fairtrade Africa 2012), a lot rides on the success of being able to impose a fair trade cooperative model on existing artisanal property relations and labour organization (cf. Fraser *et al.* 2013; Luetchford 2008) and one can question whether the cooperative model is appropriate for artisanal gold mining and market relations.

Nonetheless, fair trade, conceptualized differently, has the potential to challenge established power within mineral sector governance as it applies to artisanal mining. It is early days for the Fairtrade and Fairmined project in East Africa. As a universal prescription for enhancing producer livelihoods, fair trade is organized in ways that try to strengthen the position of small-scale producers within an international trading complex. But to succeed, the realities of local-level production and trading relations and the dynamics of social hierarchies have to be taken into account. These realities shape which producers will benefit from fair trade and which will be excluded. Ultimately entrenched power relations and unequal access to land and resources are at issue, crystallized in the Tanzanian government's artisanal mining formalization process.

Fair trade as an ideal is both a social movement and a successful global niche market. It represents a complex interweaving of social action and civic critique with business norms, practices and institutions that are necessary for participation in corporate value chains. Having moved from a market alternative into the corporate domain there is now substantial debate about the direction of the fair trade movement within this mainstreaming process and whether political commitment to radical transformation and instrumental engagement in the market can be negotiated. For some this tension has diminished the capability of fair trade as a vehicle to challenge the international trading structures that perpetuate producer marginalization (e.g. Renard 2005; Dolan 2010). Others, including ourselves, take a nuanced view, recognizing that differentiation in contemporary fair trade may permit new forms of social action and value formation to emerge within the politics of grassroots networks (e.g. Arce 2009; Fisher 2012; Fraser *et al.* 2013; Raynolds 2012).

While the character of voluntary regulation may challenge social movement radicalism, the Fairtrade and Fairmined project in East Africa is still embryonic and may nonetheless enhance governance dynamics in ways that demonstrate a different type of democracy, bringing relational values and civic action to the fore over the long term, if and when the fair trade movement is willing to address the realities of Tanzania's 685,000 non-licenced artisanal miners in addition to the miniscule number of artisanal PML claim owners who appear eligible for the Fairtrade and Fairmined project.

Notes

1   Thank you to Alberto Arce, Deborah Bryceson and Matthew Anderson for comments; all errors remain our responsibility.

2   Voluntary regulation is also referred to as 'private' or 'social' regulation. Linked to this, different classifications exist for categorizing standards, all with shortcomings. A common two-fold dichotomy is made between 'public' (i.e. state) and 'private' (i.e. an amalgamation of all-non state actors, including private enterprises and civil society organizations). We use the term voluntary standards to refer to a coordinated process within an industry or sector in which consensus is sought between key participants (government, private enterprise and civil society). In contrast, public standards are led by the state (and state representation in multilateral organizations such as the United Nations) and private standards are developed, monitored and dominated by private enterprises. While these categories are not perfect they help to capture differences in the mining sector.

3   Fair trade is 'a trading partnership based on dialogue, transparency and respect that seeks greater equity in international trade. It contributes to sustainable development by offering better trading conditions to, and securing the rights of, marginalised producers and workers – especially in the South' (FLO/WFTO 2009: 4). 'Fairtrade™' refers to the trademark of the Fairtrade International system and 'fair trade' to the wider movement and market.

4   In 1988 the World Gold Commission was formed by the anti-apartheid movement to inform people about the link between gold mining and apartheid policies, to present evidence to international bodies, and to promote the use of non-South African gold in the jewellery industry (Archives, Rhodes House, Oxford, MSS.Afr.s.2350-/101-6).

5   Provisional estimate according to Professor Crispin Kinabo of the Geology Department, University of Dar es Salaam.

References

Arce, A. (2009) 'Living in times of solidarity: Fair trade and the fractured life worlds of Guatemalan coffee farmers'. *Journal of International Development* 21 (7): 1031–41.

Arce, A. and Fisher, E. (2003) 'Knowledge interfaces and practices of negotiation: Cases from a women's group in Bolivia and an oil refinery in Wales'. in Pottier, J., Bicker, A. and Sillitoe, P. (eds) *Negotiating Local Knowledge: Power and Identity in Development.* London: Pluto Press. pp. 175–91.

ARM [Alliance for Responsible Mining] (2011) 'Analysis for stakeholders on formalization in the artisanal and small-scale gold mining sector based on experiences in Latin America, Africa, and Asia'. Available from www.communitymining.org/index.php/en/our-publications (accessed 20 February 2013).

Banchirigah, S.M. (2008) 'Challenges with eradicating illegal mining in Ghana: A perspective from the grassroots'. *Resources Policy* 33(1): 29–38.

Barreto, M.L. (2011) 'Legalization guide for artisanal and small-scale mining (ASM): Draft for discussion'. Available from www.communitymining.org/index.php/ en/our-publications (accessed 20 February 2013).

Blore, S. and Smillie, I. (2011) 'Taming the resource curse: Implementing the ICGLR Certification Mechanism for conflict-prone minerals'. Partnership Africa Canada. Available from www.africaportal.org/dspace/articles/taming-resource-curse-implementing-icglr-certification-mechanism-conflict-prone (accessed 20 November 2012).

BBC [British Broadcasting Corporation] (2013) 'Does the fairtrade label on your chocolate bar mean 100% fairtrade cocoa beans?' Available from www.bbc.co.uk/programmes/b006mg74/features/fairtrade-chocolate (accessed 20 February 2013).

Bracking, S. (2009) 'Hiding conflict over industry returns: A stakeholder analysis of the

Extractive Industries Transparency Initiative' [Working Paper 91]. Manchester: Brooks World Poverty Institute.

Bryceson, D.F., Jønsson, J.B., Kinabo, C. and Shand, M. (2012) 'Unearthing treasure and trouble: Mining as an impetus to urbanisation in Tanzania'. *Journal of Contemporary African Studies* 30(4): 631–49.

BRC (Bundesanstalt für Geowissenschaften und Rohstoffe) (2010) 'Certified trading chains in mineral production: Project outline and status'. Available from www.bgr.bund.de/EN/Themen/Min_rohstoffe/Downloads/CTC-update-Mai2010.pdf?__blob=publicationFile&v=1 (accessed 20 February 2013).

Brunsson, N. and Jacobsson, B. (2000) 'The contemporary expansion of standardization'. in Brunsson, N., Jacobsson, B. et al. (eds), *A World of Standards*. Oxford: Oxford University Press. pp. 1–20.

CAFOD (2006) 'Unearthing justice: Counting the cost of gold'. Available from www.utedecker.com/jewellery/CAFOD%20GOLD%20REPORT.pdf (accessed 20 February 2013).

Cardiff, S. (EARTHWORKS) (2010) 'The quest for responsible small-scale gold mining: A comparison of standards of initiatives aiming for responsibility'. Available from www.earthworksaction.org/files/publications/Small-scale-gold%20mining-initiatives-comparison-2010.pdf (accessed 20 November 2012).

Carnoy, M. and Castells, M. (2001) 'Globalization, the knowledge society, and the network state: Poulantzas at the millennium'. *Global Networks* 1: 1–18.

Childs, J. (2008) 'Reforming small-scale mining in sub-Saharan Africa: Political and ideological challenges to a Fair Trade gold initiative'. *Resources Policy* 33(4): 203–9.

Davenport, E. and Low, W. (2012) 'The World Fair Trade Organization: From trust to compliance'. in Reed, D., Utting, P., and Mukherjee-Reed (eds) *Business Regulation and Non-State Actors: Whose Standards? Whose Development?* London and New York: Routledge. pp. 288–99.

Dolan, C. (2010) 'Virtual moralities: The mainstreaming of Fairtrade in Kenyan tea fields'. *Geoforum* 41(1): 33–43.

Edward, P. and Tallontire, A. (2009) 'Business and development: Towards re-politicisation'. *Journal of International Development* 21(6): 819–33.

Fairtrade Africa (2012) 'Fairtrade gold kicks off in Kisumu'. Available from www.fairtradeafrica.net/news/fairtrade-gold-kick-off-in-kisumu-2/ (accessed 30 November 2012).

Fairtrade Foundation (2010) 'Fairtrade and Fairmined gold standard launched'. Available from www.fairtrade.org.uk/press office/ press releases and statements/march 2010 (accessed 20 November 2012).

FLO/WFTO [Fairtrade Labelling Organisations/World Fair Trade Organization] (2009) Charter of Fair Trade principles'. Available from www.fairtrade.net/fileadmin/ user_upload/content/2009/about_us/documents/Fair_Trade_Charter.pdf (accessed 26 July 2012).

FLO/ARM [Fairtrade International / Alliance for Responsible Mining] (2012) 'Fairtrade and Fairmined Standard for gold from ASM including associated precious metals: Detailed summary of proposed changes and background information'. Available from www.fairtrade.net/fileadmin/user_upload/content/2009/standards/documents/2012_08 _07_FTFM-v2-EN_Consultation_Annex.pdf (accessed 20 February 2013).

FLO/ARM [Fairtrade International / Alliance for Responsible Mining] (2010) 'Fairtrade and Fairmined Standard for gold from ASM including associated precious metals'. Available from www.communitymining.org/index.php/en/fairtrade-and-fairmined-standard (accessed 20 February 2013).

Fisher, E. (2012) 'The fair trade nation: Market-oriented development in devolved European regions?' *Human Organisation* 71(3): 255–67.

Fisher, E. (2008) 'Artisanal gold mining at the margins of mineral resource governance: A case from Tanzania'. *Development Southern Africa* 25(2): 199–213.

Fisher, E. (2007) 'Occupying the margins: Labour integration and social exclusion in artisanal mining in Tanzania'. *Development and Change* 38(4): 735–60.

Fisher, E. (1997) 'Beekeepers in the global fair trade market: A case from Tabora Region, Tanzania', *International Journal of Sociology of Agriculture and Food* 6(1): 109–60.

Fisher, E. and Sheppard, H. (2013) 'Pushing the boundaries of the social: Private agri-food standards and the governance of fair trade in European public procurement'. *International Journal of the Sociology of Agriculture and Food* 20(1): 31–49.

Fisher, E. Mwaipopo, R. Mutagwaba, W. Nyange, D. and Yaron, G. (2009) '"The ladder that sends us to wealth": Artisanal mining and poverty reduction in Tanzania'. *Resources Policy* 34: 32–8.

Fraser, J., Fisher, E. and Arce, A. (2013) 'Reframing 'crisis' in fair trade coffee production: Trajectories of agrarian change in Nicaragua'. *Journal of Agrarian Change*, first published online 11 March 2013.

Giovannucci, D. and Ponte, S. (2005) 'Standards as a new form of social contract? Sustainability initiatives in the coffee industry'. *Food Policy* 30(3): 284–301.

Global Witness (2008) 'Loupe holes: Illicit diamonds in the Kimberley Process'. Available from www.globalwitness.org/library/loupe-holes-illicit-diamonds-kimberley-process (accessed 20 November 2012).

Hatanaka, M., C. Bain and L. Busch (2005) 'Third-party certification in the global agri-food system'. *Food Policy* 30(3): 356–61.

Hilson, G. (2007) '"Fair trade gold": Antecedents, prospects and challenges'. *Geoforum* 39: 386–400.

Hilson, G. (forthcoming) 'Constructing' ethical mineral supply chains in sub-Saharan Africa: The case of Malawian fair trade rubies', *Development and Change*.

Hruschka, F. and Echavarría, C. (2011) 'Rock-solid chances for responsible mining'. Available from www.communitymining.org/index.php/en/our-publications (accessed 20 February 2013).

Jewellers Vigilance Committee (2013) 'Jewellers Vigilance Committee: The Industry's Guardian of Ethics and Integrity'. Available from www.jvclegal.org/ (accessed 22 February 2013).

Jomo, F. (2007) 'Middle Eastern bank invests in refinery to add value to Tanzania's gold'. Available from www.mineweb.net/mineweb/content/en/mineweb-gold-news?oid= 21260&sn=Detail (accessed 25 January 2013).

Lazaro, J. (2007) 'Dar es Salaam bank invests $1 Million in gold refinery'. *East African Business Week*. Available from http://m44: wanzanewsblog.blogspot.com/2007/05/dar-es-salaam-bank-invests-1-million-in.html (accessed 20 February 2013).

Litrell, M.A. and Dickson, M.A. (1999) *Social Responsibility in the Global Market: Fair Trade of Cultural Products*. Thousand Oaks, CA: Sage.

Luetchford, P. (2008) 'The hands that pick fair trade coffee: Beyond the charms of the family farm'. *Research in Economic Anthropology* 28: 147–70.

Lyon, S. (2006) 'Evaluating fair trade consumption: Politics, defetishization and producer participation'. *International Journal of Consumer Studies* 30(5): 452–64.

Macfarlane, M. Tallontire, A. and Martine, A. (2003) 'Towards an ethical jewellery business', [A Report for CRED]. Greenwich: Natural Resources Institute.

Marston, A. (2013) 'Justice for all? Material and semiotic impacts of Fair Trade craft certification'. *Geoforum* 44(1): 162–9.

MCEP [Mining Certification Evaluation Project] (2006) 'Final Report'. Available from www.minerals.csiro.au/sd/Certification/MCEP_Final_Report_Jan2006.pdf (accessed 20 November 2012).

MEM [Ministry of Energy and Minerals Tanzania] (2010) *Five Years of Implementing the Mining Cadastral Informal Management System in Tanzania*. Dar es Salaam: Government Printers.

OECD [Organisation for Economic Co-operation and Development] (2010) 'OECD due diligence guidance for responsible supply chains of minerals from conflict-affected and high-risk areas'. Available from www.oecd.org/fr/daf/inv/mne/mining.htm (accessed 20 February 2013).

Raynolds, L. (2012) 'Fair trade: Social regulation in global food markets', *Journal of Rural Studies* 28: 276–87.

Renard, M-C. (2005) 'Quality certification, regulation and power in Fair Trade', *Journal of Rural Studies* 21: 419–31.

Schroeder, R. A. (2010) 'Tanzanite as a conflict gem: Certifying a secure commodity chain in Tanzania', *Geoforum* 41: 56–65.

Seay, L.E. (2012) 'What's wrong with the Dodd-Frank 1502? Conflict minerals, civilian livelihoods, and the unintended consequences of Western advocacy'. Centre for Global Development WP 284. Available from www.cgdev.org/content/publications/detail/1425843/ (accessed 20 February 2013).

Tallontire, A. (2000) 'Partnerships in fair trade: Reflections from a case study of Cafedirect'. *Development in Practice* 10(2): 166–77.

Tallontire, A. (2006) 'The development of alternative and fair trade: Moving into the mainstream'. in Barrientos, S. and Dolan, C. (eds) *Ethical Sourcing in the Global Food System*. London: Earthscan. pp. 35–48.

TWIN (1990) 'Alternative Gold Jewellery', *The Network* 3(1). London: Twin Trading.

UN [United Nations] (2009) Security Council Committee established pursuant to resolution 1533 (2004) concerning the Democratic Republic of the Congo S/RES/1952 (2010). Available from www.un.org/sc/committees/1533/resolutions.shtml (accessed 20 February 2013).

UNEP [United Nations Environment Programme] (2011) 'Analysis for stakeholders on formalization in the artisanal and small-scale gold mining sector based on experiences in Latin America, Africa, and Asia: A compendium of case studies'. Available from http://new.unep.org/hazardoussubstances/Portals/9/Mercury/Documents/ASGM/Formalization_ARM/Case%20Studies%20Compendium%20Sept%2015%202011.pdf (accessed 30 November 2012).

US Congress (2010) 'H.R. 4173 (111th): Dodd-Frank Wall Street Reform and Consumer Protection Act'. Available from www.govtrack.us/congress/bills/111/hr4173 (accessed 20 February 2013).

Valerio, G. (2012) 'Open letter to Alliance for Responsible Mining and Fairtrade Labelling Organisation signed by 140 international jewellers'. Blog posted on September 28 2012. Available from www.fairjewelry.org/open-letter-to-alliance-for-responsible-mining-and-fairtrade-labeling-organisation-signed-by-140-international-jewellers-s/ (accessed 20 February 2013).

Viteri, M.L. and Arce, A. (2013) 'The negotiation of quality standards: A social interactionist approach to fruit and vegetable distribution in Argentina', *International Journal of Sociology of Agriculture and Food* 20(1): 127–46.

9 The politics of mining

Foreign direct investment, the state and artisanal mining in Tanzania

France Bourgouin

In Tanzania, the Mineral Policy of 1997 and Mining Act of 1998 (Tanzania 1997, 1998) defined the three main players forming the nucleus of the country's mining industry: the state, large-scale mining operators and artisanal miners. The state's main role was designated as promoter and regulator of the industry. The Act emphasized the importance of a private sector-led industry, with artisanal mining exclusively for Tanzanians, while allowing up to 100 per cent foreign ownership for large-scale operations. The relationships between these players are complex and ever changing, as the political-economic context in which they operate evolves. This chapter discusses the nature of the interactions within the industry and their transformation over time in light of foreign direct investment (FDI)[1] in large-scale mining.

By viewing artisanal mining from the perspective of the large-scale mining sector, the discussion will cast light on how the current nature of power relations has impacted on the formation and implementation of the Tanzanian state's approach to the mining sector. From this vantage point, an analysis of the methods introduced to govern the industry and a contextualization of the ensuing conflicts between large-scale and artisanal mining follows. After exploring the connections between multinational gold mining corporations and FDI, I turn to the artisanal miners and the policies that govern them. My key questions are: what are the relative values placed on large-scale and artisanal mining by Tanzanian policy makers? What measures has the state taken to facilitate their growth?

My analysis builds upon six months fieldwork conducted in Tanzania in 2010 that provided on-the-ground insight, which often differed from the formal policies and legislation. Dissecting external and internal political-economic pressures that catalyzed the 1998 changes in mining law (Tanzania 1998) sheds light on discrepancies between policy and practice as well as conflicts between artisanal and large-scale mining. This discussion serves as a backdrop to the transformation of policy, legislation, and economic structures in Tanzania's gold industry over the years and how these have altered the relative power of the sector over time.

The first section of the chapter traces the privatization of the mineral sector in light of Tanzania's neo-liberal policies of the 1990s, revealing the prioritization given to FDI. Thereafter, I explore how governance processes and power relations implicit in the current structure of the industry frame the triad of contesting actors and their interests: namely large-scale mining, artisanal mining and the state. Citing the example of conflict between artisanal miners and the large-scale North Mara Gold Mine underscores the consequences of Tanzanian mining policies for artisanal mining. The chapter concludes with a summary of the balance of power in Tanzanian mining, specifically with reference to the position of artisanal miners.

Contextualizing post-independence mining policy reforms in Tanzania

For the first two decades of the post-independence period the Tanzania state under President Julius Nyerere endeavoured to enable 'control of the economy by the indigenous people rather than by expatriates and others non-African in origin' (McHenry 1994: 107). The Tanzanian government nationalized many of its industries, driving out international capital from mineral extraction with the establishment of state-owned enterprises (Bastida *et al.* 2005). However, Tanzania's state mining industries generally performed poorly. There was a severe lack of capital and technical skills (Chapter 1).

Following the oil crisis of 1979, Tanzania entered a decade of economic depression. Debt-ridden, the World Bank and IMF imposed structural adjustment policies that quickly unravelled earlier attempts by Nyerere's government to suppress accumulation and to promote social equality in the name of nation-building (McHenry 1994; Wangwe 2010). Meanwhile, at the global level, in the wake of the privatization of mining in the leading mineral-producing countries and of the growing power of multinational mining corporations (MNC), the global mining industry became increasingly interested in investment beyond the US, Canada, and Australia (Naito and Remy 2001; Bridge 2004).

During the 1990s, Sub-Saharan Africa caught the eye of new international investors and experienced a growth in its share of worldwide corporate investment. Africa's mineral-rich countries with stagnant or non-existent mining industries, caught in the malaise of low national economic performance, started to appreciate the potential for multinational corporate investment in mining (Bridge 2004). Nudged by the World Bank, many Sub-Saharan African countries began altering their legal and fiscal investment frameworks to attract foreign MNCs investment in mineral extraction (cf. World Bank 1992). The process of privatization of Tanzania's mineral sector took place in the context of a surge in large-scale mining investment on the African continent (Chapters 1 and 7).

The World Bank recommendations for reform of Tanzania's mining sector focused explicitly on the underperformance of existing commercial mining and measures to facilitate foreign large capital investment in the development of the country's mineral deposits. No systematic recommendations for harnessing the potential of the artisanal mining sector and local commercial industrial development were made. Recommendations were tailored for global corporate investment, emphasizing foreign investment incentives and short-term fiscal redress. FDI was considered the unconditional necessity for spurring a properly functioning mining industry in Tanzania (Bastida 2005; Therkildsen and Bourgouin 2012).

At the turn of the twenty-first century, Tanzania, with its new favourable investment climate for foreign mining MNCs and its undeveloped world-class ore deposits, was hailed by the global gold industry to be full of lucrative opportunities, triggering the influx of FDI and a sudden increased presence of transnational mining and exploration operations. At present, the mineral industry has become the quintessential symbol of private sector development in the country (Lange 2011). Paradoxically, at the outset the anticipated revenues generated by a viable commercial large-scale mining sector were believed to be the means to gain sovereignty from donor aid and assistance (Therkildsen and Bourgouin 2012). However, a decade after the mining industry took off in earnest, Tanzania remains one of the largest recipients of aid in Sub-Saharan Africa, with over a third of its government spending being financed by foreign aid. Meanwhile, revenue generation from the mining industry has fallen far short of original expectations.

Tanzania took steps to create a policy environment that was highly attractive to foreign investors. The Mining Act of 1998, which came into force on 1 July 1999 replacing *inter alia* the Mining Act of 1979, became the principal law governing the sector. The legislation allowed 100 per cent foreign ownership, guarantees against nationalization and expropriation, and the offer of unrestricted repatriation of profits and capital, coupled with a relatively low royalty rate of three per cent and a variety of incentives such as waived import duties on mining equipment and tax exemptions. In addition, retention licenses were created which permitted companies to hold an exploration area for an extended period of time in the expectation that a discovered deposit would become economical following the completion of a business cycle. This lengthened the time that an exploration area could be held without developing it for production. More importantly from a development perspective, while the previous 1979 mining act required applicants for mining licenses to present a plan for local procurement of goods and services, such a stipulation was absent from the 1998 Act.

The change in mining policy and legislation in the second half of the 1990s defined roles for each actor in the industry that resulted in a shifting balance of power in which large-scale mining was given priority. The private sector was expected to lead all mining activities, including exploration, development, and marketing. The Government of Tanzania was accorded the task of creating a legislative, fiscal, and institutional framework that would attract private investment, ensuring that social and environmental guidelines and codes of conduct were established and adhered to as well as fostering the development of industrial infrastructure. Interestingly, it was also stated that the government would provide support to artisanal mining.

Triad politics of mining governance: Artisanal mining, large-scale mining and state relations

The mining policy and legislative reform process of the late 1990s was informed by two specific dichotomies: first, that of public versus private; and second, that of large-scale versus artisanal mining. Explicitly state-run mining enterprise and privatized mining industry were put in direct opposition to one another, reflecting thinking within the mining industry globally. In contrast, large-scale and artisanal mining scales of operation were never blatantly or purposefully opposed in Tanzanian policy. Yet, this dichotomy crept into policy implementation to the detriment of artisanal mining and had a corrosive effect on the country's mining industry generally. How this happened is important to understand. The problem is not that large-scale mining activities are prioritized *per se*, but that they are dealt with in a manner that negatively impinges on artisanal mining. Governance of interaction between large and artisanal mining is constructed as a zero-sum game to the detriment of artisanal mining in reality gain in one need not mean loss to the other (Hilson 2011). Formal policy is not necessarily undermining the potential for artisanal mining growth, but the fact that formal policy is frequently superseded by the implementation of extraordinary *ad-hoc* measures opens the door for the privileging of large-scale mining concerns.

While recent mining law reforms in Tanzania favour a standardized regulatory framework embedded in mining law, this framework has nevertheless been perceived by government as inadequate in the case of very large corporate and bank-financed projects. Tanzania joined a number of Sub-Saharan African countries that retained within their reformed mining laws the ability to auction off properties or make them available only by negotiated agreement through Mine Development Agreements (MDAs). These agreements 'may contain provisions binding on the United Republic which guarantee the fiscal stability of a long-term mining project ... and may contain special provisions to take effect in the event of a change in the applicable law' (Mining Act, Section 10.2, Tanzania 1998). An MDA represents a contract negotiated solely between the Government (in this case the Ministry of Energy and Minerals) and a mining company. In Tanzania they are only applicable in cases involving capital investment of at least US$ 100 million.

For a substantial period of time MDAs remained closed confidential documents. Although now they have been brought to increasing public attention (Tanzania Policy Forum 2008), they do not pass through Parliament nor are they part of a consultative process with civil society or communities. In essence, the legal and regulatory framework of these agreements often guarantees security of tenure and a stable fiscal agreement over the life of a mine, representing a significant avenue through which the state prioritizes the use of mineral assets for large-scale mining and foreign investors.

At the time of writing, the Tanzanian Ministry of Energy and Minerals had concluded six MDAs with MNCs engaged in large-scale gold mining. Each of the six agreements was negotiated separately, and hence there is variance between the terms and conditions of each agreement. Of the six, at least four were entered into before the Mining Act of 1998 came into force in July 1999 and three of these before the Mineral Policy of October 1997. Agreements that were entered into immediately prior to the enactment of the Mining Act ensure that the rights accrued by the companies would endure in the event that a new law would be enacted repealing the Mining Act of 1979.[2] Importantly, however, this means that a significant proportion of the current MDAs were executed at a time when the

Government of Tanzania had not yet formally set out its development strategy for the sector. Accordingly, the concluded agreements potentially do not take into account long-term development objectives as later identified in the 1998 and 2010 Mining Acts. It also means that not all six commercial gold mines are operating with reference to the legislation that was based upon the mineral policies of 1997 and 2009.

The motivation on the part of mining companies to develop a mining operation under an MDA rather than through legislation is that an MDA ensures stability, which is important given the nature of the long investment horizon of the mining industry. In terms of understanding the relations between state and MNCs they represent an opaque and individualized relationship albeit a cooperative one since the goal for both parties is FDI in the mineral sector. While discretional decision-making powers of the Minister of Energy and Minerals or Commissioner of Minerals in a MDA is not inconsistent with the Mining Act of 1998, such discretion cannot be exercised outside of the provisions of the negotiated MDA.

In essence, MDAs represent an 'informalization' of formal procedures that occur between government and MNCs. MDA negotiations involve large teams of lawyers for the drafting and redrafting of agreements, yet their success depends on the less formal quality of relationships and trust between MNC and state representatives – especially given asymmetries of information and negotiating power and historical legacies of mistrust. The process of formal negotiation of a MDA can be seen as setting the foundation for an informal relationship between the Tanzanian government and the MNC.

For the state, MDAs are viewed as a critical platform for attracting FDI. For civil society actors, however, MDAs represent a problematic and often opaque arrangement that may compromise benefits for citizens in the state's pursuit of foreign capital. Civil society organizations believe that the length of development agreements is too long, excluding the possibility of change and flexibility. This renewed provision within the Mining Act of 1998 has had the effect of constraining the Tanzanian state's future ability to introduce legislative changes aimed at advancing broad development goals.

There are four main political implications to MDA contracts in Tanzania. First, these individualized contractual arrangements decrease the likelihood of the formation of a strong business association to collectively lobby government in the interest of the industry. More importantly, the Tanzania Chamber of Minerals and Energy, representing the voice of private sector participants in the industry, remains very weak, unable to project a coherent industrial lobby. In other words, state–business relations develop under a policy system that has undercut the state's ability to use these relations to advance economic development objectives. While the privatization of state assets provides space for international mining companies to take substantial control over the mineral sector, the relations remain limited to individualized interactions between each company and government. The trade unions remain relatively weak (e.g. TAMICO, the Tanzanian Mine and Construction Workers Union), suffering from distrust between mine workers and the union leadership and without a strong national voice.

Second, MDAs have been kept out of both parliamentary processes and the public arena, which has led to mistrust of the motives of those involved. Rumour and innuendo fill the information vacuum as it is difficult to trust the outcome of an agreement – creating a process that is not considered reliable. This is against a context where the benefits of mineral sector development to Tanzanian citizens are the subject of intense debate (Curtis and Lissu 2008; Cooksey 2011; Lange 2011). During interviews, representatives of both companies and government each cited commercially sensitive information as the chief reason for restricting access to signed agreements.

Third, the affected communities' expectations are not reflected in the terms of MDAs agreed by the State and MNC representatives, which further erodes trust in the agreement making process and contributes to feelings of distrust among communities towards the company and government. This mismatch of expectations presents a real threat to the MNCs reputation and to the legitimacy of the state. In reaction to this, MNCs in Tanzania describe going beyond the terms of an MDA to meet these expectations of local communities, particularly with respect to infrastructural development and service provisioning as part of their corporate social responsibility.

Fourth, a central aspect of bias towards FDI is the profound limitation of certain types of state participation in the mining sector. My interviews with corporate executives indicated the importance to MNCs of being able to operate on the basis of competitive commercial practices – that is with the freedom to set their own cut-off grades and production levels, to hire technically competent employees (which for instance may involve hiring foreigners), to market their products directly and not through a government-imposed intermediary, and to manage their finances. In this way, the state is not able to direct its own mineral industry development; it can only regulate it (Campbell 2009).

Over time, as large-scale mining in Tanzania has developed under the MDA regimes, it has became increasingly clear to government and civil society that Tanzania is not accruing the anticipated benefits. This has fuelled on-going public debate and in 2010 led to the redrafting of the Mining Act.

The Mining Act of 2010

Tension between FDI-led large-scale mining and artisanal mining, underpinned by lack of visible socioeconomic benefits to Tanzania, has been manifested in widespread discontent and popular resistance, as well as further disagreement within government on how to direct the mining industry (cf. Cooksey 2011; Lange 2011). In 2007, the Government directed a commission headed by Justice Mark Bomani (commonly referred to as 'the Bomani Commission', which issued a report in 2008; Tanzania 2008) that investigated the mining sector and reviewed the existing MDAs with multinational companies. Their findings were instrumental in the drafting of new legislation.

On 23 April 2010, Tanzania's Parliament passed The Mining Act 2010. This tightened government control over MNCs, increased regulation in key sectors, sought to concentrate greater power in the hands of Tanzanian nationals, and encouraged inward investment. At the time of public debate about the legislation, there were expressed concerns about the reservation of mineral rights and licenses for dealing in minerals for Tanzanian citizens and corporate bodies under the exclusive control of Tanzanian citizens. These complaints were amended before the law was passed. Thus, the Act placed restrictions on non-Tanzanian participation in artisanal mining and trade in minerals and gemstones. Importantly it materially increased the levels of gold royalty payable to the government of Tanzania from three to four per cent (based on gross as opposed to net revenues). The 2010 Act authorizes the Tanzanian government to participate in the conduct and financing of mining operations for all projects exceeding US$ 100m, as well as stipulating that the government will receive a negotiated share of profits. Significantly, the Minister retains the power to prescribe a standard MDA model. The Act also introduced significant changes to the governance of artisanal mining. It gave exclusivity of resource rights to Tanzanian citizens and corporate bodies for small-scale licenses, which apply to 'Primary Mining Licences' for artisanal mining operations involving capital expenditure of less than US$ 100,000.

The thrust of government policy and legislation in both the 1997–98 and 2009–10 mineral policies and mining acts has been towards formalization, regularization and modernization of the artisanal mining sector, yet paradoxically government action has veered further away from addressing artisanal mining development. While the development potential of improvements to artisanal mining – a sector with an already large labour force – and potential multiplier effects of local accumulation for artisanal mining were both given consideration in the 2010 Act and the preceding National Strategy for Growth and Reduction of Poverty (2005–2010), these provisions have not translated into practice (cf. Phillips *et al.* 2001; Kulindwa *et al.* 2003; Fisher *et al.* 2009).

Government policy implementation is weighted towards creating an environment suitable for the private sector, in line with international financial institutions' preference for a clearly articulated mineral sector policy. Emphasis is on the role of the private sector as owner and operator and the government as regulator and promoter. The importance of creating opportunities for local capital accumulation is being blatantly disregarded (Therkildsen and Bourgouin 2012).

The Ministry of Energy and Minerals (specifically the Commissioner and Minister) holds great power in determining the development of the sector. At present, Tanzanian accumulation from mining is rumoured to be mainly related to the possession and dispossession of land and mining rights, and to real estate deals and trade (Shivji 2009). As Khan and Gray (2006: 55) opine, the increasing evidence of political competition and corruption reflects 'the growing opportunities available to political representatives in managing the non-market transfers and allocations of assets like land and natural resources' (cf. Cooksey 2011; Cooksey and Kelsall 2011).

Nonetheless, the government was committed to mining reforms in 2010 if for no other reason than it was an election year and it is largely beholden to the will of the people. Public opinion remains hostile towards foreign mining companies so legislation that offered major reform was needed and expected. The reforms implemented in the early months of 2010 were done expediently, without support from the industry. These measures did not satisfy the opposition, although the resource indigenization of artisanal mining did gain them increasing public support. Clearly, the motivation for the more balanced policy and legislative change that takes account of artisanal interests arises from Tanzanian politicians desire to win elections in the country's mining regions. Mining politics become laced with popular nationalism and patriotism at the time of elections.

Thus in Tanzania today, exploration and mining for gold, which in the post-Independence period was limited to the activities of artisanal miners and an unproductive state-run operation (Kulindwa *et al.* 2003), is now dominated by FDI by some of the world's largest mining MNCs. The labour-intensive artisanal sector is being eclipsed politically, despite the artisanal mining's rapid growth in the last three decades. Both artisanal mining and formal medium-scale capital-intensive domestic operations are not being supported in practice. Overall, the privatization of the mineral sector is not generating an economically viable and politically stable mineral industry for the benefit of the Tanzanian population in the mining regions and nationally. The immediate consequences are illustrated in the following case study.

Triangulation of contentious relationships: the case of North Mara

At the time of the 2009–10 change in mineral policy and mining legislation, large-scale mining activities in the gold sector were already well established but were experiencing an increasing challenge from artisanal miners. Protest stemmed from disagreement about artisanal miners' mining rights and local communities' residential presence in specified land areas. Furthermore, the lack of visible beneficial outcomes from large-scale mining in terms of revenue generation, employment and poverty alleviation were sources of deepening resentment.

Discontent was particularly acute in North Mara, manifested in the practice of artisanal miners' 'intrusion' on a large-scale mining site, with the intention of seizing gold (see also Chapter 11). Artisanal miners' gold-digging activities constitute a crucial underpinning for the local and regional economy of Mara, with many people in the mining settlements benefiting either directly or indirectly. However, the prospect of future growth of artisanal mining is limited, primarily due to large-scale mining's acquisition of exploration, prospecting, and mining rights. Intrusion reveals the politics of artisanal mining and large-scale mining relations and their inextricable links to mining rights, different subjective understandings of these rights, how the rights are exercised in actual practice, and how segments of Tanzania's mineral sector gain or lose legitimacy.

North Mara mine opened in 2002 under the ownership of Afrika Mashariki Gold Mines and thereafter became Placer Dome Tanzania, a subsidiary of Placer Dome Inc. In January 2006, Barrick Gold took over Placer Dome Inc. and since

2009 the mine has been operated by its spin-off – African Barrick Gold Ltd (ABG). Development of the mine led to the displacement of many artisanal mining operations and it has been subject to the critical eye of advocacy groups and civil society organizations since a cyanide spill caused the death of villagers and livestock through contamination of the water supply of neighbouring villages (Mnyanyika 2009). In 2009, Harrison Mwakyembe, a Member of Parliament, demanded that the North Mara Gold Mine be closed due to the deaths of eighteen villagers from polluted drinking water in Nyamogo.[3] In addition to this environmental scandal, the mine has been plagued by violent conflicts between both private and public security forces and intruders at the mine site.[4]

Intrusion became a regular affair at North Mara Gold Mine, involving groups of people entering the mine at night by stealth to remove gold-bearing ore from the pit as well as the practice of local people rushing onto the site immediately following a mine blast to grab gold-bearing material. A third form of intrusion, less practiced in Mara, arises from artisanal miners digging shafts in undeveloped areas of large-scale mining concessions.

In North Mara the intruders are more likely to be mining directly in the pit. Using their own dynamite for blasting, they boldly follow the same vein lines as ABG. In the evening, the intruders can be seen standing upon the high ridge overlooking the pit, ready to invade, waiting for ABG's mine staff to clear out at the end of their working day. On one night during the course of my field research, the mine management estimated that over 300 intruders were in the pit and had blasted six times. No accurate figures exist concerning the level of regular intrusion onto the site but interviews with mine personnel suggested that what I witnessed was not unusual.

Artisanal miners' intrusion practices challenge the economic, social and political order that the government's mineral sector policies aim to achieve. Artisanal miners are at loggerheads with ABG who claim the rule of law on the basis of being in legal possession of a government mining licence for the area, while the intruders claim the original rights to the mineral resources as indigenous inhabitants who were the first to prospect and mine the area.

The system of law that accompanies the Mining Act and associated Mineral Policy is premised on the rule of law. Government legislation established the rights for large-scale foreign-owned land concessions but this legal framework does not account for other registers of understanding of ownership, be it with regard to customary land rights or a proprietorial sense of moral rights to the site of one's artisanal production (cf. Lange 2011). The reality is that the government's policy, legislation and legal enforcement are understood differently from the perspectives of artisanal miners as opposed to large-scale mining interests. By law, intruders are deemed to be stealing from ABG; whereas artisanal miners see the mining company as the thief taking what they believe to be rightfully theirs.

MNCs are considered highly rational and instrumentalist. As corporate entities, they readily accept and internalize the legal norms and codes of conduct that have been legislated to serve their interests. Through mutually agreed legal discourse between the state and the MNC, their position is legitimized. Artisanal miners' interests and material position, on the other hand, are increasingly being eclipsed. Their resort to intrusion and mining in the MNC's mine pit, is a way of asserting their moral right in the political arena, based on the strength of their demographic presence.

The North Mara case dramatizes the unfolding complexity of the relations between the three core actors. The amount of theft of gold-bearing ore from the pit is marginal to the large-scale mining operation but such raids necessitate a halt in the mine's operations while engineers ensure security of the ABG's employees. This is highly disruptive to production and damaging to the reputation of the mine on financial markets vis-à-vis shareholders. The issue is not about lost profit through theft as such, but rather fear of a decreasing shareholder price. So far there has not been much evidence of political action by state actors in support of artisanal miners, despite giving them credence in policy and political discourse. Thus, artisanal miners face constricted boundaries, propelling many to resort to night raiding of the ABG pit.

Currently North Mara Gold Mine is considering relinquishing part of their concession to artisanal miners in the hope that it would, at least in part, ease the issue of intruders whose presence on the site at night disrupts their mining activities during the day. ABG has framed this as part of their corporate social responsibility programme, seeking to turn the situation around positively in terms of maintaining shareholder price. More relevant to this discussion however, is that this 'programme in the making' offers an added dimension to the relations between artisanal and large-scale mining operations, which in essence are bypassing the state. Thus artisanal mining has the potential to find some respite, not in state policy and political action, but in formal arrangements with large-scale mining operations. Other than the provisions made in the 2010 Mining Act, the predicament of artisanal mining is not being taken up directly by the Tanzanian state. And paradoxically, the letter of the law is being circumvented by all three actors in the mining arena, underlining the complexity of the relationship between them.

Conclusion

The relations that manifest themselves between the core triad of actors who form the nucleus of the mining industry in Tanzania – the state, large-scale mining and artisanal mining operators – are clearly laid out in policy and legislation, but in practice the interplay of these actors deviates considerably. The regulatory framework of the mining industry in the 1990s was based on the perceived need to attract FDI to develop Tanzania's mineral endowments. Moreover it was premised on a sectoral approach that emphasized the development of Tanzania's world-class ore bodies in the interest of the global mining industry. In the 2000s, the extractive industries took centre stage in public *fora* in response to mounting public pressure. It is the discrepancy between policy and practice that has fuelled tensions between artisanal and large-scale mining. As MNCs entered into operation, the state did not actively and visibly mediate the situation, leading to violent conflict between artisanal mining and large-scale mining operators on several occasions. In North Mara, the legitimacy of large-scale mining operators has been challenged by local artisanal miners through their intrusion tactic.

Not surprisingly, there is doubt about the efficacy of the current approach to mineral sector development in achieving development goals other than the attraction of FDI. As with the 1997 Mineral Policy and 1998 Mining Act, the focus of the most recent Mineral Policy 2009 and Mining Act 2010 is heavily biased towards FDI (Tanzania 2009, 2010). The current situation is that the MNCs have a firm presence in Tanzania, having invested large-scale capital and signed MDAs with the Tanzanian state. They hold large mining concessions and endeavour to expand the output and increase the capacity of their mines, and acquire new mineral assets to retain the value of the corporation and its share price.

Operating with another logic based on livelihood viability of hundreds of thousands of Tanzanian artisanal miners, the Tanzanian artisanal mining sector is formally recognized in policy and law, yet it remains conspicuously invisible in both past and current policy practice. Consideration of key issues confronting artisanal miners in terms of land constraints, inability to raise capital, expand operations, or improve health and safety measures is limited with little incentive for on-the-ground action. If the Tanzanian state seeks to have a balanced and productive mineral industry that contributes to all areas of its economy, it must recognize the importance of artisanal mining and foster capital accumulation in the sector.

Notes

1   FDI refers to the direct acquisition of a foreign firm, construction of a facility, or investment in a joint venture or strategic alliance with a local firm with attendant input of technology.
2   Further, the Mining Act (1998) ensures that agreements between mineral rights-holders and the Government of Tanzania under the Mining Act (1979) would remain effective.
3   In February 2010, the National Assembly of Tanzania ordered the Government to complete a study to determine the level of pollution of the Tigithe River caused by the North Mara Gold Mine and in June 2010 the Tanzanian government declared the Tigithe River to be potable and suitable for human consumption, following changes made to ABG's environmental programme (Bariyo 2010).
4   In 2008 it was reported that a group of 200 people broke into the North Mara mine site and destroyed approximately US$ 7 million worth of Barrick property. The vandalism resulted in the temporary closure of the mine's operations (Wright and Edwards 2011). Violent conflicts between security forces and intruders trespassing on the mine site, scavenging for gold-bearing material, have been prevalent over past years. Such confrontations escalated on 16 May 2011 when several hundred villagers sought to access the mine site, resulting in the deadly shooting of five intruders and the injury of several villagers (York 2011).

References

Bariyo, N. (2010) 'Tanzania clears North Mara gold mine over river pollution'. Available from www.epcengineer.com: www.epcengineer.com/news/post/406/tanzania-clears-north-mara-gold-mine-over-river-pollution-min, Dow Jones Newswires, Monday, 28 June 2010.

Bastida, E. (2005) 'Mineral law: New Directions?' in Bastida, E., Wälde, T. and Warden-Fernández, J. (eds), *International and Comparative Mineral Law and Policy: Trends and Prospects*. The Hague: Kluwer Law International. pp. 409–23.

Bastida, E., Wälde, T. and Warden-Fernández, J. (eds) (2005) *International and Comparative Mineral Law and Policy: Trends and Prospects*. The Hague, The Netherlands: Kluwer Law International.

Bridge, G. (2004) 'Mapping the bonanza: Geographies of mining investment in an era of neoliberal reform'. *The Professional Geographer* 56(3): 406–21.

Campbell, B. (2009) 'Conclusion: What development model? What governance agenda?' in Campbell, B. (ed.) *Mining in Africa: Regulation and Development*. Ottawa, Canada: IDRC.

Cooksey, B. (2011) 'The investment and business environment for gold exploration and mining in Tanzania'. London: ODI. Available from www.dfid.gov.uk/r4d/PDF/Outputs/APPP/20110606-appp-background-paper-03-brian-cooksey-june-2011.pdf (accessed 12 November 2012).

Cooksey, B. and Kelsall, T. (2011) 'The political economy of the investment climate in Tanzania'. London: ODI. Available from www.institutions-africa.org/filestream/20110606-appp-research-report-01-the-political-economy-of-the-investment-climate-in-tanzania-by-cooksey-kelsall-june-2011 (accessed 12 November 2012).

Curtis, M. and Lissu, T. (2008) *A Golden Opportunity? How Tanzania Is Failing to Benefit from Gold Mining*. Dar es Salaam: Christian Council of Tanzania (CCT), National Council of Muslims in Tanzania (BAKWATA) and Tanzania Episcopal Conference (TEC).

Fisher, E., Mwaipopo, R., Mutagwaba, W., Nyange, D., and Yaron, G. (2009) 'The ladder that sends us to wealth: Artisanal mining and poverty reduction in Tanzania'. *Resources Policy* 34(1–2): 32–8.

Hilson, G. (2011) '"A conflict of interest"? A critical examination of artisanal/large-scale miner relations in Sub-Saharan Africa'. in Botchway, F. (ed.) *New Directions in Resource Investment and African Development*. London: Edward Elgar. pp. 134–58.

Khan, M. and Gray, H. (2006) *State Weakness in Developing Countries and Strategies of Institutional Reform: Operational Implications for Anti-Corruption Policy and a Case-Study of Tanzania*. London: DFID.

Kulindwa, K., Mashindano, O., Shechambo, F. and Sosovele, H. (2003) *Mining for Sustainable Development in Tanzania*. Dar es Salaam: Dar es Salaam University Press.

Lange, S. (2011), 'Gold and governance: Legal injustices and lost opportunities in Tanzania' *African Affairs* 110(439): 233–53.

McHenry, D. E. (1994) *Limited Choices: The Political Struggle for Socialism in Tanzania*. Boulder, CO: Lynne Rienner Publishers.

Mnyanyika, V. (2009) 'Close North Mara mine-activists'. *The Citizen*. June 27.

Naito, K. and Remy, F. (2001) *Mining Sector Reform and Investment: Results of a Global Survey*. London: Mining Journal Books.

Phillips L. C., Semboja, H., Shukla, G. P., Sezinga, R., Mutagwaba, W., Mchwampaka, B., Wanga, G., Kahyarara, G. and Keller, C. (2001) *Tanzania's Precious Mineral Boom: Issues in Mining and Marketing*. Washington, DC: USAID.

Shivji, I. G. (2009), *Accumulation in an African Periphery: A Theoretical Framework*. Dar es Salaam: Mkuki na Nyota Publishers.

Tanzania, United Republic of (1997) *Mineral Policy of Tanzania* [Ministry of Energy and Minerals]. Dar es Salaam: Government Printer.

Tanzania, United Republic of (1998) *The Mining Act* [Ministry of Energy and Minerals]. Dar es Salaam: Government Printer.

Tanzania, United Republic of (2008) *Report of the Presidential Mining Review Committee to advise the Government on oversight of the Mining Sector*. Dar es Salaam: Government Printer.

Tanzania, United Republic of (2009) *The Mineral Policy of Tanzania* [Ministry of Energy and Minerals]. Dar es Salaam: Government Printer.

Tanzania, United Republic of (2010) *The Mining Act* [Ministry of Energy and Minerals]. Dar es Salaam: Government Printer.

Tanzania Policy Forum (2008) *The Demystification of Mining Contracts in Tanzania*. Dar es Salaam: Tanzania Policy Forum.

Therkildsen, O. and Bourgouin, F. (2012) 'Continuity and change in Tanzania's ruling coalition'. [DIIS Working Paper 12/06]. Available from www.diis.dk/sw47287.asp.

Wangwe, S. (2010) *The Political Economy of Tanzania: The Evolution of Policymaking*. Dar es Salaam: REPOA.

World Bank (1992) *Strategy for African Mining*. Washington, DC: World Bank.

Wright, L. and Edwards, J. (2011) 'Seven dead in clash at African Barrick Mine'. *The Star* newspaper, Tuesday, 17 May 2011.

York, G. (2011) 'In an African mine, the lust for gold sparks a deadly clash'. *The Globe and Mail*. 17/06/11. Available from www.theglobeandmail.com/news/world/in-an-african-mine-the-lust-for-gold-sparks-a-deadly-clash/article598554/ (accessed 15 January 2013).

10 *Ubeshi* – negotiating co-existence

Artisanal and large-scale relations in diamond mining

Rosemarie Mwaipopo

Ubeshi[1] is a local term that has been adopted from the Kisukuma word for a hawk (*mbeshi*), which stealthily dives down and scoops up its prey. Analogously, local people in the communities around the Williamson Diamond Mine of Mwadui stealthily swoop in and steal diamond-bearing material from within the mine 'when the owners are not looking', as described by local informants. Although today the practice of *ubeshi* is less common than before, it remains an activity that has defined the rules regarding mineral rights and power relations in diamond production and exchange in the Mwadui area of Maganzo.

Based on observations, in-depth oral accounts of local history, and discussions with mine officials, this chapter centres on the nature of *ubeshi*, dissecting its role in negotiations between several parties, notably local artisanal miners and the large-scale Williamson Diamond Mine, in their contestation over the locality's diamond wealth. I explore how the politics of power are manifested in the interface between artisanal and large-scale mining and how space is created for various actors within this arena. Beginning with the contextualization of artisanal diamond mining in Tanzania's mining sector, I proceed to consider factors leading to the emergence of *ubeshi*. The actors and networks that constitute the *ubeshi* system are then discussed, before concluding with an assessment of *ubeshi*'s overall significance.

Artisanal mining access and governance

Ubeshi is not a new practice. It has become ingrained in the Maganzo area over time, deepening into a physical conflict between artisanal and large-scale diamond mining. Artisanal mining in Tanzania and elsewhere has led to struggles about equity in the distribution of natural resource wealth (Chapter 10). What is at stake is the 'dispossession of land, territory, landscape and natural resources, property, self-governance, citizenship and cultural rights' of artisanal miners (Bebbington *et al.* 2010: 903). The negative consequences of contestations within mining are generally emphasized if not sensationalized, clouding a perception of the ways in which local people living in mineral-rich areas shape their livelihood practices as well as masking creative potentialities for co-existence that can pave the way to more humane and inclusive institutions (Lahiri-Dutt 2006; Bebbington *et al.* 2010).

Ribot and Peluso's (2003: 153) definition of 'access', as the *ability* to benefit from things, rather than, as has been conventionally claimed, the *right* to benefit from things, helps situate the analysis of the *ubeshi* practice squarely within specific mining sector processes and relationships. It is in this context that the conception of co-existence in the mineral sector in Tanzania needs to be located to reveal the property relations and multiplicity of ways that enable people to benefit from these resources.

Competing ideas about rights to resources versus the ability to benefit from resources within prevailing mineral governance systems has plagued the mineral sector, sometimes leading to conflict, amidst exclusion and acquisition, especially by people who feel disadvantaged in the process (Society for International Development [SID] 2009). When shifts in access to minerals occur, groups of people redefine their understanding of how they can benefit from these resources (Mwaipopo 2010).

In many instances, people make claims to land ownership, on the assumption that access to land is key to gaining benefits (Lahiri-Dutt 2006; Lange 2008). While land is indeed central, claims to it often rest instead on a network of relations that provide access to resources rather than ownership *per se*. This is the case with *ubeshi*, a tactic for illegally benefiting from mineral resources on the basis of multi-stakeholder entanglement that operates partly outside and partly within the established governance system. However, the conception of legality and illegality in such cases is highly contested (Mwaipopo *et al.* 2004), and incursions on Williamson Diamond Mine have become a way of resolving benefit claims by local people who realize that titling or other endowments bestowed by governance systems do not necessarily make any difference to their competing claims to resources.

The history of artisanal mining in Tanzania illuminated by Chachage (1995: 37) led him to conclude that 'the meek shall inherit the earth but not the mining rights'. Over the last two decades, the Tanzanian government adopted a more private sector and market-oriented economic development policies and has encouraged foreign large-scale investors to Tanzania for mineral exploration and mining. These policies have nonetheless been accompanied by recognition of the existence of artisanal miners, according them transferable mineral rights, the ability to mortgage mineral rights, and access to fiscal incentives (Chapters 1 and 9). This has served to boost employment in artisanal mining and increase trade and related services.[2]

The Mining Policy of 1997 addressed several constraints of the artisanal mining sector, including low levels of education, rudimentary technology, low capital for investment, poor access to market information and lack of bargaining power (Tanzania 1997; Mwaipopo *et al.* 2004). Creation of a legal regulatory framework within which licencing procedures would be streamlined and harmonized and mineral rights in order to facilitate the entry of more formalized artisanal mining ventures was also promised (Tanzania 1998).

With an increasing presence of foreign-owned large-scale mines, cooperation between large-scale mining ventures and artisanal miners was encouraged. Nonetheless, positive results for artisanal miners were disappointing. Community social service support through corporate social responsibility programmes of large-scale mining companies had a limited effect, largely based on the companies' own designs rather than being an outcome of careful consultation with the artisanal miners (Lange 2006). The few initiatives to support technology improvement for artisanal miners have had limited success due to the high costs of maintenance of machinery, and the realization that such cooperation is not making a significant impact on poverty levels (Lange 2006; Hall 2010). Most importantly, there is a feeling that reforms in the mining sector favour foreign large-scale investments rather than safeguarding the interests of local Tanzanians, including the delicate issue of resettlement of local communities to make way for large-scale mining companies' ventures (Chachage 1995; SID 2009; Hall 2010).

What has therefore been developing over the years is a troubled co-existence between artisanal and large-scale mining, harbouring conflict and despite potential for leverage, artisanal miners are facing spatial encroachment as more and more large-scale mining licences have been allocated. Their reactions to this marginalization vary. Some have sought to enter into exploration agreements or to transfer their concessions to large-scale mining for compensation, others seek co-existence with large-scale operators, and still others bitterly contest their eviction to make room for large-scale mining firms (Tanzania Chamber of Mines [TCM] 2002; Lange 2006).

Thus, while the Tanzanian government asserts its support for the co-existence of both large and small-scale sectors, artisanal miners have faced many frustrations and unpredictable outcomes. Poverty in mining communities is abundantly evident (TCM 2002; European Commission for Africa [ECA] 2008; SID 2009). On the other hand, many artisanal miners are finding minerals and benefiting financially. This is even more the case for the Tanzanian brokers and dealers serving the artisanal miners. Mining communities, which are exceptionally complex, spanning a wide range of socioeconomic differentiation, make the analysis of negotiations between large-scale and artisanal miners quite complicated.

The 2010 Mining Act makes it mandatory for the government to set aside specific areas for artisanal miners, presumably as a means of averting conflicts between them and larger mining companies. Furthermore, it is stipulated that all Primary Licences for mining of gemstones must be given exclusively to Tanzanians (Tanzania 2010). Nonetheless, access to profitable mining land is still the most contentious issue between artisanal mining and large-scale mining companies, and all other efforts to rationalize or formalize the artisanal mining sector have been taken as simply cosmetic, testifying to the general belief that co-existence in the mining sector of Tanzania is exceptionally problematic.

Livelihood pursuits in artisanal mining settlements are directed at accessing minerals as the most promising activity for poverty alleviation (Fisher *et al.* 2009). Yet, government awards of mining rights to large-scale firms in areas significantly worked by artisanal miners have raised questions about the government's true commitment to traditional bush geologists' claims for space and legal breakthroughs favouring artisanal mining (Chachage 1995; Lange 2006, 2008; Curtis and Lissu 2008; Hall 2010). It is in this context that *ubeshi* proliferates.

Ubeshi stealth

An understanding of *ubeshi* requires tracing the background to the establishment and development of Williamson Diamond Mine (WDM)[3] at Mwadui. The Mwadui Mine is one of the oldest continuously operating diamond mines in the world. It was discovered by a Canadian geologist, Dr John Williamson in 1940 and remained under his control as a private limited company, Williamsons Diamonds Ltd, until his death in 1958. Thereafter De Beers of South Africa purchased the equity, transferring 320 shares to the Government of Tanganyika in lieu of payment on Williamson's estate (Knight and Stevensen 1986). In 1971 the Tanzanian government nationalized the mine. The State Mining Corporation (STAMICO) ran the mine until 1994 when De Beers was invited back, to rectify the mine's poor performance under parastatal management, with an agreed share allocation of 75 per cent for De Beers and 25 per cent for the Tanzanian government. In 2008, Petra Diamonds acquired Williamson Diamond Mines and took over mining operations in February 2009 (SID 2009; Hall 2010).

According to oral history, the Williamson Diamond Mines started operations on the basis of negotiated agreement between Williamson, the traditional local leaders and local people. Chief Sheka Lifa, descendant of the local chief of that time, in an interview with me, recounted how Williamson developed rapport with local leaders, getting their consent to establish a mine. He constructed a house for the chief in the process.[4] In his eyes, Williamson legitimately took over control of the land, which is counter to local people's view after national independence that the WDM was unfairly occupying their land.

Diamond mining by the Tanzania Gold and Diamond Development Company in Shinyanga region had preceded Williamson in the 1920s, though with limited success. Williamson arrived in Tanzania as a prospector in 1938. According to oral history, one of his scouts informed him of people playing *bao*[5] with unusually beautiful stones in the Mwadui area. Williamson immediately suspected these were diamonds[6] and went to Mwadui to negotiate with the local chief, Makwaiya. Williamson later applied and obtained an Exclusive Prospective Licence in 1940.

Local elders in Maganzo recall that Williamson relied on a Mwanza-based Indian trader, I.C. Chopra, for financial credit and for the sale of his diamonds. In comparison to local people's suspicions about colonial government officers, Maganzo's elders reminisce fondly about their encounters with Williamson who they saw as 'a good man who blended in well with the people and learned Kisukuma'[7] In negotiations with Chief Makwaiya, Williamson allowed local people to have access to the mine's dispensary, the Shinyanga secondary school and the two dams that he constructed to service the needs of the mine employees. Songwa and Mhumbu dams, built in the 1950s, greatly facilitated Maganzo residents' domestic water needs and livelihood pursuits in the area's semi-arid environment. Chief Sheka Lifa recounts that Williamson went to the trouble of constructing water troughs for livestock and distributed water to local people by standpipes. Yet, as one of the informants observed:

Williamson taught local people how to process tailings to find diamonds. He was also a scavenger, and he used the local people to collect the tailings left by other people for him to re-work. He was the first mbeshi in Mwadui, although of a different kind...

(Simon M., Mwadui, 1 March 2009)

Mining rights in the area were granted to WDM for a 16.6 km^2 area, which included most of the primary kimberlite pipe, and another 13.1 km^2 that included alluvial and elluvial deposits.[8] The two mining licences were amalgamated into one licence covering 29.7 km^2 on 25 May 2006, which is valid to 24 May 2030 (Mutagwaba, Seegers and Mwaipopo 2006).

The area around WDM with approximate dimensions of 12 km north-south and 16 km east-west was declared a diamond protected area in 1948. It later became heavily contested in November 2001, when the Ministry of Energy and Minerals (MEM) issued Prospecting Licences covering most of the area to El Hillal Minerals Ltd, owned by a local entrepreneur (ECA 2008: 53). This led to a dispute between WDM and El Hillal Minerals Ltd, which the latter ultimately won, granting them prospecting activities.[9] By 2005, 13 applicants were granted prospecting or mining licences in the Mwadui area,[10] five of which were under El Hillal Minerals with whom local artisanal miners claimed to have a love–hate relationship. The claim owner, El Hillal Minerals allowed artisanal miners to work its areas on the understanding that the artisanal miners agreed to sell the diamonds they found to the company. This transaction was illegal, but was openly practised (ECA 2008).

At the same time, El Hillal was among those accused by local artisanal miners of having been favoured by the government in the acquisition of the mining lease that resulted in the artisanal miners' exclusion from the area. The spread of open illegal mining covered some of the holders of prospecting licences, who allowed artisanal mining operations in their licenced areas instead of doing prospecting work presumably due to lack of capital to initiate production.

Local agitation ensued from the allocation of prime areas to under-capitalized medium-scale licence-holders, disadvantaging the artisanal miners. An artisanal miners' committee was independently formed to protest against the Ministry of Energy and Mineral's allocation of mining rights that they, albeit illegally, had been working. Their protests eventually met with a positive response. The respective Minister addressed their complaints and in 2005 designated the Maganzo Exclusive Area for Primary Licences, which had 14,000 plots. The Shinyanga regional government then established an official plot allocation committee, which made 1,564 allocations by 2006. This directive also stipulated eligibility for plot allocation as: the applicant's technical competence, relevant (mining) experience, financial resources and allocation of a reasonable part of the land to people living in the mining area or vicinity (Tanzania 1998). Prior to this allocation, there had been only 138 valid PMLs for mining of gemstones (mainly diamonds) in the Shinyanga zone.

The plot allocation committee had 10 members, including an incumbent member of parliament, three appointed people and local miners' representatives.[11] This committee was entrusted to look into the issue of *ubeshi,* since it was assumed that allocation of the plots in the surrounding wards[12] would alleviate the problem of *ubeshi*. The Zonal Mining Office claimed to have carefully informed the artisanal miners and local people in the area about their eligibility for the PMLs through public discussions in 2006.

However, plot allocation records indicate that outside speculators had the possibility of applying for and being granted numerous plots. Local views were that during the second allocation exercise some individuals from the capital city, Dar es Salaam, or from nearby Mwanza, had applications for up to 50 plots. If allowed to proceed, many local people would not have received access to mining land even in the government-designated block. The designation of this block went hand in hand with the allocation of other mining licences around Mwadui mine, an exercise that was beset with complications, including PMLs being located in areas used by the public, notably the public market and school area.

What irked residents was the realization that some of the land they had owned customarily, and worked on to earn their livelihoods, was being allocated to 'foreign' people, while some were being pushed to distant or unproductive land allocations. Unsatisfactory explanations by the Zonal Office, that 'it was difficult to do otherwise' given the number of applicants, raised accusations about inequality in access to mining land despite the government's mining policy that recognizes artisanal mining rights. Many local people also challenged the allocation committee's stipulations about the eligibility of artisanal miners to secure mineral rights saying that they were being used to exclude many and give preference to a small minority of artisanal miners.

A problem was that many artisanal mining operations are based on informal lending systems, where loans are paid when success is realized, rather than through formal bank credit. It was noted that the sector operated on a local system of trust where resources circulated in exchange for labour, with stringent community-based mechanisms for monitoring against cheating. Finally and ironically, a 'first-come, first-served' basis for allocation of mining rights prevailed in which local people tended to be the last to know about allocation opportunities. They were handicapped by poor information systems, low education, hesitation and corruption, whereas urban-based people with education, information and nous were the first in line to apply. Local artisanal miners' disappointment and resentment over this state of affairs was rationalized as grounds for continuing *ubeshi* activities.[13]

Dissecting the practice of *Ubeshi*

Ubeshi became a widespread practice in the 1970s after groups of people from the surrounding villages started stealing diamond-bearing ore or tailings from within the Mwadui mines, which they sold to buyers in and around Shinyanga region.[14] Its inception is traced back to the contact that local people had with the Williamson mine employees and later ex-employees (the retrenched and retired), who had in-depth knowledge of the lease area and were able to point to places where diamonds could be found.

Epstein (1982) reports that by 1946 the Mwadui mine had about 6000 workers and 200 armed guards, all situated within a fenced encampment. Upon retirement, many of the workers settled around Maganzo and the neighbouring villages bordering the mine and stimulated artisanal mining ventures in the area (SID 2009). Subsequent waves of retirees and those retrenched from the mine joined the ranks of undercover *ubeshi* practitioners. In this way the practice was sustained side-by-side with the operations of the WDM.

This section relies on data from a Mwadui Community Development Project (MCDP) survey that the author participated in during the mid-2000s (Mutagwaba *et al.* 2006). At that time, an estimated 20,000 people resided in the nine villages surrounding the WDM, including seasonal artisanal miners, who entered the area during the off-agricultural season. Their artisanal mining activities were concentrated in the former diamond protected area around the WDM and the designated block for primary mining licences. Seventy-five per cent of the families in these areas cited artisanal mining as their most significant source of cash income, and 37 per cent of the households cited artisanal mining as their major source of employment. A majority of the population still worked in small-scale agriculture as a fall-back activity.

In the late 1990s to early 2000s, artisanal diamond mining gained momentum as people experienced success in several spots in the WDM former diamond protected area accessed by local artisanal miners. Simultaneously, people desperate to continue finding diamonds started digging in their backyards and latrines, in front of their homesteads, along the roadside, in fact, anywhere where they thought they could strike it lucky.

Ubeshi work groups

Ubeshi involves work-group-organized exploitation of target areas within the WDM often at night, but also during daylight using simple technologies, such as shovels and gunny sacks for collection of diamond-bearing gravel. Particular spots where gravel is known to be found are visited. The gravel is hastily shoved into the gunnysacks, followed by a quick escape. The sorting of the gravel is conducted back at people's homes, and surprisingly sometimes in village public space. In safer areas, *wabeshi* use locally-made sieves for sorting the gravel. Due to the crude sorting technologies, large amounts of gravel are usually handled and diamond recovery is not always certain. Hence discarded gravel in the yards of several houses is a common sight.

The *wabeshi* target remote locations in WDM, which are infrequently patrolled by security guards. The large size of the WDM lease has made it complicated to maintain effective and frequent security guard patrols.[15] The WDM is so large that there are areas with 'open routes' that are considered safe, where artisanal miners are completely at ease carrying and working with picks, shovels and sieves, out of the purview of the WDM security guards. So too another entry for *wabeshi* is the area famously called 'Kosovo' given its unruly nature. Following allocation of part of the WDM lease to various newly allocated claim owners, Kosovo is now outside the former WDM property, leaving it open for *wabeshi* entry.

Most *wabeshi* earn their living as diggers in the artisanal mining sector. However, local farmers also practice *ubeshi*. In some cases, owners of a PML engage in the actual activity of *ubeshi*, but they are more likely to be sponsors. In a 2006 study, 30 per cent of the respondents said that they mine at Mwadui, implying that they enter the WDM and earn their living as *wabeshi* (Mutagwaba *et al.* 2006).[16]

Wabeshi membership is of able-bodied people between 15–50 years. These are usually men and often young school boys and more rarely women. Women in some of the surrounding villages conduct *ubeshi* with their husbands or partners, while others participate as members of the work group. In January 2006, a heavily pregnant woman had to be rushed to the village dispensary from the WDM area after experiencing labour contractions as she was collecting gravel for diamonds.[17] School children are also known to engage in *ubeshi*. A teacher at Maganzo primary school mentioned that they sometimes trace truancy to *ubeshi* activities.

Ubeshi is normally organized in groups under a *kiongozi* (team leader) who is considered to be *mzoefu* (highly experienced). The *wabeshi* (singular: *mbeshi*) are usually local people residing within the communities that surround the WDM. They are joined by individuals who flock to Maganzo in the rainy season to try their luck in both the illegal and legal diamond-mining areas around Mwadui. The newcomers are recruited by practicing *wabeshi* or agents. The *kiongozi* serves as the agent of a 'sponsor' and is responsible for keeping track of team members '*genge*' and monitoring their haul so that the sponsor remains the sole buyer. Occasionally, individuals operate alone as *wabeshi* and are called *diba*, referring to the fact that they are not tied to any sponsor. The *diba* are highly experienced and known for their agility and strength in dealing with WDM security guards.

Wabeshi sponsors

Sponsors (*wafadhili*) operate as financiers in the *ubeshi* system, providing monetary support for *ubeshi* operations as well as informal artisanal mining work more generally. They are popularly known as *matajiri* (translated: rich people). Sponsors may be registered gold brokers, PML owners, school teachers, business people, and even government or village authorities, essentially anyone who can provide financial support for the *wabeshi* work groups. The diamond brokers tend to be the most prominent sponsors since they have the capital to maintain a work group of *wabeshi* for a longer period.

The individual *tajiri* takes the risk of first accommodating a work team of *wabeshi* in temporary lodgings in the settlements. The most common are residential blocks called *mabehewa*.[18] The sponsor organizes the daily upkeep of the *wabeshi*, including their meals and incidentals for personal hygiene, and occasional cigarettes or drinks. These costs are considered speculative investment by the sponsor and are deducted from the price of the diamonds that the *wabeshi* deliver to him. The sponsor insists on being the sole buyer of diamonds obtained by the work group. A *mbeshi* may also seek a cash loan from the sponsor, which is recovered through a separate arrangement between the two parties. Since many *wabeshi* are propertyless or come into Maganzo *'jinsi walivyo'* meaning that they have nothing to invest other than their labour, they accept these conditions. The sponsors take advantage of easily available cheap labour. In justifying the system, one sponsor had this to say:

> We play a gambling game. When I assist a *mbeshi* I rent sleeping quarters for him, I give him food, if he gets ill I pay for treatment . . . and in most cases he may work for 6 months without getting any diamonds. Or, one may get a stone and take it to another sponsor behind your back (*kupiga buti*). Or you may sponsor a *mbeshi* for a long time and he loses hope after many disappointments and just leaves you and goes back to his home without your knowledge. You are the one who incurs a loss! So since we do not have any firm agreement, or written contract, we keep track of them with these conditions. We spend a lot of money in sponsoring a team for 6–7 months before they get a good scoop. Some of us have sponsored *wabeshi* and ended up bankrupt!
>
> (Sponsor, Maganzo, 1 June 2007)

This system of client–patron relationships operates on the basis of word-of-mouth agreements and it is the social pivot, which sustains the *ubeshi* system. In 2006, the average cost that a sponsor spent on a *mbeshi* was estimated to be US$ 25 per month.

Ubeshi diamond sales

Similar to the formal sector, diamond sales in the *ubeshi* sector normally begin with information about a diamond delivery to a sponsor. Once a diamond *'ng'ana'* has been found, the *ubeshi* work team leader contacts the sponsor. Sponsors, on forewarning of the possibility of a good haul, are likely to accompany the *ubeshi* group as far as possible.[19] Normally, once a significantly sized diamond is discovered, the transaction will commence with the team leader and sponsor examining its quality and weight in private, making assessments of the stone's value. The sponsor's offer price to the team leader is based on the assessed value of the stone minus the costs he has incurred in financing the mining activities.

Many *wabeshi* prefer to sell to other buyers than to sponsors, but tight networking among buyers, most of whom are also financial sponsors, means that it is difficult for a miner to renege on the agreement that they have already made with their sponsor. Nonetheless some desperate *wabeshi* are tempted to sell a stone for immediate cash, a practice called *kupiga buti*,[20] which is done in extreme secrecy, involving a group of *wabeshi* and an external buyer. The *wabeshi* assume that they will get a better price than selling to a sponsor who deducts all their preceding maintenance costs, while the undisclosed buyer reckons on offering a relatively low price to take advantage of the desperation of the miners who fear being caught by their sponsor. Indeed news of the *wabeshi's* treachery often reaches a sponsor. In any case, the miners' inaccessibility to information about diamond prices and their lack of experience in evaluating the worth of specific stones, makes them vulnerable to exploitation by buyers.

An informant at Maganzo gave the example of the transaction of a 25-carat diamond stone with a pyramid shape obtained at the New Alamasi area in 2006. He said the buyer bought the stone for Tsh 60 million (US$ 37,500) from the team leader, but sold it for more than Tsh 200 million (US$ 125,000) to a mineral dealer. Notwithstanding the actual value of the stone, given the limitations that local miners have in estimating actual market value, this case indicates how miners are under-remunerated in diamond transactions.

Maganzo: Hub of Ubeshi

Maganzo settlement, located along the Shinyanga-Mwanza highway and bordering WDM, serves as the residential hub of itinerant miners and the management headquarters of *ubeshi*. The existence of Maganzo in the vicinity of Mwadui mine exemplifies the uneasy co-existence of large-scale and artisanal mining.

Maganzo began as a labour camp for people who sought work within WDM. Its development into a permanent settlement has taken place during the post-independence period since 1961. Maganzo today is an expanding settlement, with modern residences and thriving businesses located predominantly along the highway. The economic vibrancy of Maganzo has allowed affluent in-migrants to buy land for residences, sometimes pushing out those who were originally settled in the area.

The settlement's major constraint is an inadequate water supply for its growing population. In 1972, a reservoir was constructed by the government, which broke down in 1980. Maganzo's existence as the hub of *ubeshi* is a continuous source of frustration to the WDM management. It was recounted by Maganzo informants that one irritated WDM official responded to the community's request for a piped water facility from the mine with the remark 'giving water to you is like giving blood to an enemy'. However, Maganzo residents have been able to survive by accessing WDM's dams.

The settlement has about 90 per cent of its adult population engaged directly or indirectly in mining. In 2006, the population was estimated at 11,868 people, up from 9,272 people recorded in the 2002 National Population Census. Of these, 4,519 were females and 7,349 were males, residing in approximately 2,502 households.[21] This skewed population structure is a result of the many males who are attracted to Maganzo for legal and illegal mining activities. Many of the women in Maganzo and the surrounding villages serve as traders, food vendors or sponsors for *ubeshi,* rather than engaging in *ubeshi* themselves. The resident population fluctuates sharply during the rainy season when many miners come to

Maganzo because of the availability of water, which facilitates diamond-sorting activities.

Maganzo is also the centre of diamond marketing, with several brokers and various unregistered mineral traders resident there. In 2006–07 it was estimated that there were approximately 20 licenced brokers working independently in Maganzo who controlled about 7.5 per cent of all the diamonds produced in the area. Roughly 75 per cent of the artisanal miners sell their diamonds to local buyers in Maganzo, compared to 21 per cent selling to a distant buyer and only 4 per cent are sold to a company (Mutagwaba *et al.* 2006).

Persistence of Ubeshi

Ubeshi is seen as 'a way of life'[22] that is practised by men, as well as some women and children. A local informant explained 'My grandfather was a *mbeshi*, my father and mother were *wabeshi*, and my children will be *wabeshi*. The persistence of *ubeshi* relates to: first, the sponsor's enticement to engage in *ubeshi*. Sponsors are in the habit of offering motorcycles or cellphones to the *ubeshi* team leaders. Team members are offered bicycles and beer and promises to bail them out from remand if they get caught. Second, there are diamond brokers and dealers in Shinyanga town who specialize in buying the small-sized diamonds that are obtained by reworking the WDM diamond tailings. Third, *ubeshi*'s enabling environment is facilitated by what Duffy (2005) calls complex clandestine or shadow networks. These networks include relationships that are maintained by local community members and leaders, the security personnel and sometimes even WDM employees in and around Mwadui.

Wabeshi have often worked in collaboration with WDM's contracted security guards and people of responsibility in the ward and village governments surrounding the mine (Mutagwaba *et al.* 2006). It is claimed by the *wabeshi* that some WDM-contracted security guards, either in fear of reprisal, threats, or in need of extra income, enter into agreements with the *wabeshi*. Such collusion allows the *wabeshi* to criss-cross the WDM without fear, sometimes in broad daylight. This circumstance is greatly facilitated by Maganzo buyers and sponsors bribing the guards with payments of Tsh 50,000–100,000 (approximately US$30–60) per entry. The *wabeshi* and security guards prearrange when and for how long the *wabeshi* can enter the WDM area within the time slot of the security guards' work shifts. If a security guard instructs 'you enter from 9 pm to 1 am and then leave!', the *wabeshi* work group must strictly adhere to this timing. Otherwise, they may find the security dogs attacking them.[23]

Clearly, *ubeshi* is an integral part of the local economy and a regular source of household income. Government ward and village officials do not deny knowledge of *ubeshi* and the silence that one encounters from the local authorities when seeking ideas on how to address *ubeshi* is telling. Population pressure on declining natural endowments, prolonged droughts, poor soils and shrinking land holdings have reduced agricultural livelihood options, perpetuating *ubeshi*'s attraction as a source of income for local households.

Mwadui mine's attempts to control *Ubeshi*

Owing to continuous incursions by *wabeshi*, the WDM area has jokingly been termed *shamba la bibi* (lit: grandmother's farm), referring to the relative freedom of entry that the *wabeshi* enjoy. Usage of this term mocks its derivation from a term coined during German colonial rule when Kaiser Wilhelm II gave the Selous Game Reserve to his wife; later, under British colonial rule, the term referred to forest and wildlife reserves preserved in the name of the Queen of England. Today, however, it is used to refer to 'harvesting at no cost' or 'harvesting where one has not sown'.

WDM has employed several strategies to address *ubeshi*, usually involving the police at Maganzo and at regional headquarters in Shinyanga. WDM's contracted security company in the first instance handles incursions, apprehending ubeshi work teams, but this is hampered by collusive practices. In some cases *wabeshi* have fought violently against arrest causing injury to the guards on duty. More recently, the WDM management has instituted unexpected changes in the guards' work shifts, which has led to *wabeshi* being more likely to get caught and arrested. In mid-2007, a troupe of almost 100 *wabeshi* entered the WDL and could not be controlled until the WDM management called in the police force. About 60 were seized and sent to Maganzo police station.[24]

Negotiations between WDM and the *wabeshi* were inordinately compounded by the fact that there was little basis for distinguishing the local community from the *wabeshi*. They were largely one and the same. Even though WDM had initiated an *ujirani mwema* (good neighbourhood) policy in consultation with the Maganzo community, to serve as a forum to iron out differences and for extending company social responsibility to the neighbouring communities, the policy was undermined by a lack of trust on both sides. Nonetheless WDM supported a number of community projects in the surrounding communities.

In 2006, De Beers, who owned the majority share of WDM, initiated the Mwadui Diamond Partnership Project (MCDP), designed to be the model for accelerating socioeconomic development and alleviating poverty around the mine through the development of a multi-stakeholder approach. To facilitate the implementation of the project, De Beers provided seed money for an in-depth appraisal of the artisanal diamond-mining activities and the socioeconomic setting of the communities around the mine. A diagnostic study was conducted between August and December 2006. The MCDP studies identified various strategies to assist the nine surrounding artisanal mining settlements through participatory engagement with the people. In addition, the study identified potential livelihood activities that could be developed and social programmes that could be supported in the area (Mutagwaba *et al.* 2006).

In collaboration with WDM, the MCDP study identified blocks within the WDM lease area that could be made available for training diggers in improved methods of mining (Mutagwaba *et al.* 2006). The project was expected, in its initial pilot phase, to take three years after which individual groups of miners would have attained sufficient expertise to run their own small-scale diamond mining enterprises. If the pilot was successful, the project was intended to be extended to areas outside the WDM lease and encompass areas in other private mining company leases (Mutagwaba *et al.* 2006; ECA 2008). A building was set aside for use as a training centre for the project, and efforts were planned to ensure fair diamond prices for artisanal miners.

Potential scenarios for co-existence through benefit-sharing and support system modalities were intensively discussed, but before they could be implemented De Beers sold WDM to Petra Diamonds in 2008. Petra Diamonds has not committed itself to implementing the MCDP recommendations. Maganzo miners, whose hopes had been raised during the 2006 planning activities, expressed disillusionment during my 2010 follow-up visit.[25]

The 2006 diagnostic study[26] had singled out several key community needs in the Mwadui area, namely: better access to land, fair diamond markets and prices, technology, knowledge regarding the diamond business, health, safety and environmental management and related issues. The MCDP interviews revealed i) local people's belief that the diamond potential of the area was high and ii) their hope that they could gain employment and direct access to markets to improve their livelihoods. However, the fact that about 75 per cent of the population around the WDM, especially in Maganzo were directly dependent on artisanal mining meant that many acknowledged that such beliefs and hopes had to be moderated by the reality of numbers. A concept of delimitation crept into the discussions, in the form of 'identifying eligible miners' to be included in the project area, alongside WDM's aims to alter the mindset of the people. Given their history of contested interaction with the mine, many were well aware of the need for an institutional framework, which could be used as mutually agreed parameters for the sustainable co-existence between artisanal and large-scale mining (Semboja *et al.* 2006). However, delicate questions about mineral resource governance and equity remained unanswered, while the oft assumed 'cure' through social responsibility measures to quell social unrest in the mineral-rich areas in and around Maganzo and WDM has yet to materialize. These issues simmer on, mired in an uneasy sense of ambiguity involving both distrust and hope for a better future (Lahiri-Dutt 2006). Meanwhile *ubeshi* continues to prevail.

Conclusion

Drawing on Ribot and Peluso's (2003: 173) analysis of how certain social and political-economic contexts shape people's ability to draw on 'bundles of power', this chapter illustrates how artisanal miners around the WDM navigate their access to diamonds in a situation of deepening legal exclusion from surrounding diamond-bearing areas. For artisanal miners, access to profitable land is one of the most contentious issues, but lack of land ownership is partially compensated by networks of relations that provide informal or illegal access to the land and its mineral resources through the system of *ubeshi*.

This chapter has attempted to trace the chain of agents and mechanisms that facilitate the illegal value chain of diamond production and exchange across the interface between artisanal and large-scale mining. The fluidity with which artisanal miners move in and out of formal and informal spheres of production creates confusion and a disarming sense of normalcy regarding clandestine networks and shadowy practices that transgress several local and formal governance norms. In such situations it has become difficult if not impossible for WDM to control *ubeshi* in its environs.

Patron–client relations between the brokers and dealers who benefit most from the system, and the *tajiri-mbeshi* support system serve to sustain the practice. The *wabeshi* who scoop up the diamonds from the WDM tailings receive the lowest financial returns but take the greatest risks in terms of being arrested and occasionally seriously injured in skirmishes with security guards.

Ultimately, *ubeshi* exemplifies the co-existence of different perceptions and discourses about mineral governance that are woven between the government, the corporate world, and local communities in mineral rich areas. The distribution of mining profits are not always what they seem, just as the boundaries between legality and illegality are difficult to decipher when trying to discern the agency of everyone involved *ubeshi* in Maganzo.

Notes

1   *Ubeshi* derives from the Sukuma language, denoting the activity, process or system of conducting *ubeshi*. *Mbeshi* (pl. *wabeshi*) refers to the practitioner/s of *ubeshi*.
2   Interview with a mining surveyor at Tan Discoveries, a company involved in a government-led initiative to provide miners with affordable equipment on credit, 5 January 2012.
3   Williamsons Diamond Mine is the world's largest economic kimberlite mine by surface area: 146 hectares. http: petradiamonds.com (accessed 9 January 2012). Of the roughly 60 diamondiferous kimberlite pipes in Tanzania, approximately half are located in and around the WDM (Mutagwaba *et al.* 1997). WDM mine was taken over by Petra Diamonds in 2008.
4   Personal communication, Chief Lifa Shekha, Mwadui-Utemini, August 2006. This building was nationalized after independence and is used to house local government officers.
5   A local board game played with markers on a grid of two or four rows.
6   There are different local versions of the story of Williamson's diamond discovery breakthrough. Another claims that a large piece of ilmenite found in a trench dug by the Geological Survey of Tanganyika team was brought to Williamson from the village of Luhumbo (Knight and Stevenson 1986).
7   Personal communication, Chief Lifa Shekha, Mwadui-Utemini, August, 2006
    8   Mining Lease No. 224 under New Alamasi (1963) Ltd, a wholly owned subsidiary of WDM.
9   Government Notice No. 528 published in the *Official Gazette* (3 December 2004) designated a 1400 km2 block in the southern part of the WDM licence as an exclusive area for primary licences.
10   Interview with WDM officials, 1 September 2006.
11   Records of *Kamati ya Wachimbaji Wadogo*, Kishapu, obtained from the Chairperson, 1 June 2007.
12   These included: Ibadakuli, Kolandoto, Mwadui and Songwa wards of Kishapu District.
13   '*Hata wengine walioomba maneneo ya kuchimba kwenye maeneo yao ya asili hawak-*

ufanikiwa, hivyo watu wanaendelea na ubeshi'. Translated: 'Even people who asked for plots in their places of origin did not receive them'. They see this state of affairs as a justification for continuing to practice *ubeshi*.

14 Consultations with former Mwadui Mine employees when under STAMICO, 1 March 2010.

15 The New Alamasi mine area is 3,007 acres in size.

16 The Mwadui Community Development programme study (2006) remains unpublished to the present.

17 This experience is used by local people to emphasize the significance of women's involvement in *ubeshi*.

18 Translated: 'rail car' given the block appearance and cramped nature of the accommodation.

19 The author observed the daring with which the sponsors monitor their 'haul' during a visit to Idukilo village (September 2006). A work team of *wabeshi* were observed sitting, waiting for the sponsor to arrive. After a few minutes, a 4-wheel drive dark blue vehicle came speeding into the village, followed by a brief verbal exchange between the sponsor and the team. The team then burst into jubilation indicating a successful diamond haul.

20 *Kupiga buti* literally means to kick a person with a strong boot, graphically indicating the significance of double-crossing the sponsor by selling diamonds behind his back.

21 Maganzo Ward Executive Officer records, August 2006.

22 Local Village Government member, Idukilo village, Kishapu District, 2006.

23 Authors' interviews with *wabeshi* informants, 1 September 2006.

24 Personal observation during fieldwork for Mwadui Community Development Project (MCDP), Maganzo Shinyanga, June 2007.

25 One of the artisanal mining leaders who wanted the good-neighbourhood initiative to be revived stated: '*Tulijua mnatudanganya*' (we knew that you [the MCDP] were deceiving us) referring to the mismatch between the promising engagement of the MCDP at the time it was implemented and its subsequent outcome (Personal communication with Mzee S. Maganzo, 22 May 2010).

26 The MCDP appraisal aimed at tracing efforts to support artisanal and large-scale diamond-mining relied on insights from Lahiri-Dutt's (2006) research on mining in India.

References

Bebbington, A., Hinojosa, L., Humphreys, D., Bebbington, A., Burneo, M.L. and Warnaars, S. (2010) 'Contention and ambiguity: Mining and the possibilities of development'. *Development and Change* 39(6): 887–914.

Chachage, C. S. (1995) 'The meek shall inherit the earth but not the mining rights: The mining industry and accumulation in Tanzania'. in Gibbon, P. (ed.) *Liberalised Development in Tanzania*. Uppsala, Sweden: Nordiska Afrikainstitutet. pp. 37–108.

Curtis, M. and Lissu, T. (2008) 'A golden opportunity? How Tanzania is failing to benefit from gold mining'. Dar es Salaam: Christian Council of Tanzania (CCT), National Council of Muslims in Tanzania (BAKWATA) and Tanzania Episcopal Conference.

Duffy, R. (2005) 'Global environmental governance and the challenge of shadow states: The impact of illicit sapphire mining in Madagascar'. *Development and Change* 36(5): 825–43.

European Commission for Africa (ECA) (2008) 'Promoting mineral clusters: The case of Tanzania'. Brussels: European Commission for Africa.

Epstein, E.J. (1982) *The Diamond Invention*. London: Hutchinson and Co.

Fisher, E., Mwaipopo, R., Mutagwaba, W., Nyange, D. and Yaron, G. (2009) 'The ladder that sends us to wealth: Artisanal mining and poverty reduction in Tanzania'. *Resources Policy* 34(1): 15–22.

Hall, A. (2010) 'Tanzania's gold sector: From reform and expansion to conflict?' [Foundation for Environmental Security and Sustainability (FESS) Issue Brief]. Available from www.fess-global.org/Publications/issuebriefs/Tanzanias_Gold_Sector.pdf (accessed 8 January 2012).

Knight, J. and Stevenson, H. (1986) 'The Williamson Diamond Mine, De Beers, and the colonial office: A case-study of the quest for control'. *Journal of Modern African Studies* 24(3): 423–45.

Lahiri-Dutt, K. (2006) '"May God give us chaos, so that we can plunder": A critique of "resource curse" and conflict theories', *Development* 49(3): 14–21.

Lange, S. (2006) 'Benefit streams from mining in Botswana, Namibia, Mali and Tanzania. Lessons from studies conducted in 2005'. Bergen, Norway: Chr Michelsen Institute.

Lange, S. (2008) 'Land tenure and mining in Tanzania'. Bergen, Norway: Chr Michelsen Institute, CMI. Available from http://bora.cmi.no/dspace/bitstream/10202/401/1/Report%20R%202008-2.pdf (accessed 4 December 2011).

Mutagwaba, W., Mwaipopo-Ako, R. and Mlaki, A.L. (1997) 'The impact of technology on poverty alleviation: The case of artisanal mining in Tanzania'. [Research Report 97.2]. Dar es Salaam: Research on Poverty Alleviation.

Mutagwaba, W., Seegers, J. and Mwaipopo, R. (2006) 'Mwadui Community Diamond Partnership project'. Paper presented at the 6th Annual Communities and Small-scale Mining (CASM) Conference, November 11–15, 2006, Antsirabe, Madagascar.

Mwaipopo, R., Mutagwaba, W., Nyange, D. with Fisher, E. (2004) 'Increasing the contribution of artisanal and small-scale mining to poverty reduction in Tanzania: Based on an analysis of mining livelihoods in Misungwi and Geita districts, Mwanza region'. London: DFID.

Mwaipopo, R. (2010) 'The use of critical discourse analysis in understanding claims for legitimacy in marine protected area management at Jibondo Island, Mafia Tanzania: The memoirs of Mzee Popote'. *Utafiti* (Vol 82). University of Dar es Salaam.

Ribot, J.C. and Peluso, N.L. (2003) 'A theory of access'. *Rural Sociology* 68(2): 153–81.

Semboja, H.H., Selejio, O. and Silas, J. (2006) 'Partnership for economic development and poverty reduction: The Mwadui Community Development Partnership in Tanzania'. Available from unglobalcompact.org/NewsAndEvents/event_archives/ghana_2006/MCDP.pdf. (accessed 20 November 2009.

Society for International Development (SID) (2009) 'The extractive resource industry of Tanzania: Status and challenges of the mining sector'. Nairobi: Society for International Development. Kenya. Available from www.sidint.net/docs/TZ_ERI_Report.pdf. (accessed 9 January 2012)

Tanzania Chamber of Mines (TCM) (2002) 'Relationship between small and large-scale mining in Tanzania'. Paper presented at the Miners' Workshop, Tanga, 13 October, 2002. Newsletter 19, Tanzania Chamber of Mines, October 2002.

Tanzania, United Republic of (1997) *The Mining Policy* [Ministry of Energy and Minerals]. Dar es Salaam: Government Printer.

Tanzania, United Republic of (1998) *The Mining Act* [Ministry of Energy and Minerals]. Dar es Salaam: Government Printer.

Tanzania, United Republic of (2010) *The Mining Act* [Special Bill Supplement of 10 April, 2010]. Dar es Salaam: Government Printer.

Part III

What future for artisanal mining?

11 Artisanal mining's democratizing directions and deviations

Deborah Fahy Bryceson and Eleanor Fisher

Artisanal miners tend to be portrayed in the literature and media as 'rough diamonds', people who work and play hard and are likely to cross the boundaries of appropriate behaviour through pursuit of wealth and flamboyant living, often at the cost of local environmental damage. An alternative image is of marginalized labourers, driven by poverty to toil in harsh conditions, pursuing mining livelihoods in the face of national governments' and large-scale mining companies' subversion of their land and mineral rights. Both views reflect partial realities, but are inclined to exaggerate the position of miners as mischief-making rogues or downtrodden victims. Through documentation of the multifaceted nature of Tanzanian artisanal miners' work and home lives during the country's ongoing economic mineralization, we have endeavoured to convey a balanced rendering of their aspirations, occupational identity and social ties. Our emphasis has been on their working lives as artisans, the ways they contend with occupational risk, their social interaction and the influence of government policy and large-scale mining interests on their mining pursuits.

Against charges of artisanal miners as adventurers transgressing the boundaries of acceptable society, we are suggesting that artisanal miners may be injecting a new sense of distributive justice and democracy. Rather than corrupting the social order, or continually being trounced by state and corporate mining interests, they have the potential to uplift their local communities and stimulate democratic principles. But this will not always be the case.

Our conclusion explores both the positive and negative sides of artisanal miners' transformative role in mineralization, asking when and why democratic tendencies thrive as opposed to where autocratic tendencies are likely to come to the fore. We defined democratization in Chapter 1 as a process of occupational and residential community formation around the principles of freedom of movement, egalitarian opportunity and local self-governance. The following analysis outlines the intricate interconnections between economic, political and social change embedded in Tanzanian artisanal mining's occupational formation, and then relates it to other parts of mining Africa through the construction of a typology of African mining complexes.

Reconfiguring social order

There is abundant evidence that Tanzanian society and culture are being realigned in the process of mineralization. We have argued that hundreds of thousands of artisanal miners and mining settlement residents are swaying this process towards more egalitarian distribution of the country's mineral wealth. Democratizing tendencies are embedded in the evolution of artisanal mining organizational structures and lifestyles, which contrast sharply with rural communities in the surrounding countryside. The democratic influence challenges autocratic tendencies of rural gerontocracy at the local level and may forestall inequities of resource wealth distribution arising from the conflicting interests of large-scale mining's profit-seeking and state revenue generation and value transfers at the national level (Moody 2007; Campbell 2009; Cooksey 2011). The democratizing tendency is composed of several interwoven paths traced below.

Egalitarian frontier entry

Collier and Venables (2008a) note that Africa's enormous surface area and relatively unexplored geological resources represent a vast potential reserve of wealth. In the case of Tanzania, its mineral wealth remained largely untapped until recently. Now it exists as mineral frontier below ground posing a great unknown with respect to the magnitude of wealth it harbours. Above ground most of the frontier is already utilized for cultivation, grazing, hunting, wildlife, forestry or settlement, making it liable to conflicts of interest between existing users and incoming men and women bent on establishing a new social order centred on mineral extraction. Thus, quandaries over artisanal miners' quest for extractable deposits in the face of the unknown location of mineral wealth, its layered depth and the interests embedded in other forms of surface land use abound.

As autotelic producers, artisanal miners are breaking new ground, pioneering uncharted work lives, experimenting with novel lifestyles and forming urbanizing communities in a frontier economy. Their self-making is manifested at the outset in the migrant's individual ambition, willingness to engage in arduous labour and can-do versatility to take on demanding tasks and harsh living conditions with the aim of economic gain. Most of the men and women living in Tanzania's mining settlements have migrated from rural backgrounds to the mining frontier. There they enter a multi-ethnic, cosmopolitan experience removed from the pressures of an ascriptive age and gender hierarchy (Chapter 2). Distanced from rural elders' regulation of marriage and brideprice payments, sexual relations and marriage are casualized with decision-making regarding sexual relations exercised by women as well as men (Chapter 4).

Social hierarchies that previously ordained rank and privilege are being levelled and replaced with market relations. People are scrambling for economic profit and status in the reconfiguring social order. Gold mining is a relatively open entry activity. Diggers do not require a large amount of starting capital. They are advanced their subsistence by the claim owners, pit holders or mineral buyers in lieu of future produce (Chapters 2, 3 and 7).

Labour flexibility arises from the changing composition of work teams digging, blasting and hoisting the hard rock from the pit. Temporary work shifts are formed for a limited duration of up to approximately four weeks (Chapter 7). Apart from the claim owner who usually remains aloof from pit production, there is a lack of outward social differentiation amongst miners at the pit site. Miners espouse a sense of camaraderie that relates in part to the fact that they are exposed to physical danger in the pit and recognize the need for cooperation to ensure survival.

Although the pit holders act as 'bosses' directing digging operations, a spirit of teamwork is generated by the fact that everyone is vulnerable to ever-changing mining fortunes. Pit holders may join the ranks of diggers if and when their resources to finance digging operations contract. Maintaining good relations with other miners is vital to the smooth operation of digging shifts, inclusion in future shifts and mutual assistance in times of need.

A sense of artisanal pride can arise from the demonstrated skill and material output from pit work (Chapter 1). Miners are only too aware of the occupational hazards that threaten life and limb, and the need for developing effective production techniques to find and excavate minerals. The extent of their success is reflected in mineral strikes and good hauls of mineral-bearing ore.

Pit power politics

Becoming and being a miner is a process of proving oneself to one's colleagues, demonstrating that one is skilled, hardworking, disciplined, trustworthy, and cooperative. Occupationality is of the essence. Professionalism and collegial ties, in addition to the luck of finding minerals form a major part of one's success in mining. Beyond succeeding within a shift and movement between shifts, miners' interact and network to exchange information about new strike sites, prices of minerals and business opportunities in general. Collegial ties foster a democratic interplay reflected in a sense of collective endeavour, fairness and egalitarianism.

Family and patron–client relations are likely to be less pronounced than those pervading agrarian settlements because miners are judged on their group cooperation and work performance in the pit rather than who they are related to or know. Claim owners, on the other hand, frequently ask trusted family member to supervise their investments when they are away from the pit site. Also, it is at the claim-owning level that Tanzania's educational hierarchy is evident. Claim owners tend to be white-collar, relatively educated people who have social access to official government circles at local, regional and sometimes national levels. In this way, they are the first to hear of claim availability and have the 'know how' and political connections to formalize the claim (Chachage 1995; Cooksey 2011).

Given that titled claim owners are largely tangential to the actual mining production process, it is ironic that they are considered the only artisanal miners with defensible legal mining rights under Tanzanian law. This state of affairs ignores complex labour relations and access to mineral resources provided by an informal system of 'sub-contracting' pits by claim owners to pit holders in return for a percentage of the ore that is produced or proceeds from its sale (Chachage 1995; Fisher 2008). This reality generates a tension between the *de jure* 'titled miners' and the *de facto* 'pit holders' who are physically engaged in mineral production and shoulder most of the financial risk in mining operations (Chapter 5).[1]

Although men in possession of a private mining licence may engage in mining labour, particularly when their exploitation of a claim is not successful, the widespread practice of sub-contracting means that the claim owner is the outlier who does not participate in artisanal mining's democratic tendencies, pointing to the fundamentally skewed nature of Tanzanian law with respect to artisanal mining. Official artisanal miners (i.e. with a private mining licence) are typically not 'real' artisanal miners, in terms of engaging in mining labour as discussed in Chapter 3 and 5. Constituting a tiny minority of the artisanal mining population, with a mere 3,932 people owning private mining licences in 2010 (Tanzania, Ministry of Energy and Minerals 2010), claim owners are an anomalous category. They form part of Tanzania's entrepreneurial capitalist class, lodged between the state and the 'real' miners with 'hand, head and heart 'engagement in the artisanal mining sector.

Thus, 'at the rim' of the pit, relations between the claim owner and pit holder may be tense, whereas in the pit amongst pit holders and diggers, relations tend to have a collaborative 'we are all in this together' quality, by virtue of the physical and financial hazards of mining. Digging teams endeavour to succeed collectively. Every miner knows that very broad collegial ties are necessary to ensure a steady stream of work and to help smooth the boom and bust pattern of mining. Friends to lean on are essential for long-term economic survival in mining.

In this regard, sharing good times, especially after a mineral strike, forms an important part of group bonding. Miners have a reputation for heavy drinking. They congregate at bars in the evenings (Chapter 4). On the occasion of a mineral strike, striking miners may treat their mining colleagues to lavish largesse, with a continuous flow of drinks, accentuated by expenditure on foreign beer, sometimes demonstratively displayed by piling crates of beer to heights beyond head level, a phallic representation of prowess. A performative show of generosity follows with everyone invited to drink with gusto. Alternatively, the lucky host might occasionally treat all his friends to a stay in the best hotel in town or indeed in the nearest city to create a memorable occasion for social bonding.[2]

At the level of the individual, however, ostentatious displays of acquired wealth are frowned upon. A miner who manages to accumulate large sums of money is most likely to use it for building a house, but rarely in the mining settlement, where the house would be a permanent landmark testifying to his success. Instead he generally chooses to build somewhere distant, be it in his home area, a nearby market town or the regional capital, where his wealth accumulation will go unnoticed by his colleagues. Such habits preserve a sense of community egalitarianism as well as representing good economic foresight since no one knows if the mineral wealth of the mining site will persist. Interestingly, gold and diamond buyers are the exception to this general behavioural pattern, since they need to demonstrate affluence in order to attract local miners to them. The success of their business depends on continuously residing at the site of production, as exemplified by the existence of a highly affluent enclave of diamond merchants in Maganzo in Tanzania's northwestern Shinyanga region.

Democratic trends in local governance

With an absence of governmental authority at fresh strike sites, and a quite minimalist presence at many more mature sites due to the remoteness of most mining sites, miners have developed a strong tradition of relatively autonomous self-governance. Apart from claim owners, who are more likely to have direct contact with government officials, many miners are unaware of the Tanzanian legislation governing artisanal mining.

In any case, Tanzanian officialdom is erratic in its implementation of the law as illustrated by the case study of mining rights in Mgusu, Geita region where regional authorities turned a blind eye to the existence of artisanal mining in a forest reserve and the irregularities of local claim ownership (Chapter 5). At national level, on the other hand, pro-artisanal mining legislation, intended to reserve areas for artisanal production, has been barely implemented, in effect reneging on promises to increase artisanal miners' mining opportunities.

There are several reasons for the deficiencies of policy implementation. The Ministry of Minerals and Energy is centralized at national level in Dar es Salaam, very distant from the ring of gold and scores of other gold, diamond and gemstone mining sites and hence not readily at hand to govern (Bryceson *et al.* 2012). The eight Zonal Mining Officers in charge of Tanzania's vast mining terrain do not have coordinated links with other line ministries. Artisanal mining only accrues small revenues for central government relative to large-scale mining and therefore tends to be ignored. Thus, at local and regional levels, lack of government personnel on the ground and light-touch policy-enforcement in the regions generally gives artisanal miners the opportunity to occupy promising mining areas (Jønsson and Fold 2011).

Under these circumstances, artisanal miners gravitate towards self-governnce of an informal nature at mineral rush sites. Under Nyerere's leadership, soon after national independence, the election of village chairpeople assisted by committee members replaced tribal chiefs' local governance. Artisanal miners have adopted and adapted this institutionalized structure to their needs at rush sites. Miners from the initial migrant cohort are likely to be the first to be elected and may continue to dominate both elected and appointed leadership positions. Various committees are formed, usually on a voluntary basis, to oversee health and safety, the environment, security and tax collection. When a system of tax collection is not already in place, the local leadership at rush sites is likely to start taxing the many on-site businesses. Although the mining settlement leadership is usually not officially recognized, expediency leads Zonal Mining Officers to gravitate towards them for local negotiations and problem solving in the settlement.

Despite democratic election or some other selection procedure involving group approval, it is not uncommon for the mining population to exercise votes of no confidence on the part of the mining rank and file, prompted by dissatisfaction with the leadership's performance. These dismissals are often colourful, reflecting the emphatic rejection of the leader on the part of the mining community. At Londoni mine rush site in Singida region, for example, the population felt that the settlement's leadership was becoming increasingly undemocratic and callous. Their demise followed an incident in which a miner was accused of stealing gold-bearing gravel. He was arrested, locked up, severely beaten and died in custody during the night. News of this catalyzed miners to demonstrate and riot against the leadership's thuggery. The leadership fled; the chairman fearing for his life escaped, disguised as a veiled Muslim woman. The secretary, who was identified as the person who physically beat the victim causing his death, was imprisoned.

In the gold rush site of Ikuzi in Shinyanga region, residents became increasingly frustrated with the leadership's practice of charging money to resolve disputes. When a miner was killed, attempting to steal gold-bearing ore by entering a tunnel immediately after a blast, the miners blamed the leadership for his death. At the same time, the Ikuzi artisanal miners' cooperative, formed in the nearby pre-existing agricultural village of Ikuzi, had been gaining in strength and legitimacy. Seizing the opportunity, they replaced the discredited mining camp leadership.

In general, the mining settlement leadership is expected to be instrumental in facilitating the adequacy of the market response to the settlement's basic needs for supplies of water, food, wood for building the mine shafts and mining inputs. After a mineral discovery, entrepreneurial migrants and nearby villagers are quickly on hand to sell provisions as well as luxuries, attracted by the miners' superior purchasing power relative to rural dwellers in the surrounding countryside. In most cases, villagers receive much needed cash income by selling foodstuffs to the miners and some young village men gain lucrative incomes by becoming miners.

However, relations between the mining settlement and nearby village/s are a delicate matter that the leadership have to monitor. Mining settlements' utilization of raw material supplies is problematic. Villagers are naturally upset about the miners' deforestation and pollution of nearby water supplies. These issues are dealt with through: i) negotiated bargaining to effect the exchange of goods and services of mutual benefit, ii) money transfers to villagers or iii) bribes to village leaders.

The balance of power in the mining settlement tends to be weighted towards charismatic miners as opposed to officials from the over-stretched formal regional governance structure. Still less influence is exerted by 'Dar es Salaam', the distant national headquarters of the Ministry of Energy and Minerals. It is therefore no surprise that there is a large divergence between government laws, policy and actual practice.

When artisanal miners clash with large-scale mining interests, miners act collectively to defend their interests in legal and extra-legal ways (Chapter 5, 9 and 10). As relatively large population concentrations exist in many mine sites, their numbers can be strategic in swaying decisions regarding mining company investment.[3] However miners' occupational solidarity is put to the test when companies employ divide and rule tactics to drive a wedge between them and local residents (Lange and Kolstad).

In the case of government evictions, the leadership, supported by the settlement's most influential miners, usually takes the lead. Daily incursions against large scale mines, such as *ubeshi* (Chapter 10), tend to involve the participation of individual miners rather than general community involvement and may be part of criminalized networks, arranged and sponsored by diamond merchants, rather than artisanal miners or their leadership. These practices have led to violent confrontation with large-scale mining companies, in some instances reflecting a form of social protest, although in other localities they constitute organized theft that cannot be equated with artisanal mining.[4]

Miners also collectively act in politically astute ways to further their interests in less confrontational settings. They are known to opportunistically use party politics to gain amenities or favourable decisions on mining rights especially during national election campaigns (Chapter 7).

Social contradictions and diversions

While pointing to democratic tendencies in Tanzania's artisanal mining settlements, it should not be assumed that artisanal mining is intrinsically democratic nor that the Tanzanian context is essentially more democratic than other countries in Sub-Saharan Africa. Rather we are arguing that intricate amalgams of social, economic and political influences within and surrounding Tanzanian artisanal mining settlements serve to foster democratic tendencies at the local level with reverberations for regional and national levels (Chapter 1). However, we would be the first to admit that there is no iron-clad certainty about this direction. Several foreseen and unforeseen circumstances are capable of redirecting or thwarting democratic tendencies. These include technological constraints, political and economic pressures diverting the course of artisanal mining away from its egalitarian leanings, and displacement of artisanal miners' mineral access to make way for large-scale mining, as discussed in the following.

Resource curse undermining democracy?

There is a voluminous literature on the resource curse in Africa and worldwide (Le Billon 2001; Bannon and Collier 2003; Weszkalnys 2011; Hujo 2012). One of its central tenets is that mineral wealth, in the hands of poorly governed states, provides the means for states to circumvent dependency on taxation from its citizenry, allowing them to bypass responsiveness to their electorate. These outcomes are premised on the state's role in granting mining concessions to large-scale mining companies, a process that is assumed to set in train the displacement of democratic processes and increasing state autocracy with respect to the distribution of the nation's resource wealth.

Economists argue that mineral booms have short-term positive effects but long-term negative implications. When there are insufficient institutional safeguards to avert a bonanza atmosphere, private and public consumption escalate (Collier and Goderis 2007; Humphreys *et al.* 2007). The country's exchange rate becomes over-valued with an escalation of imports likely to ensue leading to 'Dutch disease', a syndrome in which the non-mineral-producing sectors of the national economy become uncompetitive. Shrinking employment and the maldistribution of incomes and revenues from mineral production usually follow, with the net effect of a widening gap between haves and have-nots (Auty 1993; Karl 1997; Mkandawire and Soludo 1999).

Political scientists are less interested in the mechanisms of the resource curse and instead stress the shortfalls of state decision-making and management. They are concerned with possible leanings towards authoritarianism as well as tensions linked to the concentration of mineral wealth in specific areas of a country capable of causing regional economic imbalances (Ross 1999; Rosser 2006; Haber and Menaldo 2010; Dode 2011). Despite its detractors (Brunnschweiler and Bulte 2006), the resource curse thesis remains influential in discussions on governance and violent conflict in Africa (Bannon and Collier 2003; Watts 2004; Le Billon 2001) and how neo-liberal techniques of governance are linked to political order and disorder across the African continent (Ferguson 2006; Reno 2004).

Luong and Weinthal (2006) argue that the experience of resource curse rests heavily on the specific form of mine ownership, asserting that domestic private ownership is less liable to a resource curse predicament than domestic public or foreign private ownership. What is overlooked in their argument and indeed in the resource curse literature generally is that mining can be artisanal as well as large-scale. Accepting Luong and Weinthal's assumption that domestic private ownership is more beneficial to the country's population, given greater decentralized accessibility to mineral management and the population's direct gains from mineral production, and then adding the fact that artisanal mining involves employment for far more of the national population than large-scale mining, the democratic participation quotient could rise by a very large margin, challenging the applicability of the resource curse thesis to artisanal mining.

Resource materiality and the social imaginary of migrants seeking mineral wealth

Literature on the materiality of natural resources has proliferated during the recent global commodity boom (Bakker and Bridge 2006; Reyna and Behrend 2008; Bridge 2009; Weszkalnys 2013). Richardson and Weszkalnys (forthcoming) associate resource materiality with forms of sociality connected with people's exploration and extraction of resources, and the continually altering potentiality of the resource in terms of people's abstraction, signification and valuation of natural resources as physical substances, ultimately influencing their expectations of access to natural resource wealth. In the case of Tanzanian mineralization, producers, traders, consumers, as well as citizens and residents more generally have an interest in what extracted and commodified minerals hold in store for them.

The materiality of minerals is conditioned by their illusive physical availability and their non-renewable nature once extracted. As miners experience Sennett's (2008) process of 'becoming and being artisans', mineral wealth's creation is being reflexively achieved through miners' discovery, excavation and processing of natural sediments and hard rock into mineral commodities. The agency of artisanal miners transforming natural rock into a commodity destined for an international value circuit is situated within the specific historical and political context of a Tanzanian mineral boom, spurred by favourable international prices.[5]

Appadurai's (1996) work on the 'social imaginary' refers to transnational migrants' acute awareness of cultural relativity and their consequent creative construction and mobilization of differences to generate a new collective cultural identity. Similarly Bryceson and Vuorela (2002) refer to a process of 'relativising' in the process of selectively forming a sense of a transnational family that spans national borders. Both terms signify migrants' exercise of social imagination to generate a sense of social belonging following social dislocation.

Artisanal miners generally have not crossed international boundaries but the sense of dislocation is similar to transnational migrants. At the outset, their displacement is two-fold as they arrive in a new place and embark on a new occupation. Stimulated by a combined sense of social vacuity and economic opportunity, they find that they share a commonality of purpose; all are seeking to economically benefit from mining. Their reflexive construction of an artisanal mining sub-culture reflects their mutuality of interests. In neo-liberal Tanzania, the discovery of high value minerals and the ensuing mineral rushes testify to the power of the imaginary as a motivating force for economic, political and social value transformation. Mass migration to the country's precious mineral sites has been triggered by artisanal mining migrants' belief that they will succeed in prospecting and extracting minerals that will bring enrichment, despite many never having previously experienced living and working in a mining community.[6]

Over time, this belief is tempered by experience of the real probabilities and risks involved in mining, the exceptionally hard work it entails and the market practices and price fluctuations that can undermine the miner's earnings. Nonetheless, even at the stage of greater awareness of the pitfalls, an imaginary of 'anyone can get rich', may continue to prevail because it is observed that some do succeed.

As the naïve egalitarian hope that all migrants can enrich themselves recedes, it is replaced by a 'frontier democracy of the deserving' social imaginary, in which it is assumed that 'real miners' with the artisanal skill, work commitment and *de facto* or, in fewer instances, *de jure* access to mineral-rich land will gain their 'just deserts'. It is at this stage that artisanal mining comes into its own, with collegial appreciation of evolving craftsmanship (Sennett 2008). It is also the case that in gold mining communities, where the largest number of artisanal miners are concentrated, extremely poor men and women may secure more regular and higher income through mine-related work and services than they might otherwise gain from employment in other rural activities (Fisher *et al.* 2009).

Poverty dynamics and wealth creation

In the 1990s amidst rapid expansion of artisanal mining across the continent and international donor and national government formulated policies to encourage foreign direct investment, a number of high profile studies drew the socioeconomic, health and environmental problems of artisanal mining to international attention (e.g. ILO 1999; Hentschel *et al.* 2002). These studies fed into a dominant discourse on 'artisanal and small-scale mining' being a 'poverty driven' activity. All too often artisanal miners have been portrayed as caught in a 'vicious cycle of poverty' or 'poverty trap' (Barry 1996; Hilson 2009, 2012; Labonne 2002; Sinding 2005; UNECA 2003; World Bank 2005). While such discourses may play an important role in focusing policy attention on artisanal mining, there is a growing body of evidence, including the data on miners' lives and livelihoods presented in chapters of this volume, which suggests the need to interrogate simplistic assumptions about the processes that drive people to enter artisanal mining or to stay within the occupation.

Certainly in the case of Tanzania, a close correlation between artisanal mining and poverty should not be assumed for all artisanal settings. There are several interlinked processes of both wealth creation and impoverishment taking place between artisanal miners and mineral brokers. As the number of artisanal mine rush sites diminish over time, competition between miners for mining opportunities is likely to generate clear winners and losers. Tracing democratizing tendencies within artisanal mining requires being alert to ever changing circumstances of mineral availability and evolving organizational features of artisanal mining to discern who is benefiting and who is being marginalized.

The dynamics of vulnerability and security as well as inequality and equity are always in flux. In this regard, mounting evidence from different African countries becomes invaluable for drawing out intricate linkages between artisanal mining and agriculture (Hilson and Garforth 2012; Hilson and Van Bockstael 2012; Maconachie 2011; Maconachie and Binns 2007), urbanization (Bryceson *et al.* 2012; Maconachie 2012) and poverty reduction (Fisher *et al.* 2009), which are bound to impact on processes of wealth creation and impoverishment. This suggests the need for evidence on nuanced spatial and longitudinal dynamics that challenge blanket notions of African artisanal mining being linked to a self-perpetuating lack of development (e.g. Noetstaller *et al.* 2004).

Mining rights and wrongs: Democratic or autocratic public policy

Venturing into the myriad of ways that artisanal mining's democratic tendencies can go off course, one must take cognizance of the progression of the artisanal mining cycle, and the fact that as the geological depth of mining approaches technological limits, artisanal miners are often looking for exit options, either moving to a more promising mine site or switching to another form of income-earning, often facilitated by saved earnings from mining.

Access to artisanal mining rights

Tanzania's mining frontier has the force of mass numbers, which imparts democratic potentiality. A recent World Bank study estimated that the country's artisanal mining sector comprised 685,000 people living in settlements in the ring of gold and dotted elsewhere, but the livelihoods of most of them are lodged on metaphorical shifting sands given the paradoxical nature of artisanal mining's legalization.[7] Less than 4,000 of this multitude hold titled private mining licence (PML) claims and only they are officially recognized as 'artisanal miners' (Tanzania, MEM 2010). This is the most fundamental impediment to the democratic trajectory of the masses of Tanzanian artisanal miners. Analysis of their position, however, is complicated by the large gap between the letter of the law and its practice.

In fact, many PMLs are owned by small groups of partners. Most PMLs are lying idle, either because the owner does not have adequate capital to develop the claim; the PML was acquired primarily for speculative purposes; or the PML's mineral content remains unknown. Most critically, the vast majority of artisanal miners are legally liable to eviction at any time because they do not own PMLs. Closing the gap between reality and legality, zonal mining authorities have devised various *de facto* ways of accommodating their presence (Chapter 7). This gives artisanal miners room for manoeuvre, albeit spaces harbouring a great deal of ambiguity and uncertainty.

Collier and Venables (2008a, 2008b) consider the democratic role of the state to be that of regulator of mining rights, tax collector and distributor of mining revenue. In a genuine democracy, the state's custodial rights over mineral wealth are held on behalf of the citizenry who are the collective owners. The state's obligation to regulate mining rights, both the granting of prospecting rights and mining claims for excavation, and the distribution mining revenues, entails impartial, egalitarian conduct of business with the aim of maximizing benefits to the citizenry.

Fairness and impartiality are prickly matters given that mineral endowments are spatially uneven and require different levels of capital investment depending on the depth and scale of extraction. From the outset, hierarchical priorities have been inscribed in the law. The state holds all the mineral rights and arbitrates the granting of mining licences. Mining rights override agricultural user rights to land, so licenced miners are privileged over farmers.

Under the Tanzanian Mining Act of 2010, individual artisanal miners defined as small-scale operators with capital investments under US$ 100,000 are legally allowed to apply for PMLs up to a maximum of 10 hectares. The licence fee costs US$ 6 per hectare with a rent of US$ 6 per year. The artisanal miner is restricted to the ownership of a maximum of 20 PMLs costing US$ 42 per hectare. Thus, an artisanal miner can legally own a full 200 hectares (2 km^2) costing US$ 840 for the seven year duration of the PML. The claim is subject to renewal thereafter.[8] This is an exceptionally reasonable price. The hitch is that artisanal miners rarely hear about the availability of PMLs before the information has already been acquired by private speculators and mining corporations, especially junior companies.

In the recent past, artisanal miners' agitation to be allocated dedicated artisanal blocs of PMLs has occasionally been rewarded in specific areas. The 2010 Mining Act allows government to formally reserve blocs of mining tracts for partition into PMLs, however, by 2013 most of Tanzania was covered with a patchwork of already licenced land for prospecting, monopolized by medium and large-scale mining interests. The legislation has provisions for the relinquishment of such licences if the holders do not live up to their prospecting or exploration responsibilities as specified in the Act. This has not hitherto been enforced; but, at the time of writing, there are indications that the Ministry of Energy and Minerals may be moving towards more active pursuit of such measures. If so, artisanal miners would have an opportunity to expand their operations.[9]

The setting up of blocs of reserved land for artisanal mining, gives licenced small-scale miners the potential opportunity to gain claims speculatively that they would be free to mine until their licence expiry or onward sale of their PML rights to other artisanal miners, junior companies or large-scale mining companies. It is well-known that many PML owners are tempted by the latter. In these cases, the PML claim owner benefits from the sale at the expense of the existing pit holder and diggers who are actually working the claim, as illustrated in the Mgusu case study (Chapter 5; Chachage 1995; Fisher 2008).

Reading the 2010 Mining Act suggests that Tanzanian artisanal miners have an enviable legal position regarding the acquisition of claims, but in practice it is extremely difficult for them to obtain PMLs. Taking this into account, zonal mining authorities have instituted compensating extra-legal arrangements that, in effect, double-book licences on individual claims where the existing legal claim owner, notably junior companies and mining companies, are not working the claim. If and when the original claim owners decide to utilize their claim, the artisanal miners with secondary claims are likely to be evicted promptly. This happens in areas where prospecting and exploration licences are already allocated.

This muddled situation accords with Collier and Venables' (2008a) observation that low state regulation and a 'finders keepers' principle, encourages speculative licence purchase of large tracts of claim holding that are then inefficiently left unutilized, similar to what prevailed in the nineteenth century American 'Wild West'. The ironic twist is that the state, large-scale mining and artisanal miners each seem to benefit, at least in the short run, from this chaotic state through the institution of extra-legal double-booking of claims. The state collects double fees on land claims enhancing their revenue, the artisanal miners are availed claims to work to depths that they are capable of reaching, and the mining companies save money on prospecting their vast tracts of claims by simply watching where the artisanal miners concentrate their diggings. They then know where to invest their capital and start mechanized mining when the artisanal miners' licence expires or they hit a depth at which they can no longer proceed with their tools and low-powered water pumps. Of course matters do not always work out so conveniently. The 'real miners' namely the pit holders and diggers, may come to deeply resent the arrival of large-scale mining interests intent on taking over and fiercely retaliate because their interests are not synonymous with that of the claim owner. After all, they lose their livelihood while the 'artisanal' claim owner benefits from the sale of the PML.

After the mineral rush stage, the principle of 'finders keepers' becomes increasingly challenged by legal entitlement. As the availability of minerals diminishes and mining depths descend, the state, anticipating the mining revenues that they could gain from different categories of miners, is likely to privilege junior companies and mining companies over artisanal miners in the purchase of claims, despite legislation drafted in the spirit of fairness and equitable access (Chapter 9; Curtis and Lissu 2008; Lissu 2008; Cooksey 2011). It is debatable whether this is technological realism or if, with more effort, some licenced artisanal miners could extend their capitalization and literally 'dig deeper'. In either case, mechanization and job loss is inevitable for large numbers of artisanal miners over the medium and long term.

Ethical trade

How ethical trade initiatives enter African artisanal mining has the potential to exacerbate rather than moderate the long-term tendency towards marginalization of unlicenced artisanal miners if they only favour the trading position of licenced PML owners, as is currently the position of the Fairtrade and Fairmined gold certification scheme discussed in Chapter 8. The potential for new forms of social economy to emerge for the benefit of artisanal miners may be lost in a normative alignment with existing policy prescriptions. Under the guise of good intentions, conflicts of interest and unequal power relations can be obscured by a language of liberal consensus (Bracking 2009).

The forthcoming implementation of the Minamata Convention,[10] which is intended to internationally ban the use of mercury in mining, will pose a major constraint on artisanal gold production. In the short term, the ban will criminalize thousands of artisanal miners, who are unaware of alternative gold extractive methods. For these miners, the ban will increase the gap between themselves and Tanzania's formal mining sector, and push them further outside the formal economy. In the longer run, and in view of the health interests of the mining and general population, the ban hopefully could facilitate a shift to cleaner production methods.

At this stage, the democratic character of artisanal mining is facing mounting challenges. New market-oriented initiatives, intended to benefit marginalized producers, may unintentionally reinforce rather than counter-balance these challenges. The mining frontier is fading. Artisanal miners fighting to save their livelihood and mining identity may increasingly resort to *ubeshi*, encroaching on large-scale mining concessions where they hope to gain access to the company's ore and tailings, sometimes risking life and limb in the process of doing so, as documented by Mwaipopo (Chapter 10) at Mwadui diamond mine. Activity, there, tends to be pursued by individuals or small groups. At the Barrick gold mine in North Mara, years of covert entry for tailings has become a protracted collective struggle against the mine, which has veered increasingly towards violent encounters and an escalating casualty list, as described by Bourgouin (Chapter 9).

Public distribution of mineral wealth

Moving to the state's role in democratically distributing revenues derived from mineral wealth, legislation regarding corporate mining taxes, repatriation of profits, collusion between mining companies and government officials are at issue. Royalties and revenues from large-scale mining far exceed that from artisanal mining, tempting the state to forego artisanal miners' egalitarian concerns for equal opportunities in claim distribution and the labour-absorbing employment of hundreds of thousands of self-made miners in favour of revenue maximization.

As large-scale mining displaces artisanal mining, there is one compensation: large-scale mining's payment of royalties and revenues provides potential finance for state subsidies. Ideally, the subsidies would be directed at addressing inequities generated by bias against artisanal mining as well as provisioning the infrastructural and service needs of the national population generally.

The government's Tanzanian Minerals Audit Agency reported receiving US$ 162 million in corporate taxes from Geita gold mine alone over the three years preceding 2013. By contrast it faced rampant revenue loss from non-collection of royalties from small and medium-scale miners engaged in smuggling.[11] Like large-scale mining companies, artisanal miners are liable to payment of four per cent royalties in addition to their PML fees and annual rent. PML fees are collectable but the small number of licenced artisanal miners and enormous number of unlicenced artisanal miners, combined with the low monetary value of their transactions and their varied selling points throughout the country, make it logistically challenging for government revenue collectors.

State management of mining revenues are discussed at length elsewhere in the large-scale mining literature (Campbell 2004; Otto *et al.* 2006; Campbell 2009; Bush 2010; World Bank 2011; Gajigo *et al.* 2012) and – given limited space and our artisanal mining focus – are outside of the scope of this book. Suffice to note that at present royalties earned by the Tanzanian state are low compared to mining company earnings, a state of affairs encouraged by investor-friendly contracts (Lange 2011).

However, as Tanzania has progressed towards an advanced stage of large-scale mining expansion, one matter is worth mentioning that pertains to egalitarianism and mass democracy. Mineral-rich countries, particularly ones with small populations such as Botswana and the Arab Gulf states have invested heavily in improving the living standards of their citizens through the provision of superior infrastructure and welfare measures. This in combination with a shortage of labour in the economy attracts international migrants. Such societies tend to be identified with a two-tier policy whereby citizens have legal entitlements to an array of benefits while immigrants attracted to employment opportunities and higher salaries than in their home areas obtain temporary work permits but labour in inferior work conditions. The outcome is one of inequity and lack of democracy. Tanzania, however, does not face this situation given that public investment based on mineral revenues has not been pronounced and a mass influx of foreign immigrants does not exist. Cross-border miners and service providers, notably from the DRC and Kenya, are occasionally found in the country's mining settlements. However, the problem of a two-tiered citizen and denizen dichotomy challenging democratic principles of state welfare distribution is not an issue given the lack of government-provisioned welfare subsidies derived from mining revenues.

Gender divides and the question of democracy

In contrast to the mutualism and egalitarian orientation of artisanal mining, the gender division of labour within mining communities militates for deep inequalities. Women's access to mineral wealth is more indirect than that of men. The notable exception is a small percentage of women who have gained ownership of formal mineral claims through inheritance following the death of a spouse. Some of these women have accruedwealth and leadership roles in civil society, but they are very exceptional. Other women pan for gold, but virtually no women engage in pit mining. Male miners believe women's presence in a mining pit willbring bad luck. Instead women are usually relegated to the menial casual labour of processing minerals, notably the laborious crushing of ore-bearing rocks,. In doing so, they are exposed to the inhalation of mercury fumes and fine dust.

Are women missing out on mining's democratic dividend in mining settlements? They are deriving direct income from mineral processing through payment for performance of task-based work. This differs from pit miners' more fluctuating earnings, which depend on the uncertainty of mineral discovery. Women's access to male mining income is primarily through the indirect channel of conjugal relational ties with men – be it as wives, girlfriends or lovers (Chapter 4, Bryceson *et al.* 2014). The income that flows from male miners to women has a strong multiplier effect. In turn, women tend to invest their earnings in service sector provisioning, gaining income for themselves and often using it to provide material support for their mining husbands or boyfriends who otherwise depend on erratic earnings from mining. Women's more regularized daily income helps to smooth their male partners' income spikes.

Young single women enjoy freedom of movement similar to men, confirmed by the fact that most women in mining settlements are migrants who have arrived in the settlement under their own volition. However, once women give birth to children, their mobility is greatly reduced, unlike that of male miners whose occupational *modus operandi* is one of frequent movement (Chapters 2 and 4). It is at this point in the male–female relationship that the democracy dividend seriously deteriorates for women. If men leave their female partner and children, there is no certainty that they will be providing financial support to them. Conjugal relationships are highly casualized and thus it is virtually unthinkable for a woman to formally divorce and seek alimony for herself and her children. Unless she finds another miner or some other man willing to contribute to her family's support, she could face hard times given the absence of extended family assistance or recourse to state welfare.

Democratic selection of women for leadership positions within mining settlements is relatively rare. The fact that the earliest arrivals in the mining settlement are men and that there is a tendency for charismatic men to be elected to leadership positions, does not auger well for women's political voice being heard within the settlement. However, it must be noted that women tend to be grossly underrepresented in leadership positions generally at the local level in Tanzania.

Trajectories of change in Sub-Saharan Africa: Interplay of states, artisanal mining and large-scale mining

Chapter 1 reviewed three successive eras of Sub-Saharan African mining over the past century: i) Southern African apartheid-influenced mining; ii) the conflict mineral mining of strife-ridden post-independence countries; and iii) the current era of widespread continental mineralization stimulated by a global mineral commodity boom. Moving back to a continental level of analysis, this section poses the question of how relevant the Tanzanian experience is to understanding continental artisanal mining patterns, then proposes a typology of democratic versus autocratic mining tendencies. In light of the tripartite relationship between the state, large-scale mining and artisanal mining, four African mining complexes are delineated on the basis of the presence or absence of democratizing trends.

The Tanzanian experience: Unique or ubiquitous?

To this point we have argued that democratic tendencies emanate from artisanal miners, be it through their livelihood pursuits and associational ties, or far less likely through the state, in relation to the equitable distribution of mining claims and mining revenues, or some combination of the two. The emergence of Tanzanian mineral frontier and the opening it provides for artisanal miners' creative self-making is certainly not unique. Mineralization is underway in several African countries catalyzing large-scale migration to artisanal mining areas (see Appendices 1.1, 1.2 and 1.3). The perception of cultural difference, the social imaginary associated with mining as a new occupation and the political tensions surrounding mineral access shapes the emergence of a new open-ended but nonetheless identifiable group identity. Wherever an artisanal mining identity is coalescing, it is readily distinguishable from the hierarchical age and gender identities of the agrarian communities in the surrounding countryside.

Artisanal miners, most of whom have migrated from tradition-bound agrarian settlements, represent a mass movement of risk-taking labourers seizing and shaping economic opportunity and social freedom on a relatively equitable footing. They are, however, doing so on the basis of profound personal and group insecurity vis-à-vis the vagaries of the global market and unequal access to mineral rights in the national context. In this sense, they are part of a worldwide precariat (Standing 2009, 2011), working with hopes of the eureka moment, postponing thought of their long-term fate as marginalized miners.

Miners in large-scale mining, by contrast, face far less risk. They receive regular wages and work in a contractually defined hierarchical relationship vis-à-vis their employers. Democratic tendencies, nonetheless, may surface if and when they can form collective unions to further their interests or, less formally, where they assert their will collectively against a mining management on issues of justice.

Moving to the national level, where the processes of democracy are manifested in more indirect ways, there are five main criteria: i) the democratic election of political leaders; ii) legislation and implementation of just principles of the rule of law; iii) commitment to equality of opportunity; iv) the bureaucratic calibre of state officials and their degree of resistance to bribery and corruption; and v) judicious investment decisions over mining revenues for the benefit of the present and future national population.

We argue that the broad outline of mineralizing and democratizing Tanzania is relevant to several other mineralizing countries in Sub-Saharan Africa. However, democratic tendencies are likely to be highly varied. We propose that such differences can be usefully compared by delineating African mining complexes on the basis of the relative institutional dominance of the state, artisanal mining and large-scale corporate mining. The precise form of the complex in any specific country will be intimately influenced by the type and availability of minerals and the stage of the mining cycle from artisanal prospecting, to excavation, diminishing mineral resources and declining economic viability at increasing depths of artisanal production. Despite differences between nation-states, the gradual displacement of artisanal mining by large-scale mining[12] will almost inevitably arise in every country given the non-renewable nature of mineral resources. As this happens, artisanal mining populations are likely to increasingly resort to raiding large-scale mining sites for tailings in the absence of other livelihood options.

The strength and nature of the state as a regulator over artisanal and large-scale mining and the relative presence of artisanal as opposed to large-scale mining are the defining characteristics of the complexes. The nexus between the state, artisanal and large-scale mining can be represented as a triangular relationship with the size and shape of the triangle depicting the relative strength of each of the three realms.

Figure 11.1 diagrammatically depicts the varying nature and degree of control exerted by the nation-state over mining. Triangle (a) represents circumstances in which artisanal and large-scale mining are equally important in terms of output and operations vis-à-vis the regulatory state. This is unlikely anywhere. In the evolution of newly mineralizing states, as exemplified by Tanzania's recent mineralization, the artisanal mining sector coalesced and grew in the 1980s,

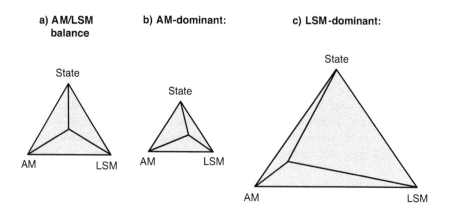

Figure 11.1 State, artisanal (AM) and large-scale mining (LSM) complexes

Source: Authors' depiction

gaining a legitimated presence during the 1990s as the state started sanctioning its existence and attempted to impose some regulatory control over it. This is represented by the small (b) triangle suggestive of the relatively minimal interaction of the coalescing artisanal mining sector with the state prior to the large-scale mining boom.

Over time, as mineral rushes gradually decline in number, artisanal mining's growth slows and output and employment stagnates or contracts. Meanwhile, the large-scale industrial mining sector experiences heavy investment and spatial expansion, compounding the erosion of the artisanal sector, which compensates the loss of mineral rush opportunities with fringe encroachment on the large-scale mining company's stock-piled tailings. As this stage becomes generalized across the country, the dominance of artisanal and large-scale mining is reversed and the relationship between the state and large-scale mining gains dominance, as depicted in triangle (c).

While the relationship between the state and large-scale mining can be two-way with the regulatory force of the state becoming dominant, there is also the possibility of the reverse. This becomes the case if large-scale mining gains influence over state decision-making, through infiltration of the state policy-making process by bribery and corruption of state agents. Furthermore, corruption is not restricted to the state/large-scale axis of the triangle. State officials can also become involved in artisanal mining investments counter to Weberian bureaucratic ethics.

It should be noted that in the Tanzanian case, the state has an egalitarian legacy dating back to the Nyerere period evident in the adoption of populist policy stances to facilitate the poor's basic needs for food security and livelihood (Bryceson 1990; 1997). Nonetheless the long-term material interests of state agents lie in their alignment with large-scale corporate mining, which is a rich source of both public and private accumulation (Curtis and Lissu 2008; Lissu 2008; Cooksey 2011). There are increasing safeguards being instituted to combat corruption in African mining exemplified by the Tanzanian government's recent agreement to be subject to an annual international transparency review (Economic Commission for Africa 2011).[13] Time will tell if they prove to be effective.

Government accountability to the public and judicious utilization of revenues from large-scale mining is vital to a democratic future (Collier and Venables 2008b). An equally strong case can be made for the welfare-enhancing influences of artisanal miners' livelihoods and the accompanying wide dispersion of purchasing power engendering local-level economic development and popular democracy. These developments can be viewed as a counterbalance to the problems of light taxation of artisanal miners.

Continental comparisons

We define mining complexes as delineated configurations of the tripartite relationship between the state, large-scale mining and artisanal mining associated with varied social outcomes on a gradient between autocracy and democracy. Table 11.1 differentiates four stylized African mining complexes.

Our paradigm is constructed with the following provisos. First, we are not suggesting that African nation-states can neatly be accommodated into a single category. Individual countries will represent amalgams of the different complexes but can nonetheless usually be primarily identified with a specific complex to facilitate analytical comparison.

Second, our main aim is to get beyond the exceptionally narrow narratives that portray African mining as: i) intrinsically autocratic, dominated by a state/large-scale authoritarian regime and/or corrupt tangles of state and corporate interests that monopolize the material gain from mining at the cost of present and future generations of the country, or ii) anarchic and violence-prone artisanal mining led by rival political forces vying for state power and primarily using mineral wealth for bankrolling military campaigns and personal enrichment.

The dynamics of the above four stylized complexes can be illustrated with mention of specific countries that exemplify aspects of one or another category: the first being the 'absent state' complex, which veers towards anarchy and what could be characterized as the law of 'might is right'. Artisanal miners often face highly exploitative conditions as witnessed presently in the DRC and previously in Liberia, Sierra Leone and Angola. This situation has already been described in Chapter 1 with respect to the conflict minerals era.

Second, the 'weak state' complex affords artisanal miners the most room for manoeuvre, as illustrated in Tanzania. Tanzania has been fortunate insofar as it has remained relatively politically stable throughout the passage of neo-liberal mining legislation and the increase of international corporate investment in the

Table 11.1 Democratic and autocratic tendencies in African mining complexes

State-mining complex	Nature of state	Artisanal mining presence	Large-scale mining presence	Degree of egalitarianism, democracy and welfare
Absent state				
With coerced and/or physically insecure labour conditions.	Anarchic context of war with lack of legitimated state power hence absence of social contract between state and people (formerly Angola, DRC, Sierra Leone).	Usually dominant.	Generally difficult to operate without very heavy investment in on-site security.	Deplorable working and living conditions on artisanal mine sites.
Low-level state control				
With voluntary labour, usually in an early stage of frontier mining development.	Weak state, with lack of regulatory presence in mining areas, affording glimmers of egalitarianism (e.g. Tanzania).	Dominant at outset, representing a historical interlude that wanes over time as mineral rushes and resource accessibility declines.	Growing presence over time, reducing mine labour absorption in the national economy.	Dichotomous between large and artisanal mining, with the latter affording possibilities of economic advance for artisanal miners that erodes as LSM gains ground.
Autocratic state control				
Strong political and economic linkages between state and mining corporations usually prevalent.	Highly regulatory and discriminatory, favouring special interest groups and often in coalition with industrial mining interests (e.g. apartheid-influenced states of Southern Africa).	Either negligible existing on the fringes of LSM with theft of tailing or state outlawed.	Dominant.	Employment and housing of employees is geared to profit maximization with non-democratic, elitist bias in state distribution of mining revenues.

Table 11.1 continued

State-mining complex	Nature of state	Artisanal mining presence	Large-scale mining presence	Degree of egalitarianism, democracy and welfare
Democratic state control	Non-discriminatory regulation with aims of fair distribution of state mining revenues to national population (e.g. Botswana).	Relatively negligible employment, usually based on LSM tailing recycling or more favourably specially designated AM zones.	Dominant.	Egalitarian spread of state's mining revenue expenditure evenly across the population, sometimes with special provisions for population in mining zones.

Source: Authors' categorization. LSM = large-scale mining; AM = artisanal mining.

country. The 'weak state' label is applicable in light of the tenuous nature of governance of mineral production and trade given its patchy coverage and over-centralization of policy decisions in Dar es Salaam.

Other new or revived mining nations following neo-liberal policy reforms, such as Benin, Burkina Faso, Ghana, Mali and Niger in West Africa as well as Uganda and Mozambique in East and Southern Africa, have generally implemented neo-liberal policies to encourage international investment and revised their mining laws in accordance with World Bank recommendations. They are now experiencing the increasing dominance of international mining firms alongside artisanal mining (Werthmann 2003; Hilson and Potter 2005; Banchirigah 2006; Luning 2006; Grätz 2009). This may enhance democracy at the grassroots or alternatively be a source of discontent if exacerbated by national governments, which neglect to invest mining revenues for the welfare of the national population (Arezki and Gylfason 2013). Most at risk will be countries where mineralization has been very rapid causing mining to become overwhelmingly dominant in the national economy with insufficient time for gradual social adjustment and necessary institutional reform. Such circumstances could propel a country along the road towards inexorable state autocracy.

Third, the 'autocratic state' refers to countries that are mineral-rich, receive high natural resource rents, generally have small or negligible artisanal mining populations and have leaderships that have consistently refrained from investing their countries' mineral wealth in the welfare of the population. This is indicated by the low percentage income share held by the poorest 20 per cent of national populations of some well-known mineral-rich countries: Central African

Republic (3.4 per cent), Namibia (3.0 per cent), South Africa (2.5 per cent), Angola (2.0 per cent) and it is likely that this would also apply to Equatorial Guinea which has no published figures[14] (World Bank 2012). However, it should be noted that the Angolan government is making a conscious effort to deploy some of its vast mineral wealth for national infrastructural building and poverty alleviation (Soares de Oliveira 2013).

Our fourth category, the 'democratic state' complex is most clearly illustrated by the Botswanan experience. This large country with a small population and vast diamond wealth implemented an enlightened welfare investment strategy for the national population under its first president Sir Seretse Khama (Gwebu 2012). It nonetheless has its critics. Good (2008) argues that subsequent presidents have swayed the state away from beneficence, with rising influence and corruption of the rich and powerful who are undermining the country's democratic tendencies. The deteriorating situation is affected by the leadership's growing awareness of the country's diminishing diamond wealth. Mineral-funded democracy and welfare are indeed difficult to achieve, as Zambia came to learn after its second decade of independence when the price of copper plummeted on the world market (Mususa 2012).

Conclusion

It has been argued that artisanal mining may offer a pivotal interlude in a nation-state's mineralizing history, when the windfall gain of mineral discovery can potentially be accessed by large numbers of the population with minimal capital investment barriers. In the process, those willing to contend with the risks of arti-sanal mining are afforded potential economic advance, social mobility, cultural creativity and political democracy.

The extent to which this is achieved depends largely on the African state's sense of justice, fair play and a genuine will to maximize the distribution of mining benefits to the population at large during mineralization. When the state has the political will and integrity to choose this path, the central question is how this window of opportunity can be optimized and prolonged technically, econom-ically and politically for the benefit of artisanal miners, local mining settlement residents as well as the regional and national economy. Leaving artisanal miners with room for manoeuvre ensures labour absorption and personal savings accu-mulation on the basis of people's direct involvement in artisanal mining.

However, as the depth of the nation's mineral wealth reaches downwards beyond the 'artisanal frontier', the question of how the state will manage the inevitable transition from artisanal to large-scale mining arises. The influence of the artisanal democratic tendency wanes as corporate mining becomes domi-nant and an important phase of the country's political and economic history ebbs away. Large-scale mechanized mining is inevitably enclave-based, restricted primarily to the employment of limited numbers of highly skilled workers. As the inclusivity of artisanal mining's hundreds of thousands of self-made miners eclipses, the state has the enormous challenge of effecting a smooth transition to a mineral-endowed country with new forms of inclusivity via the creation of alternative labour absorption, increased skill capability and economic diversification. The risk of political instability is very high when the self-made artisanal mining sector is displaced without new sources of labour-absorbing economic dynamism. Large-scale mining wealth and the country's continuing growth should be leveraged to ensure economic welfare for the population. Enormous effort needs to be devoted to innovative economic policy design in this regard.

Meanwhile, socially and politically, artisanal mining has profoundly altered social relations and embedded seeds of democracy in the politics and cultural foundations of local mining communities and regions, which percolate to the national level. The question is how deep will the roots of democracy have reached in the short space of time that artisanal mining has managed to thrive. Will this historical interlude remain a vibrant legacy for the future of the African nation-state?

Tanzania is not a special case but a clearer case than most, given its mineral history which progressed from a long interlude under Nyerere when world prices for minerals were not attractive and state policies were not focused on the country's mineral wealth to the recent rapid expansion of extractive industries in the context of economic liberalization and a booming global mineral market. It is true that Nyerere's influence as father of the nation steered the country towards popular democracy and the prioritization of basic needs of the masses. However, over the last three decades, the presence of the country's many artisanal mineral rush settlements and the occupationality of mining frontiersmen and women charting new mining livelihoods and lifestyles has been, and continues to be a vital conduit through which hundreds of thousands participate in democratizing processes of social, political and economic transformation.

The exploitation of mineral wealth has an extremely paradoxical potentiality depending on which amalgams of state, market and mining labour agencies shape it. Minerals do not have an essentialist character that ordains the outcome of mineral production and distribution. Nor does mineralization in African countries inevitably follow the same path. At all historical junctures, it is the reflexive interaction of conflict, cooperation and regulation between the state, artisanal mining and large-scale mining, which moulds social mobility or immobility, economic welfare or want, political harmony or discord and the underpinning cultural values of the society. The existence of mineral wealth is both enabling and constraining but never ultimately determining the direction of social transformation.

Notes

1   In some established artisanal mining settlements, pit holders sometimes have contestable long-term informal claims over pits that precede claim formalization.
2   Expensive merrymaking is not pursued by all striking miners. Others prefer to save their strike earnings for housing and other major investments.

3   For example, Barrick mining corporation has been considering selling their North Mara Gold Mine due to a state of protracted insecurity.
4   See Freund (1982) for an interesting historical example of social protest in Nigerian tin mining.
5   This is an observation which accords with theoretical constructions of resource materiality, the notion of the spirit of commodities (Appadurai 1986), as well as Marxist value theory (Bryceson 1983; Bridge 2009).
6   This phenomenon is similar to De Toqueville's (2003 [1835]) description of the material expectations of Americans and the 'pioneering spirit' associated with migrating westward across the early American frontier during the nineteenth century.
7   Personal communication with Prof. Crispin Kinabo (November 2012), one of the members of the investigative team.
8   Typically renewal poses no problems if the miner is actively mining and makes his renewal application in time.
9   However, it should be noted that implementation could be double-edged by affecting any artisanal claim owners not actively mining their claims.
10   'Minamata Convention agreed by nations: Global mercury agreement to lift health threats from lives of millions world-wide', *UNEP News Centre*, 19 January, 2013. Available from www.unep.org/newscentre/default.aspx?DocumentID=2702& ArticleID=9373 (accessed 17 March, 2013).
11   'Tanzania Mineral Audit Agency faces uphill tasks of recovering billion of shillings from small-scale miners', *The Citizen*, Dar es Salaam (2013), 19 January 2013.
12   This is especially true for mineral ores whereas small-scale gemstone mining is likely to endure longer given that it tends to be more localized and is of less interest to corporate investment.
13   Over the last two years the government has been compliant with most of the transparency review stipulations but discrepancies in government revenue records indicate that accountability remains problematic. The first Tanzania Extractive Industries Transparency Initiative (TEITI) valuation covering 2008–2009 reported that several transparency indicators were met, notably the establishment of a work plan and stakeholder group, but the reconciliation and validation of government-audited accounts were marred. The Validator noted that the original figures appeared to be 'made up' followed by a lack of confidence in the figures later provided (Adam Smith International 2011: 20). The government reporting standards indicator was not met again in the following year. A reported Tsh 424.6 billion was paid by extractive industries whereas the government's reported receipts were Tsh 419.6 billion, a discrepancy of Tsh 5 billion explained as declaration errors and differences in recording periods (TEITI 2012: 85).
14   The poverty measure is not available for Equatorial Guinea for any years between 2000 and 2012 in the World Development Indicators 2012.

References

Adam Smith International (2011) *Tanzania Extractive Industries Transparency Initiative: Validation Report Final Draft*. March 2011.

Appadurai, A. (1986) *The Social Life of Things: Commodities in Cultural Perspective*. Cambridge: Cambridge University Press.

Appadurai, A. (1996) *Modernity at Large: Cultural Dimensions of Globalization*. Cambridge: Cambridge University Press.

Arezki, R. and Gylfason, T. (2013) 'Resource rents, democracy, corruption and conflict: Evidence from Sub-Saharan Africa'. *Journal of African Economies* advanced access, published 4 January, 2013, 1–18. Available from http://ezproxy.ouls.ox.ac.uk:3324/

content/early/2013/01/04/jae.ejs036.full.pdf+html?sid=668a1659-fd31-488d-a929-0e204b4855f2 (accessed 28 January 2013).

Auty, R. (1993) *Sustaining Development in Mineral Economies: The Resource Curse Thesis*. London: Routledge.

Bakker, K. and Bridge, G. (2006) 'Material worlds? Resource geographies and the "matter of nature"'. *Progress in Human Geography* 30(5): 5–27.

Banchirigah, S.M. (2006) 'How have reforms fuelled the expansion of artisanal mining? Evidence from sub-Saharan Africa'. *Resources Policy* 31(3): 165–71.

Bannon, I. and Collier, P. (eds) (2003) *Natural Resources and Violent Conflict: Options and Actions*. Washington, DC: World Bank.

Barry, M. (1996) 'Regularizing informal mining: A summary of the proceedings of the International Roundtable on Artisanal Mining'. Washington, DC, 17–19 May 1995. Available from www.commdev.org/regularizing-informal-mining-summary-proceedings-international-roundtable-artisanal-mining (accessed 14 January 2013).

Bracking, S. (2009) 'Hiding conflict over industry returns: A stakeholder analysis of the extractive industries transparency initiative'. University of Manchester, BWPI Working Paper 91.

Bridge, G. (2009) 'Material worlds: Natural resources, resource geography and the material economy'. *Geography Compass* 3(3): 1217–44.

Brunnschweiler, C.N. and Bulte, E.H. (2006) 'The resource curse revisited and revised: A tale of paradoxes and red herrings'. *Journal of Environmental Economics and Management* 56: 248–64.

Bryceson, D.F. (1983) 'Use values, the law of value and the analysis of non-capitalist production'. *Capital and Class* 20: 29–63.

Bryceson, D.F. (1990) *Food Insecurity and the Social Division of Labour in Tanzania, 1919–1985*. London: Macmillan.

Bryceson, D.F. (1997) *Liberalizing Tanzania's Food Trade: Public and Private Faces of Urban Marketing Policy, 1939–1988*. London: James Currey Publishers.

Bryceson, D.F., Jønsson, J.B., Kinabo, C. and Shand, M. (2012) 'Unearthing treasure and trouble: Mining as an impetus to urbanisation in Tanzania'. *Journal of Contemporary African Studies* 30(4): 631–49.

Bryceson, D.F., Jønsson, J.B. and Verbrugge, H. (2014) 'For richer, for poorer: Marriage and casualized sex in East African artisanal gold mining settlements', *Development and Change*, forthcoming.

Bryceson, D.F. and Vuorela, U. (2002) *The Transnational Family*. Oxford: Berg.

Bush, R. (2010) 'Conclusion: Mining, dispossession and transformation in Africa'. in Fraser, A. and Larmer, M. (eds), *Zambia, Mining and Neoliberalism*. London: Palgrave MacMillan, pp. 237–67.

Campbell, B. (2004) *Regulating Mining in Africa: For Whose Benefit?*. Uppsala, Sweden: Nordiska Afrikainstitutet.

Campbell, B. (2009) *Mining in Africa: Regulation and Development*. New York: Pluto Press.

Chachage, C.S.L. (1995) 'The meek shall inherit the earth but not the mining rights: Mining and accumulation in Tanzania'. in Gibbon, P. (ed.) *Liberalised Development in Tanzania*. Uppsala, Sweden: Nordic Africa Institute, pp. 37–108.

Collier, P. and Goderis, B. (2007) 'Commodity prices, growth, and the natural resource curse: Reconciling the conundrum'. Oxford University, Available from http://economics.ouls.ox.ac.uk/13218/1/2007-15text.pdf (accessed 15 January 2013).

Collier, P. and Venables, A.J. (2008a) 'Managing the exploitation of natural assets: Lessons for low income countries'. Oxford: University of Oxford, Oxford Centre for the Analysis of Resource Rich Economies (OxCarre). Available from www.oxcarre.ox.ac.uk/images/stories/papers/ResearchPapers/oxcarrerp200811.pdf (accessed 19 January 2013).

Collier, P. and Venables, A.J. (2008b) 'Managing resource revenues: Lessons for low income countries' [OxCarre research paper 15]. Oxford: University of Oxford, Oxford Centre for the Analysis of Resource Rich Economies. Available from http://economics.ouls.ox.ac.uk/14313/1/ManagingResourceRevenues.pdf (accessed 19 January 2013).

Cooksey, B. (2011) 'The investment and business environment for gold exploration and mining in Tanzania' [Africa Power and Politics Background Paper 03]. London: Overseas Development Institute.

Curtis, M. and Lissu, T. (2008) 'A golden opportunity: How Tanzania is failing to benefit from gold mining'. Dar es Salaam: Christian Council of Tanzania, National Council of Muslims in Tanzania and Tanzania Episcopal Conference.

De Tocqueville, A. (2003 [1835]) *Democracy in America* (translator Bevan, G.E.). London: Penguin Books.

Dode, R. (2011) 'The political economy of resource curse and the Niger Delta crisis in Nigeria: Matters arising'. *Afro Asian Journal of Social Sciences* 2(2.1): 1–15.

Economic Commission for Africa (2011) *Minerals and Africa's Development*. Addis Ababa: United Nations Economic Commission for Africa.

Ferguson, J. (2006) *Global Shadows: Africa in the Neoliberal World Order*. Durham, NC and London: Duke University Press.

Fisher, E. (2008) 'Artisanal gold mining at the margins of mineral resource governance: A case from Tanzania'. *Development Southern Africa* 25(2): 199–213.

Fisher, E., Mwaipopo, R., Mutagwaba, W., Nyange, D. and Yaron, G. (2009) 'The ladder that sends us to wealth: Artisanal mining and poverty reduction in Tanzania'. *Resources Policy* 34(1): 15–22.

Freund, B. (1982) 'Theft and social protest among the tin miners of northern Nigeria', *Radical History Review* 26: 68–86.

Gajigo, O., Mutambatsere, E. and Ndiaye, G. (2012) 'Gold mining in Africa: Maximizing economic returns for countries' [African Development Bank Group Working Paper no. 147], March 2012.

Good, K. (2008) *Diamonds, Dispossession and Democracy in Botswana*. Woodbridge: James Currey.

Grätz, T. (2009) 'Moralities, risk and rules in West African artisanal gold mining communities: A case study of Northern Benin'. *Resources Policy* 34: 12–17.

Gwebu, T. (2012) 'Botswana's mining path to urbanisation and poverty alleviation'. *Journal of Contemporary African Studies* 30(4): 611–30.

Haber, S. and Menaldo, V. (2011) 'Do natural resources fuel authoritarianism? A reappraisal of the resource curse'. *American Political Science Review* 105(1): 1–26.

Hentschel, T., Hruschka, F. and Priester, M. (2002) *Global Report on Artisanal and Small-Scale Mining*. London: IIED.

Hilson, G.M. (2009) 'Small-scale mining, poverty and economic development in sub-Saharan Africa: An overview'. *Resources Policy* 34(1): 1–5.

Hilson G.M. (2012) 'Poverty traps in small-scale mining communities: The case of Sub-Saharan Africa'. *Canadian Journal of Development Studies* 33(2): 180–97.

Hilson G.M. and Garforth, C.J. (2012) '"Agricultural poverty" and the expansion of artisanal mining in Sub-Saharan Africa: Experiences from Southwest Mali and Southeast Ghana'. *Population Research and Policy Review* 31(3): 435–64.

Hilson, G.M. and van Bockstael, S. (2012) 'Poverty and livelihood diversification in rural

Liberia: Exploring the linkages between artisanal diamond mining and smallholder rice production'. *Journal of Development Studies*. 48(3): 416–31.

Hilson, G.M. and Potter, C. (2005) 'Structural adjustment and subsistence industry: Artisanal gold mining in Ghana'. *Development and Change* 36(1): 103–31.

Hujo, K. (2012) *Mineral Rents and the Financing of Social Policy: Opportunities and Challenges*. London: Palgrave.

Humphreys, M., Sachs, J. and Stiglitz, J.E. (2007) *Escaping the Resource Curse*. New York: Columbia University Press.

International Labour Organization (ILO) (1999) 'Social and labor issues in small-scale mines. Report for discussion at the tripartite meeting on social and labor issues in small-scale mines'. Geneva: ILO.

Jønsson, J.B. and Fold, N. (2011) 'Mining 'from below': Taking Africa's artisanal mining seriously'. *Geography Compass* 5(7): 479–93.

Karl, T.L. (1997) *The Paradox of Plenty: Oil Booms and Petro-States*. Berkeley: University of California Press.

Labonne, B. (2002) 'Synthesis report: Seminar on artisanal and small-scale mining in Africa, Yaounde, 19–22 November'. Paris: Centre for Training and Exchanges in the Geosciences.

Lange, S. (2011) 'Gold and governance: Legal injustices and lost opportunities in Tanzania'. *African Affairs* 110(439): 233–52.

Lange, S. and Kolstad, I. (2012). 'Corporate community involvement and local institutions: Two case studies from the mining industry in Tanzania', *Journal of African Business* 13(2): 134–44.

Le Billon, P. (2001) 'The political ecology of war: Natural resources and armed conflict'. *Political Geography* 20: 561–84.

Lissu, T.A. (2008) 'Not all that glitters is gold: How Tanzania's mining boom has impoverished communities, violated rights'. Dar es Salaam, Research report prepared for the Norwegian Church Aid, Tanzania.

Luning, S. (2006) 'Artisanal gold mining in Burkina Faso: Permits, poverty and perceptions of the poor in Sanmatenga, the "land of gold"'. in Hilson, G.M. (ed.) *Small-scale Mining, Rural Subsistence and Poverty in West Africa*. Rugby: Practical Action. 135–47.

Luong, P.J. and Weinthal, E. (2006) 'Rethinking the resource curse: Ownership structure, institutional capacity, and domestic constraints'. *Annual Review of Political Science* 9: 241–63.

Maconachie, R. (2011) 'Re-agrarianizing livelihoods in post-conflict Sierra Leone? Mineral wealth and rural change in artisanal and small-scale mining communities'. *Journal of International Development* 23(8): 1054–67.

Maconachie, R. (2012) 'Diamond mining, urbanisation and social transformation in Sierra Leone'. *Journal of Contemporary African Studies* 30(4): 705–23.

Maconachie, R. and Binns, T. (2007) '"Farming miners" or "mining farmers"? Diamond mining and rural development in post-conflict Sierra Leone'. *Journal of Rural Studies* 23(3): 367–80.

Mkandawire, T. and Soludo, C.C. (1999) *Our Continent, Our Future: African Perspectives on Structural Adjustment*. Trenton, NJ: Africa World Press.

Moody, R. (2007) *Rocks and Hard Places: The Globalization of Mining*. London: Zed Books Ltd.

Mususa, P. (2012) 'Mining, welfare and urbanisation: The wavering urban character of Zambia's Copperbelt'. *Journal of Contemporary African Studies* 30(4): 571–87.

Noetstaller, R., Heemskerk, M. Hruschka, F. and Dreschler, B. (2004) *Program for Improvements to the Profiling of ASM in Africa and the Implementation of Baseline Surveys*. Washington, DC: CASM Division, World Bank.

Otto, J., Andrews, C., Cawood, F., Doggett, M., Guj, P., Stermole, F., Stermole, J. and Tilton, J. (2006) *Mining Royalties: A Global Study of their Impact on Investors, Government, and Civil Society*. Washington, DC: World Bank.

Reno, W. (2004) 'Order and commerce in turbulent areas: 19th century lessons, 21st century practice', *Third World Quarterly* 25(4): 607–25.

Reyna, S. and Behrend, A. (2008) 'The crazy curse and crude domination: Towards an anthropology of oil'. *Focaal* 52: 3–17.

Richardson, T. and Weszkalnys, G. (forthcoming) 'Resource materialities: New anthropological perspectives on natural resource environments'. [Special Issue of] *Anthropological Quarterly*.

Ross, M. (1999) 'The political economy of the resource curse'. *World Politics* 51(2): 297–322.

Rosser, A. (2006) 'The political economy of the resource curse: A literature survey'. Institute of Development Studies. University of Sussex.

Sennett, R. (2008) *The Craftsman*. London: Penguin Books.

Sinding, K. (2005) 'The dynamics of artisanal and small-scale mining reforms', *Natural Resources Forum* 29(3): 243–52.

Soares de Oliveira, R. (2013) *Magnificent and Beggar Land: Angola since the Civil War*. London: Hurst.

Standing, G. (2009) *Work after Globalization: Building Occupational Citizenship*. Cheltenham: Edward Elgar.

Standing, G. (2011) *The Precariat: The New Dangerous Class*. London: Bloomsbury.

Tanzania, (MEM) Ministry of Energy and Minerals (2010) *Five Years of Implementing the Mining Cadastral Informal Management System in Tanzania*, Dar es Salaam: Government Printers.

Tanzania Extractive Industries Transparency Initiative (TEITI) (2012) 'Short Version of the Second Reconciliation Report, Year ending June 30, 2010'. Available from www.teiti.or.tz/news_images/news50581073bb67f.pdf (accessed 29 January 2013).

The Citizen, Dar es Salaam (2013) 'Tanzania mineral audit agency faces uphill tasks of recovering billion of shillings from small-scale miners'. 19 January, 2013.

United Nations Economic Commission for Africa (UNECA) (2003) *Report on Selected Themes in Natural Resource Development in Africa: Artisanal and Small-Scale Mining and Technical Challenges* [Committee on Sustainable Development Meeting, Oct. 7–10, 2003]. Addis Ababa: UNECA.

Watts, M. (2004) 'Resource curse? Governmentality, oil and power in the Niger delta, Nigeria'. *Geopolitics* 9(1): 50–80.

Werthmann, K. (2003) 'The president of the gold diggers: Sources of power in a gold mine in Burkina Faso'. *Ethnos* 68(1): 95–111.

Weszkalnys, G. (2011) 'Cursed resources, or articulations of economic theory in the Gulf of Guinea'. *Economy and Society* 40(3): 345–72.

Weszkalnys, G. (2013) 'Oil's magic: Contestation and materiality'. in Strauss, S., Rupp, S. and Love, T. (eds) *Cultures of Energy: Anthropological Perspectives on Powering the Planet*. Walnut Creek, CA: Left Coast Press, pp. 267–83.

World Bank (2005) *The Millennium Development Goals and Small-Scale Mining: A Conference for Forging Partnerships for Action*. Washington, DC: World Bank.

World Bank (2011) *Doing Business 2012: Doing Business in a More Transparent World*. Washington, DC: World Bank.

World Bank (2012) 'World development indicators'. Available from http://databank.worldbank.org/ddp/home.do?Step=12&id=4&CNO=2 (accessed 28 January 2013).

Appendices

Appendix 1.1 African metallic mineral-producing countries' mining contribution index*

Rank and country	Mining contribution index (MCI)	2010 % Mineral export contribution	2005–2010 % Change in mineral export contribution	Total % Mineral export contribution	2010 Production value (US$ million)	Change in production value 2000–2010	2010 Production value as % of 2010 GDP
1 Zambia	97.7	83.6	19.7	84.2	3,850	524	23.8
5 Mauritania	95.3	60.4	11.1	72.2	1,778	461	48.9
7 Mali	94.2	54.8	17.6	55.4	1,445	305	15.6
10 D.R.C.**	93.2	78.3	8.1	90.5	2,191	837	16.7
13 Congo, Rep.	91.5	39.1	16.9	39.1	—	—	—
14 Somalia	91.3	33.4	28	34.2	—	—	—
16 Burkina Faso	90.2	40.7	38.7	40.7	794	3134	9.0
19 Liberia	89.2	20.6	17.9	29.5	—	—	—
25 Namibia	86.5	53.4	12.3	53.9	352	278	2.9
27 Ghana	84.9	25.4	7.0	28.1	3,964	290	12.7
28 Gambia	84.7	15.6	12.3	15.7	—	—	—
30 Tanzania	82.3	40.7	4.3	43.0	1,340	500	5.8
31 South Africa	81.2	37.4	3.6	47.5	27,116	114	7.5
32 Malawi	80.9	11.1	10.8	11.3	—	—	—
36 Benin	77.4	11.1	5.2	28.9	—	—	—
37 Madagascar	77.1	10.3	5.4	13.7	—	—	—
38 Togo	76.2	15.2	3.2	28.1	—	—	—
47 Senegal	67.6	8.1	3.8	32.4	181	2230	1.4
53 Guinea	65.3	65.2	−18.7	86.4	1,174	51.2	26
55 Gabon	64.2	6.8	1.2	85.3	323	279.0	2.5
57 Djibouti	63.7	14.5	0.9	24.1	—	—	—
59 Botswana	61.9	83.7	−2.8	84.0	741	237.6	5.0
63 Ethiopia	59.1	8.9	3.2	8.9	143	83.9	0.5
64 Zimbabwe	58.7	26.8	−10.2	31.1	1,098	154.4	14.7
70 Kenya	56.1	4.3	1.5	8.6	—	—	—

71	Niger	55.9	19.4	0.1	30.5	71	1003.7	1.3
89	Sierra Leone	51.3	54.3	-3.9	55.0	24	–	1.2
98	Sudan	49.4	5.7	2.7	94.2	76	1.5	0.1
99	Mozambique	49.3	57.0	-9.9	72.0	–	–	–
110	C.A.R.***	45.5	35.8	-9.0	36.6	–	–	–
114	Rwanda	44.5	27.4	-12.4	28.4	52	6.5	0.9
120	Lesotho	43.2	10.8	-1.0	10.8	–	–	–
130	Burundi	38.9	14.6	-12.8	16.3	–	–	–
138	Cape Verde	35.4	0.9	0.8	0.9	–	–	–
143	Equatorial Guinea	34.2	0.8	0.8	95.5	–	–	–
146	Eritrea	33.5	2.6	0.1	2.6	–	–	–
153	Ivory Coast	31.3	0.8	0.3	33.4	181	351	0.8
155	Uganda	30.7	5.4	-4.0	6.3	–	–	–
162	Nigeria	28.6	1.2	1.0	91.7	33	52	0.0
167	Cameroon	27.7	3.7	-1.2	52.8	38	194	0.2
168	Guinea-Bissau	27.6	0.9	0.2	7.1	–	–	–
177	Comoros	24.1	1.2	0.0	1.2	–	–	–
183	Seychelles	22.2	0.4	0.1	12.2	–	–	–
186	Swaziland	19.8	1.5	-1.8	1.8	–	–	–
190	Chad	18.4	0.1	0.0	90.9	–	–	–
192	Angola	17.2	1.1	-2.1	99.7	–	–	–
193	Sao Tome and Principe	15.6	0.2	-0.2	0.2	–	–	–
194	Mayotte	14.9	0.0	0.0	0.3	–	–	–

Source: ICMM (International Council on Mining and Minerals) (2012), pp.12–15

*The MCI is calculated on the basis of three variables: mineral export contribution in 2010; the increase/decrease in mineral export contributions between 2005–2010; and mineral production value as a percentage of GDP in 2010 (ICMM 2012, p. 8). It should be noted that Southern Sudan and Zimbabwe, both mineral-producing countries have been omitted from the listing due to an absence of published data.

** Democratic Republic of Congo.

*** Central African Republic.

Appendix 1.2 Production of world's top 20 diamond-mining countries in 2010

African countries	Carats*	Non-African countries	Carat*
Botswana	25,000	Russia	17,800
Angola	12,500	Canada	11,733
D.R.C.**	5,500	Brazil	200
South Africa	3,500	Guyana	144
Namibia	1,200	China	100
Guinea	550	Australia	100
Lesotho	460	Armenia	50
Ghana	300		
C.A.R.***	250		
Sierra Leone	240		
Tanzania	77		
Total carats	49,627		30,203
Percentage	62%		38%

Source: United States Geological Survey (2010) *Mineral Commodity Summaries*. Available from
    http://geology.com/articles/gem-diamond-map/, (accessed 15 November, 2012)
* In thousands.
** Democratic Republic of Congo.
*** Central African Republic.

Appendix 1.3 Estimated artisanal and small-scale mining (ASM) populations in Sub-
           Saharan Africa

Country	Estimate	Population		% of population economically dependent on ASM:		Source
		Low	High	Low	High	
Sahel						
Burkina Faso	200,000				8	Hayes
Chad	100,000	50,000	150,000	2	6	CASM
Mali	200,000	150,000	300,000	6	10	CASM
Niger	200,000	300,000	500,000	20	25+	CASM
Sudan*	200,000	150,000	300,000	2	6	CASM
Horn of africa						
Eritrea	400,000	150,000	300,000	20	25+	Hayes
Djibouti	10,000				12	CASM
Ethiopia	500,000	300,000	500,000	2	6	CASM
Somalia	10,000	5,000	50,000	0	2	CASM
East Africa						
Burundi	50,000			2	6	CASM
Kenya	100,000			0	2	CASM
Rwanda	50,000			2	6	CASM
Tanzania	550,000	500,000	2,000,000	6	10	CASM
Uganda	150,000			2	6	CASM

Appendix 1.3 continued

Country	Population Estimate	Population Low	Population High	% of population economically dependent on ASM: Low	% of population economically dependent on ASM: High	Source
Southern Africa						
Angola	150,000	50,000	150,000	2	6	CASM
Botswana	10,000	5,000	50,000	2	6	CASM
Lesotho	20,000			2	6	CASM
Mozambique	200,000	150,000	300,000	2	6	CASM
Madagascar	300,000	300,000	500,000	6	10	CASM
Malawi	60,000				3	Hayes
Namibia	20,000	5,000	50,000	2	6	CASM
South Africa	27,500	5,000	50,000	2	6	CASM
Swaziland	10,000			0	2	CASM
Zambia	60,000	50,000	150,000	2	6	CASM
Zimbabwe	350,000	300,000	500,000	10	20	CASM
Central Africa						
Central African Republic	200,000	150,000	300,000	20	25+	CASM
Democratic Republic Congo	2,000,000	500,000	2,000,000	10	20	CASM
West Africa						
Benin	10,000	5,000	50,000	0	2	CASM
Cameroon	30,000	5,000	50,000	0	2	CASM
Congo	25,000	5,000	50,000	10	20	CASM
Cote d'Ivoire	100,000				3	Hayes
Equatorial Guinea	10,000	5,000	50,000	6	10	CASM
Gabon	25,000	5,000	50,000	6	10	CASM
Gambia	5,000				2	CASM
Ghana	250,000	150,000	300,000	6	10	CASM
Guinea	100,000	50,000	150,000	6	10	Hayes
Guinea Bissau	5,000	5,000	50,000	0	2	CASM
Liberia	100,000	50,000	150,000	10	20	CASM
Nigeria	100,000	50,000	150,000		1	CASM
Senegal	10,000	5,000	50,000	0	2	CASM
Sierra Leone	300,000	300,000	500,000	20	25+	CASM
Togo	15,000	5,000	50,000	0	2	CASM
Sub-Saharan Africa	7,312,500	3,830,000	9,960,000			

Sources:
1. CASM (Communities and Small-scale Mining) (2008): Available from
https://www.artisanalmining.org/casm/minersmap (accessed 30 December 2012)
2. Hayes, K. (2008). 'Artisanal and small-scale mining and livelihoods in Africa'. Amsterdam:
Common Fund for Commodities.
* Note that these estimates predate the establishment of Southern Sudan.

Index

For Product Safety Concerns and Information please contact our EU
representative GPSR@taylorandfrancis.com
Taylor & Francis Verlag GmbH, Kaufingerstraße 24, 80331 München, Germany